Books by Charles A. Madison

Jewish Publishing in America

Irving to Irving:
Author-Publisher Relations

Eminent American Jews

Yiddish Literature:
Its Scope and Major Writers

Book Publishing in America

The Owl Among Colophons

Leaders and Liberals
in 20th Century America

American Labor Leaders

Critics and Crusaders

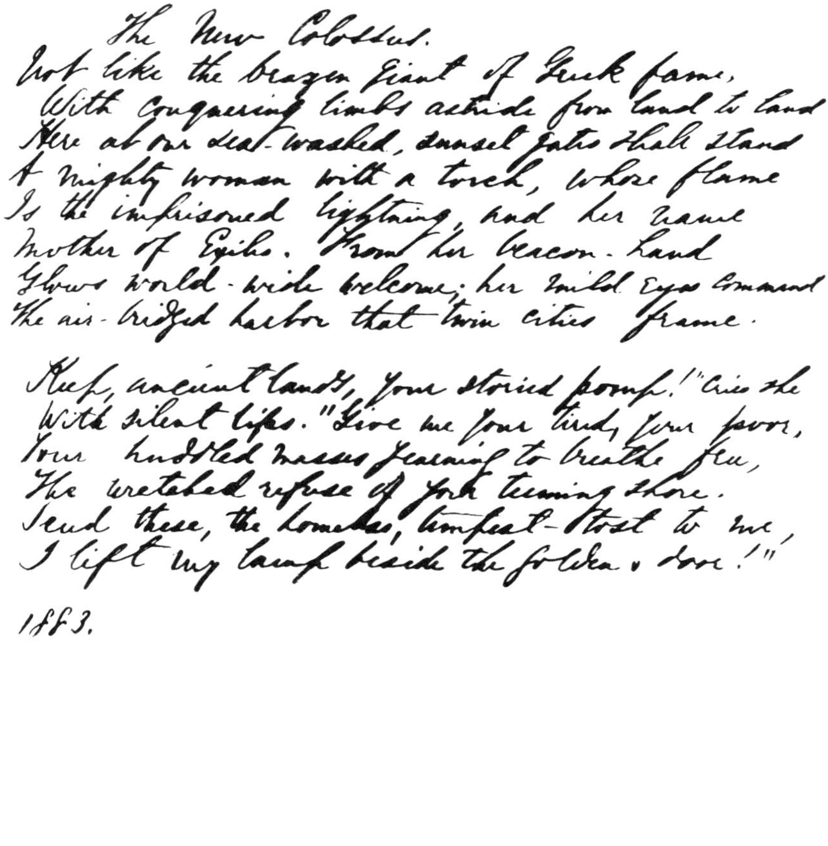

The New Colossus.
Not like the brazen giant of Greek fame,
With conquering limbs astride from land to land;
Here at our sea-washed, sunset gates shall stand
A mighty woman with a torch, whose flame
Is the imprisoned lightning, and her name
Mother of Exiles. From her beacon-hand
Glows world-wide welcome; her mild eyes command
The air-bridged harbor that twin cities frame.

"Keep, ancient lands, your storied pomp!" cries she
With silent lips. "Give me your tired, your poor,
Your huddled masses yearning to breathe free,
The wretched refuse of your teeming shore.
Send these, the homeless, tempest-tost to me,
I lift my lamp beside the golden door!"

1883.

This famous sonnet by Emma Lazarus (written in her own hand) expresses a truly Jewish spirit of compassion and hope.

CHARLES A. MADISON

Jewish Publishing in America

The Impact of Jewish Writing on American Culture

Sanhedrin Press

NEW YORK

SANHEDRIN PRESS

a division of Hebrew Publishing Company
79 Delancey Street, New York, N.Y. 10002

Library of Congress Cataloging in Publication Data

Madison, Charles Allan.
Jewish publishing in America.

Bibliography: p.
Includes index.
1. Jews in the United States–Publishing–History. 2. Yiddish literature–United States–History and criticism. 3. Jewish periodicals–United States–History and criticism. 4. United States–Intellectual life. I. Title.
Z473.M214 071'.3 76–21272
ISBN 0–88482–902–2

Designer: Ernst Reichl

PRINTED IN THE UNITED STATES OF AMERICA

Contents

To the

Jewish tradition

of

עם הספר

"The People of the Book"

Preface

Conceived as a tribute to the American Bicentenary, this book has concerned itself with the remarkable contribution of the Jews to American literary culture. It begins with a reminder of the early Puritan admiration for Hebraic writings. Contemporary Jewish writing was of minor consequence until after the Civil War, mainly because there were few Jews in this country until well into the nineteenth century. Thereafter, with the increase of Jewish immigration, Jewish writing and publishing increased significantly. A survey of this activity is given in the first chapter.

After 1900 Jewish literary performance became dynamic. The Jewish Publication Society, founded in 1888, energetically brought out works of both European and American scholars and writers. Somewhat later other Jewish organizations, religious and secular, were active in the production of liturgical and pedagogic books for use by their members as well as by the entire Jewish community. Concurrently a number of Jewish commercial publishers issued books of similar content. These various writing and publishing activities are discussed in the three chapters that follow.

Yiddish is a major factor in Jewish publishing. East European Jews began after 1880 to migrate to the United States in ever-increasing numbers, in excess of two million by the time the restrictive quota system became law in 1924. Most of them were

Yiddish oriented and traditionally Orthodox, but among them were a good many young educated radicals. They soon began to issue newspapers, magazines, and books in their mother tongue. For a time Yiddish was despised by "enlightened" intellectuals as a "jargon," but both radicals and conservative journalists, eager to reach the majority who knew only Yiddish, long used it for their propaganda purposes. Subsequently writers of authentic talent and literary ideals strove to purify and enrich it as a literary medium, and over the years Yiddish overcame the prejudice against it. Indeed, it gradually broke down its confines on the lower East Side and entered the concourse of world literature. The chapters dealing with this literature describe the rise of popular newspapers, literary and political magazines as well as its numerous writers—with emphasis on the major authors—and the peculiar nature of Yiddish book publishing.

The penultimate chapter considers the character and content of contemporary Anglo-Jewish magazines. The book ends with an examination of the salient influence of Jewish general publishers on American publishing over the past half century. Stress is placed on their revolutionary enterprise which resulted in greatly expanded book reading and the liberation of writers from the constraint of censorship. All told, the book makes evident that the Jewish contribution to American culture is vastly greater than that of any other ethnic group.

I am of course greatly indebted to many persons and libraries. Without the resources of the Jewish Division of the New York Public Library or the help of Dinah Abramovitz in the YIVO library this book could not have been written, and I am grateful to both. I also wish to thank the persons who have advised me on specific matters or who have read critically one or more chapters, among them Chaim Bass, Norman Blaustein, Edward Booher, Bernard Postal, Sylvia Smith, and Moshe Spiegel. I am of course indebted to Lawrence Werbel and David Olivestone of Hebrew Publishing Company for encouraging me to write the book and for valuable editorial comments.

C.A.M.

Jewish Publishing in America

1

Early Publishing by and about Jews

The pervasive influence of the Old Testament among Protestant Christians, firmly established in humanistic Europe, was especially strong on American Puritans. More than most Englishmen of the seventeenth century they treasured the Holy Scriptures as their God-ordained guidance to a virtuous life. John Fiske, in *The Beginning of New England,* indicated how this came about:

> At a time when there was as yet no English literature for the common people, this untold wealth of Hebrew literature was implanted in the English mind as in a virgin soil. . . . The aim of Winthrop and his friends in coming to Massachusetts was the construction of a theocratic state which would be to Christians, under the New Testament dispensation, all that the theocracy of Moses and Joshua and Samuel had been to the Jews in Old Testament days.

Emerson similarly stressed the affinity between the Old Testament and the Puritans. In his essay, "The Man of Letters," he stated:

> The Hebrew nation compensated for the insignificance of its members and territory by its religious genius, its tenacious beliefs; its poems and histories cling to the soil of this globe like the primitive rocks. . . . In Puritanism, how the whole of the Jewish history became flesh and blood in those men, let Bunyon show.

This powerful appeal of Hebraic religious and ethical concepts long affected the lives of New Englanders. Governor William Bradford, for instance, knew several ancient and modern languages, but so awed was he by Hebrew that he studied it diligently in his resolve "to see with my owne eyes something of that most ancient language and holy tongue . . . in which God, the angels, spoke to the patriarchs of old time." And on his tombstone are graven the Hebrew words "ה״ עזר חיי" (the Lord is the sustainer of my life). This interest in the people of the Old Testament was firmly articulated by Increase Mather in *The Mystery of Israel's Salvation Explained and Applied* (1669).

The high regard for Hebrew caused the more educated Puritans to study it and to possess books in it. Mather wrote of John Cotton: "The Hebrew he understood so exactly and so readily that he was able to discourse in it." A knowledge of Hebrew was considered essential for Puritan ministers, and at Harvard College it was a basic course; in its daily exercises the Old Testament was read through serially each year. The Hancock Professorship in Hebrew was the college's third oldest chair, established in 1764, and of which the incumbent must be "of the protestant reform'd Religion." When Yale and other early colleges were founded, they too organized courses in Hebrew. President Samuel Johnson of King's College, later Columbia, was passionately fond of Hebrew, and his *An English and Hebrew Grammar* was "the first short Rudiments of these two languages, Taught Together." President Ezra Stiles of Yale College was also an ardent student of Hebrew and cultivated the friendship of several rabbis, particularly Rabbi Hayim Isaak Karigal of Hebron. So well versed was he in Hebrew, that when Isaak Hart of Newport received a letter in that ancient tongue from Hebron, he had Stiles translate it for him.

This admiration for Hebrew writings was manifested in early books published in America. The first volume printed in this country, *The Whole Booke of Psalms,* appeared in Cambridge in 1640. Importations and reprints from England included, in addition to the Bible, histories of ancient Jews. Josephus's *Wars of the Jews* was first printed in 1719 and again in 1721, and several other printings appeared later. Philo's writings were equally in demand.

Indeed, numerous books, essays, and lectures devoted to Israel and Hebrew writings were widely circulated throughout the eighteenth century.

However much Colonial Americans paid homage to Hebrew religious writings, they and their early descendants were generally inhospitable to the relatively few Jews who sought asylum in the new land. Most of them assumed that Christianity was in essence a continuation of Judaism enhanced by the divinity of Jesus, and that the Jews after him who persisted in their faith were cursed by God. This prejudice, coupled with the alien appearance and strange practices of the few isolated Jews who came to their attention, tended to dissociate them in their minds from the ancient Hebrews they admired.

An instance of this attitude was evidenced in their behavior toward Judah Monis on his arrival in Boston about 1720. Although obviously a young man of scholarly attainment, he was treated as an undesirable alien. It was only when he was persuaded by the Reverend Increase Mather to convert to Christianity that Bostonians accepted him as a welcome member of the community. On March 27, 1722, his baptism was the subject of a discourse by Benjamin Coleman, held in College Hall at Harvard College. Later that year this talk together with three discourses by Monis appeared in a printed volume. Moreover, Monis was appointed by Harvard College as a teacher of Hebrew, and he remained on the faculty until his retirement nearly forty years later. In 1735 he published *A Grammar of the Hebrew Tongue*, which became a standard text for many years.

The antipathy toward Jewish newcomers remained passive so long as their number was small—there were only around three thousand Jews in all the Colonies at the time of the Revolution. Early in the nineteenth century, however, with the influx of Jews becoming sizable, the concern of pious Christians for the spiritual salvation of these benighted aliens greatly increased. In 1812 Hannah Adams, a learned and pious Bostonian who sought to convert Jews to Christianity, published *The History of the Jews from the Destruction of Jerusalem to the Nineteenth Century*, a work of little merit but quite popular. Soon agencies were formed to seek Jewish conversion. Following the example of such organizations in England, an association was formed entitled The American Society for Evangelizing the Jews. Somewhat later, in order to satisfy the requirements for a charter, the name was changed to The American Society for Ameliorating the Condition of the Jews. Jewish immigrants, being poor and in need of succor, were approached by members of the Society with offers of assistance and with pious talk of conversion. To further their propaganda, these missionaries in 1823 began to issue a monthly periodical called *Israel's Advocate.*

Public-spirited Jews resisted this insidious proselytizing. In 1820 Abraham Collins, provoked by this missionary zeal, published *Israel Vindicated*, in which he refuted the claims of the missionaries. A more persistent and more effective response was made by Solomon Henry Jackson, one of the early Jewish printers in New York. On the appearance of *Israel's Advocate* he determined to nullify its effectiveness by issuing *The Jew.* On the masthead of this monthly he stated its purport: "Being a Defender of Judaism against all the adversaries, and particularly against the insidious attacks of *Israel's Advocate.*" In each issue he made a point-by-point defense against the editorials and sermons printed in *Israel's Advocate.* He demonstrated that numerous quotations from the Old Testament were mistranslated or quoted out of context in an effort to distort the truth in favor of Christianity. (As was the custom of Orthodox Jews at that time, Jackson never printed the letters for the name Christ but used five dots for that part of a derivative term.) "By perverting the word of God out of its real and proper signification," Jackson declared, "they made the text appear contradictory, and sometimes even blasphemous, and thereby give a handle to the disbeliever in revelation to turn the whole into ridicule." He further explained that his aim was to controvert the texts in dispute and that "the whole [was] to be conducted with candor, temper and moderation, the language to be always such as should not offend any, even our opponents; derision will never be permitted." He kept himself on this high plane month after month, taking up in each issue the material printed that month in *Israel's Advocate,* answering each controversial statement, and making evident the folly of the missionaries in their attempt to convert Jews to Christianity. When *Israel's Advocate* ceased publication in 1825, Jackson stopped issuing *The Jew.*

The American Bible Society also actively pursued this missionary goal. In its building it displayed a sign—"Jews' Society, Room 36"—with the aim of attracting Jews to its quarters. When an unsuspecting Jew entered Room 36, he was met by a missionary who did his utmost to convert him. The Society subsequently published a magazine, *The Jewish Chronicle,* with the aim of demonstrating the validity and advantages of Christianity. When Rabbi Isaac Meyer Wise started *The Israelite* in 1854, in which he attacked missionary propaganda, the Society responded with *The Israelite Indeed* in its effort to nullify the rabbi's charges. To the same end it issued pamphlets with Jewish titles.

Joseph Samuel C. F. Frey, a converted Jew, likewise strove zealously to bring Jews to the Christian fold. In 1837 he began to publish the *Jewish Intelligencer,* a monthly magazine which he distributed to Jews in the effort to persuade them to follow his example. His thesis was: "Ancient Judaism had God for its author, truth for its matter, and the Messiah for its object; but modern Judaism has the Rabbins for its authors, error and superstition for its matter, and opposition to Christianity for its object." He was no more successful, however, than the missionaries who had preceded him—or those who were later to be very active on the lower East Side. And as late as the 1890s the Chicago Hebrew Mission published *The Jewish Era* in the futile effort to win Jewish converts.

With the increase of the number of Jews in the Colonies, there arose the need for religious printed matter. With the Sephardic Jews in the majority, prayer books in accord with their ritual began to be printed—when it was not readily importable. The first such volume, *The Evening Service of Rosh Hashanah and Kippur,* was published in 1761 by W. Weyman of New York. Five years later Isaak Pinto, finding Hebrew "being imperfectly understood by many, by some not at all," translated *Prayers for Sab-*

bath, Rosh-Hashanah and Kippur, and had it printed by John Holt of New York. Somewhat later I. S. Cohen, an English Jew, prepared a book on the Jewish religion, *Elements of Jewish Faith,* and had it printed in Richmond, Virginia. Still later, Solomon Henry Jackson served existing congregations with their printing needs, and also issued a Sephardic prayer book in 1826.

The end of the Napoleonic wars brought a period of political reaction in the German lands. Jewish rights, improved under French domination, were soon curtailed, and oppressive rule made life difficult for many Jews, especially those living in small towns and villages. With the United States having become known as a land of plenty and personal freedom, more and more of these Jews began to migrate to it. Most of these newcomers were very poor, with little general education, unmoved by liberal ideas or cultural aspirations. In their quest for security they settled mostly in the South and Middle West, although a good many remained in New York and other eastern cities. They began to earn their living as tradesmen and peddlers. At first with packs on their backs, and later with a horse and wagon, many of them went to farms and villages and sold the inhabitants goods not readily available locally. Their observance of Jewish ritual was of necessity haphazard, but as they prospered and settled in towns and cities, they in time formed congregations, lodges, and other religious and social institutions. Immensely grateful to their adopted land for benefits received, they gradually gave up their European way of life and adapted themselves to the social habits and activities of their Gentile neighbors. Yet few of them actually lost their Jewish identity by way of assimilation or apostasy.

After the failure of the revolutions of 1848, Jewish immigrants from Germany were not only better educated than their predecessors but were influenced by the ideals of current liberalism. Having been attracted to the advocates of Reform Judaism in their native land, they adhered to the liberalized ritual in their new home. Among them, moreover, were several rabbis who quickly became leaders in the establishment of Reform and Conservative Judaism in the United States.

Even earlier Isaac Leeser emerged as an outstanding rabbinic leader. He had migrated to Richmond in 1824 and joined an uncle in a business enterprise. One day in 1828 an article in the English *Quarterly Review* highly critical of the Jews so provoked him that he responded with a vigorous defense. His paper so impressed the officers of Mikveh Israel Congregation in Philadelphia that in 1829 they offered him the post of reader and cantor. Although Leeser was not an ordained rabbi, he soon became very active in the promotion of Judaism. He wrote much on liturgical subjects, and among his early publications was *The Jews and the Mosaic Law* (1833), with the subtitle indicating its content: "A defense of the Revelation of the Pentateuch, and of the Jews for Their Adherence to the Same." The volume was issued by Cary and Hart in Philadelphia, and included four essays on the relative importance of Judaism and Christianity, two of them by a "Professor of Christianity." In 1838 he brought out his *Hebrew Primer for Children.* Ever eager to spread the seeds of Jewish culture, in 1845 he helped to establish the first Jewish Publication Society, which brought out a number of books on Jewish subjects. Another of his achievements was the translation of Rabbi Joseph Schwartz's *Descriptive Geography and Brief Historical Sketch of Palestine* (1850), the first work of Jewish scholarship to be published in America.

In 1843 Leeser began to publish *The Occident and the American Jewish Advocate*, the first Jewish periodical since the demise of *The Jew* in 1825 and the only important one until 1854, when Rabbi Wise started *The Israelite.* The masthead stated that it was "a monthly periodical devoted to the Diffusion of Knowledge on Jewish Literature and Religion." In March 1859 it began to be issued weekly, but after April 1861 it again became a monthly. Its importance as a Jewish organ was evidenced by its wide readership. Among the frequent contributors were some of the most eminent Jews of the time. Leeser's own writings were first serialized in it before they were published in book form. Among the books by others to appear as serials in *The Occident* were De Rossi's *Dictionary of Hebrew Authors,* translated by Mayer Sulzberger, and Benjamin Dias Fernandes' *Evidences of Christianity* in a series of twenty-eight letters.

Although Leeser was one of the early rabbis to introduce preaching in English, he limited his innovations to the mild reforms of the Conservative ritual. Over the years he wrote much on Jewish subjects, but his major achievement was the translation of the Old Testament, which took him seventeen years to complete but which was widely read from its appearance in 1854 until the publication of a new and improved translation in 1917.

Rabbi Isaac Mayer Wise was the outstanding leader of the Reform movement during the second half of the nineteenth century. Born in Germany in 1819, he studied for the rabbinate and became an exponent of Reform Judaism. He reached the United States in 1846 and was soon engaged by a congregation in Albany. At his first opportunity he introduced family pews, sermons in German, and a mixed choir. Eager to establish these reforms on a wide basis, he wrote articles in their favor in *The Occident* and *The Asmonean.* When his radical innovations created a schism in the membership of the congregation, his admirers founded a new temple for him, and he remained their rabbi until 1854, when he accepted a call to Cincinnati. During this period he had striven to stabilize the chaotic character of the rituals then in practice by preparing *Minhag America* in 1847 and promoting it as a book of daily prayer. In 1855 it was approved, with a few changes, by the Cleveland rabbinical conference and remained in wide use until the adoption of the *Union Prayer Book* in 1894.

Within a month after he took charge of Cincinnati's Reform congregation, Wise decided to establish *The Israelite,* a weekly periodical favoring Reform Judaism. What he wanted in particular was to reach the relatively isolated Jews west of the Alleghenies in order to keep them informed about Jewish affairs. In his effort to obtain financial support for the weekly, he received many promises which were largely unkept. Eager to start it anyway, he arranged with his young brother-in-law, Edward Bloch, to form the Bloch Publishing Company to print it. Years later he described how he went about preparing the magazine's prospectus:

> I struggled very hard that night until I reached the following decision: come what may and how it may, I will not swerve a hair's breadth from my convictions. Either I will build up a Judaism suited to the age and breathing the atmosphere of American freedom, or I

Isaac Mayer Wise was the dominant proponent of Reform Judaism.

will be buried beneath the ruins of the old Judaism. I do not wish to be rich nor honoured, nor recognized, nor beloved. I will do my duty. I will remain true to my conviction.

Then I wrote the prospectus—short, concise, clear and fearless. I promised Judaism a sharp weapon. I promised progress, enlightenment, spiritual striving, a fearless organ.

Although the prospectus was received favorably, subscriptions were slow in coming. After a month of personal solicitation, less than five hundred persons agreed to subscribe. The initial issue consisted of a poem, various news items, Wise's sermon, and several articles of current interest. "I knew full well," he subsequently reminisced, "that every beginning was difficult; but I had no idea that the establishment of a Jewish weekly would prove as difficult as it did. Three things particularly were wanting, viz., confidence in the editor, secondly, writers, thirdly, readers."

When no novels came forth, as he had hoped, he decided to write them himself. Composing a chapter weekly despite his busy schedule, he in time completed *The Convert* and *The Shoemaker's Family*. He also wrote vigorous editorials on current affairs of Jewish interest. For years he agitated against a tacit assumption of political leaders that the United States was a Christian country, stressing the fact that the Constitution avoided any religious inference. He also opposed the teaching of religion in public schools, laws against doing business on Sunday, and various Blue laws. A summary of his position appeared in the issue of October 27, 1876; "This is a Democratic Republic and must be governed by honest men without hypocrisy or insolence, without religious lies and imposition, and also without Blue Laws, Sunday Laws, Puritan holidays, God's spiritual police hereabouts, Bible fanatics or other fanatics."

The Israelite (after 1874, *The American Israelite*) effectively fought Swiss prejudice against Jews; it also consistently opposed Russian oppression of Jews. When General Grant in 1862 thoughtlessly issued Order No. 11 excluding civilian Jews from army lines, Rabbi Wise quickly aroused opposition to it until President Lincoln rescinded it. While defending Jews and Judaism wherever slighted, he maintained that a Jew was Jewish only in his religion and American in every other way. During the

THE ISRAELITE.

A weekly Periodical, devoted to the Religion History and Literature of the Israelites.

PUBLISHED BY CHAS. F. SCHMIDT & CO., OFFICE: NO. 21, EAST THIRD STREET.

יְהִי אוֹר "LET THERE BE LIGHT"

EDITED BY ISAAC MAYER WISE, RESIDENCE: NO. 143, EAST THIRD STREET.

Vol. I. Cincinnati, O., July 15., 5614 A. M., 1854 A. C. No. 1.

THE CONVERT.

Chapter I.

At the eastern end of the Eger valley in Bohemia, and on the right bank of the river of the same name, a rock rises almost perpendicularly, forming the basis of the high plain, on which the old town of Koenigsberg proudly rests. The steeples of its churches are visible far beyond the Eger valley to the mountainous region, forming the boundary between Bohemia, Saxony and Bavaria. At the western end of Koenigsberg, perpendicularly above the Eger river, a few streets are located, which are inhabited by Jews, whose progenitors sought refuge in that solitary corner of Germany, when the crusaders made havoc among their brethren on the Rhine. In this town we enter [illegible]

[illegible] now converted into a [illegible] not even painted or ornamented, a small looking glass, a Misrach (marking the east side of the house for the purpose of prayer), and a book case [illegible] by the folio testimonies of Jewish industry were the contents of the room which together with two anti-chambers and a kitchen made the residence of Isaac Baum and his family.

Mother Hannah, a woman of about fifty-five years of age, sat at the table, gazing at an open letter which was rendered illegible by her tears, which still gushed forth in an unrestrained current. By her chair leaning stood a maiden in the prime of years; her rich and black curls falling around a pale but beautiful countenance, formed a peculiar contrast to her black and glittering eyes, in which a soul innocent and kind, now sorrowful and troubled, was reflected. Two or three times she opened her rosy lips, revealing two rows of pearls, attempting in vain to speak to her mother; but she never succeeded, affliction and surprise had bereft her of the kind words which she wished to address to her mourning mother. In the north-eastern corner of the room stood father Isaac Baum, with his face turned to the East and reciting the Minchah (afternoon prayer) with a loud and distinct voice, as if each word was intended to produce an effect before God. When repeating the answer, but the most painful emotions manifested themselves upon his troubled countenance. Rachel, however, who had stood motionless behind her mother, now spoke to her, praying her not to forget that two more children besides the one whose loss she was lamenting, loved her dearly, and were desirous to see her happy and submit piously to the incomprehensible decrees of Providence. Her voice trembled, she could speak no farther, and covering her eyes with a lily-white hand she stood again as a statue behind her mother.

Father Isaac was done praying, and sat down silently at the side of his consort. He had just opened his lips to speak, when the door was slowly opened and an old man [illegible]

[illegible]

"It has pleased the Lord" [illegible] Baum, "to [illegible] son; and I have called you to [illegible] in performing the mourning ceremonies as our sages have ordained, to invite the people to my house to prayer (Minyan) and to learn Shiur for him" (reading a portion of the Mishnah and reciting a prayer for the benefit of the departed). "Your son," exclaimed the old Rabbi, "the Doctor Moses Baum, that promising young man is dead? What [illegible] what is our life?" Then the old Rabbi directed his eyes towards heaven and said: "Blessed art thou Lord our God who is a truthful judge," and two tears rolled down the cheeks of the old sage. "O, that he was dead," exclaimed mother Hannah in the accents of wild agony. "O that the first son whom I bore unto my heart was dead, and I would pray for him day and night; but now not even the consolation of prayer is left to the bereft mother, I cannot pray for a Meshumed!" (an apostate). The silence of the grave reigned again in the room, the old Rabbi looked more like a petrified mummy than a living being; Isaac Baum had not the courage to lift up his eyes; mother Hannah leaned motionless on her daughter.

"I have nourished and brought up children and they have rebelled against me." Here his voice failed, but after a short pause he continued, "Your eldest son and my pupil whom we have brought up in the ways of righteousness and piety, and who was fondly loved by all and [illegible] has forsaken the ways of the Lord, abandoned his aged parents, and heaped upon them mountains of grief; he has abandoned his nation, and has no longer a part and possession in Israel. [illegible] I are innocent, our hands have not [illegible] the innocent blood, the God of Abraham, Isaac and Jacob will have mercy on you, and bless you with strength, to bear piously this misfortune, and [illegible]

[illegible]

of the mourning meal, the prayers were recited, the guests retired, and the family were left alone with their grief.

Zodek, the youngest son of Isaac Baum, was out on business. It was late in the evening when the young man returned home. "Shema Yisroel," exclaimed the young man on entering the room, and finding his parents and sister sitting silently and mournfully on the floor; and there he stood motionless for awhile. The old man pointed to the open letter on the table. Zodek seized anxiously the paper, and read for awhile, until it fell on the floor, and Zodek repeatedly exclaiming "My brother a Meshumed" ran violently about the room, finally he put off his boots, tore his coat and threw himself on the floor without saying one word more.

After Hannah and her daughter had repaired to the anti-chamber for the purpose of enjoying a night's rest, as well as a mourning mother and a weeping sister are able to partake of that blessing, Isaac Baum rose from the floor, and standing opposite his son, said with a troubled voice, "Zodek, I fear that I, and by thy advice, have driven my son to succeed in building up a reputation in the next three or four years. The [illegible] of Israel are always ready to make splendid promises to those whom [illegible] they lead astray; they have the power and the money, and we are feeble and but few in number; my son was lead astray, his circumstances pleased him [illegible] a step which he repents. Zodek, Zodek, I have driven my son to the Shmad, [illegible] by thy advice." Zodek gazed [illegible] unsteadily, not venturing to look [illegible] father's face; he was for awhile [illegible] to answer; the melancholy [illegible] his father had cut him through the heart and the consciousness of guilt had bound his tongue. It took him some time [illegible]

[illegible]

"We are [illegible] land to reside in this town, because we are born here, [illegible] there is no way for us in this [illegible] earn a piece of bread, we [illegible] Eger on Sunday and return on Friday, live there among strangers, far from our relatives an object of scoff and persecution to our neighbors. We are forced to pay a heavy tax for the privilege of getting a hard living by the sweat of our brows, again because we are Jews. If we abjure our religion, we may settle in Eger or elsewhere, may do what business we choose, and live [illegible] and respected, but God knows, I never forgot one of the three daily prayers, we lay Tephilin (phylacteries), wear Tzitzith (fringes), keep our Sabbaths and Holidays, and have never transgressed one of the six fasts. We never thought of abjuring our religion for earthly [illegible] Why did my brother not betray the same firmness?"

The old man was apparently dissatisfied by the force of this argument. Still after some deliberation he replied, "Whoever is where there his neighbors, is also more exposed to the temptations of

The Israelite, started by Rabbi Wise in 1854, was the most important of the early Jewish periodicals.

Civil War he was silent on the question of secession, as he had friends on both sides, so that he only prayed for peace. He continued to edit his weekly to the end of his life in 1900; his son Leon succeeded him as editor.

A year after he had begun to publish *The Israelite* Wise realized that a good many Jews he had hoped to reach were still unable to read English. For their benefit he brought out *Die Deborah,* an eight-page weekly in German, in which he included personal news, articles on various topics, and replies to foreign correspondents. In 1874–75 he serialized his *Reminiscences* in it, bringing it up to 1857. The weekly ceased to appear shortly after his death.

One of Rabbi Wise's great accomplishments was the founding of Hebrew Union College in 1875, which became the official seminary of Reform Judaism. The college also became a center for the study of Judaism, and many of its graduates not only filled numerous pulpits but also distinguished themselves as scholars and Jewish leaders. At present the college maintains the American Jewish Archives, which gathers valuable materials of all kinds relating to Jewish history and culture. Its numerous publications maintain a high standard of scholarship and further notably the research into Jewish thought and tradition.

With the rapid increase in Jewish population, the need for communication stimulated the establishment of numerous periodicals. In 1849 *Israel's Herold* was started in New York, edited by Isidor Busch, a recent arrival. Lack of funds, however, forced its suspension after several months. Another New York publication, *The Jewish Messenger* (1857), was started by Samuel Isaaks with the motto: "A messenger of good tidings, publishing salvation." Two years later Rabbi Jonas Bondi began to issue *The Hebrew Leader,* a weekly in English and German.

The fast-growing Jewish settlement in the area of San Francisco made possible the establishment of four periodicals: *The Hebrew Observer* (1855), a German and English weekly edited by William Saalburg; *The Gleaner* (1856), edited by Rabbi Julius Eckman; *The Jewish Times and Observer* (1858); and *The*

Pacific Messenger (1860). None had much circulation or influence and gradually disappeared, to be replaced by others much later.

A periodical of merit and influence, *The Asmonean,* was founded in 1849 by Robert Lyon, an immigrant from England. Its masthead proclaimed it as "A Journal of Commerce, Politics, Religion, and Literature, Devoted to the Interests of American Israelites." Lyon claimed it to be "the first American Jewish weekly of its kind." And at that time it probably was. It published poems, stories, articles on various Jewish subjects—but also on non-Jewish topics—odd items of news, and letters. Maintaining a relatively high cultural level, it included, for instance, a lengthy essay on Percy Bysshe Shelley from *The Edinburgh Review,* an incisive article on the then troubled relations between Russia and Turkey, and other pieces of similar import, copied from current periodicals. It also reprinted stories from such magazines as *Godey's Lady's Book;* an article from *The Southern Christian Advocate* entitled "The Unity of Human Races: Latest Views of Professor Agassis"; an essay titled "What Is Eastern Europe?" from *The British Quarterly Review.* Despite this serious intellectual fare, or perhaps because of it, the weekly's popularity began to wane after 1855 and was suspended after Lyon's sudden death in 1858.

Reform Judaism was notably affected by Rabbi David Einhorn. Born in Germany in 1809, he received his rabbinical credentials at the age of seventeen from the Orthodox seminary in Feurth. His enrollment in a local university antagonized his rabbinical teachers, as they feared it to be a first step to apostasy. For a decade, therefore, he was unable to obtain a rabbinical post. In 1842 a small Reform congregation employed him; but he continued to involve himself in controversy, and in 1852 he left for Pest, Hungary, to fill a post in a Reform congregation. After two months, however, the government closed the temple, charged with being inimical to the state. For the next two years he worked on a book entitled *Das Prinzip des Mosaismus,* but completed only the first volume when he received a call from Har Sinai Congregation in Baltimore. Assuming that in his new home he would be freed of conservative opposition, he proceeded to expound the aims and principles of Reform Judaism as he perceived them. The vigor and vehemence of his exposition quickly won him a position of leadership, but also the open opposition of less radical Reform rabbis—and Rabbi Isaac Mayer Wise in particular, who feared that Einhorn was endangering the unity of the Reform movement.

Rabbi Einhorn scorned any compromise with principle and persisted in his effort to radicalize Reform Judaism. In 1856 he began to publish *Sinai,* in German, in the hope of furthering his views. He at once encountered Rabbi Wise's opposition in *The Israelite.* Seeking unity and harmony within the movement, the latter attacked Einhorn's criticism of the Talmud as "slanderous and false." The two leaders aired their disagreements in their respective periodicals. Although Wise in time acquiesced in his opponent's position, Einhorn failed of dominance largely because of his insistence on expressing his views in long-winded German and failing to harmonize them with American conditions. Dr. Kaufmann Kohler later stated that the theological principles expounded by Einhorn in *Sinai* "are a mine of profound thoughts for the student . . . written in ponderous German and frequently in most involved sentences, placing them beyond the comprehension of the average reader."

In his effort to advance his kind of Reform Judaism, Rabbi Einhorn prepared a prayer book which combined the best elements of the ancient ritual with the ideals and needs of the modern Jew. Completed in 1858, the volume stressed Israel's world mission as a people of God and dwelt on the ideas of repentance and divine forgiveness. Because it was written in German, it failed of wide acceptance because by that time most Reform congregations preferred a Hebrew text with English translation. This handicap was later removed when Dr. Hirsch brought out an excellent English version. Rabbi Wise, impressed by its essential merit, included much of the material in the officially adopted Union Prayer Book.

Ever the crusader, Einhorn published religious and social articles in *Sinai* which attacked hypocrisy and fanaticism wherever they manifested themselves. He was an ardent opponent of slavery and condemned it as a crime not only against human freedom but also against God. At the start of the Civil War the mob spirit in Baltimore endangered his life, so that a bodyguard of friends had to help him flee the city on the night of April 23, 1861. He went to Philadelphia and was soon appointed rabbi of Kneseth Israel Temple. For a year thereafter he continued to edit and publish *Sinai,* and on its suspension he stated that "it died in the battle against slavery."

In Philadelphia, he published *Ner Tamid* (The Everburning Lamp), subtitled "The Teachings of Judaism for School and Home." The volume explained the subjects of revelation and prophecy. In 1866 he moved to New York to serve as rabbi of Adath Jeshurun Temple. In his sermons he dwelt longingly on an idea he had long cherished: the establishment of a Hebrew high school and a theological seminary.

Still the crusader, and continuing his effort to consolidate the principles of Reform Judaism, in 1869 he launched *The Jewish Times,* with Moritz Ellinger as editor. There he sought to give his ideas wider appeal, and prepared for it a series of lectures on his lifelong beliefs. He died in 1879.

The middle decades of the nineteenth century brought tens of thousands of Jews to the United States, primarily from German lands. New Jewish settlements were established in numerous towns and cities across the continent. It was natural for these newcomers to cling together as much as they were able and to form institutions and organizations to meet their specific needs. To bring them news of other Jewish communities in this country and in other parts of the world, they started periodicals—the nature of which depended largely on the men editing them. Some of these weeklies and monthlies have already been mentioned. Because their support remained precarious, a good many failed to survive more than a few months or several years; a number merged with those more firmly established.

On the Pacific coast *The Hebrew,* a German and English periodical started in 1863, continued to function to the end of the century. The first literary review, *The New Era,* was launched in 1871 and lasted four years. Also in 1871 Zwi H. Bernstein began issuing a Hebrew weekly which continued to appear regularly until 1905. Later other Hebrew periodicals were published for brief periods. In 1875 Henry Jones started *The Jewish Record* and kept it going for eleven years. Through the 1870s *The Hebrew Review,* another literary monthly, appeared in Cincinnati. In 1881 *The Hebrew Standard* was founded in New York to further Conservative Judaism and to favor the Democratic party during election periods. Henry C. Morais, son of the noted rabbi and drama critic of *The New York Ledger,* began in 1887 to publish *The Jewish Record* in association with Charles Hoffman. About the same time the early Zionists started *The Maccabean* as their political organ. The Independent Order of B'nai B'rith, in existence since 1843, founded *The Menorah* as a monthly magazine for the Jewish home. A later periodical, first called *B'nai B'rith Magazine,* then changed to *The National Jewish Monthy,* continues to the present to provide its large membership with news, articles, and discussions of interest to it. Frank J. Cohen, of Atlanta, was an exception among Jewish editors in his tolerance of lynching, dwelling on it favorably in *The Jewish Sentinel* from 1894 to 1900. An interesting phenomenon at the time was the appearance of *The American Jewess* in Chicago. It was published and edited by women, and contained fiction, verse, and general articles relating to women. Started in 1895, the periodical moved to New York in 1899, where it lasted another four years.

The foregoing list of periodicals merely exemplifies the media catering to Jewish readers during the second half of the nineteenth century. By 1900 these weeklies and monthlies had totaled 140 in English, 18 in German, 104 in Yiddish, and several in Hebrew—most of them ending their existence after a relatively brief period of fruitless struggle.

A notable exception was *The American Hebrew,* which was started in 1871 by Philip Cowan with the aid of F. De Sola Mendes. Cowan, who edited the weekly for twenty-seven years, stated at the outset: "Its editorial staff comprises men of diverse shades of opinion on ritualistic matters in Judaism, but men who are determined to combine their energies for the common cause of Judaism." Although he favored Orthodoxy over Reform editorially, he devoted the weekly's columns mainly to Jewish news the world over. He also sought to foster good will between Jews and Christians. In 1890 he devoted an issue to "A Concensus on Prejudice," with prominent scholars, writers, and religious leaders participating in the colloquy. Some years later, when news of Jewish persecution came from Rumania, Cowen sent David Blaustein to investigate the actual conditions, and his findings appeared in several lengthy reports. Firmly established as the leading Jewish periodical, *The American Hebrew* over the years absorbed *The Jewish Chronicle* of Baltimore (1880), *The Jewish Reformer* (1886), Rochester's *Jewish Tidings* (1895), and *The Jewish Messenger* (1902).

In his volume of reminiscences, *Memoirs of an American Jew* (1932), Cowan discussed his editorial activity at great length. Ready to retire in 1906, he sold *The American Hebrew* to a group of wealthy Jews. For the ensuing decade it was edited by the noted scholar Joseph Jacobs, who was a co-editor of *The Jewish Encyclopedia.* In 1916 he was succeeded by Herman Bernstein, a prominent journalist. Two years later Isaac Landman took over the editorship, and continued in that post until 1937, when Louis Rittenberg replaced him. By that time the weekly's circulation and influence had greatly diminished, and after a reorganization with the *Jewish Messenger* in 1956, it began to appear as *The American Examiner.* Never recovering its earlier prestige and stability, it was in 1970 absorbed by *The Jewish Week,* which in 1976 had the largest audited circulation of any English language Jewish periodical.

It should be stressed that the ephemeral nature of many Jewish periodicals was due not only to inadequate financial support but also to a lack of professional guidance. Most editors were men of good will or personal ambition but lacking in journalistic skill and breadth of view; eager to further the cause of Judaism but too inclined to please their patrons to adhere to journalistic independence. On balance, however, the influence of these periodicals on the Jewish communities they served was positive and salutary.

Bernard Postal, a veteran editor, stressed this effectiveness in his essay, "The American Jewish Press after 150 Years":

> A number of the editors of these papers have pointed out that the American Jewish newspaper, privately or publicly owned and regardless of its frequency of publication, is in effect the largest pulpit in town. No rabbi reaches a fraction of the number of people into whose homes the Jewish newspaper comes.

Books about Jews and Judaism continued to appear with more or less frequency during the first century of the Republic. Most of them were the work of pious Christian scholars who treated their subject with respect and even dedication but with the prevailing bias. The following two publications are fairly typical: *Hebrew and English Lexicon of the Old Testament Including the Biblical Chaldee* (1844), translated from the Latin of H. F. Genesius by Edward Robinson; and *Notes, Critical, Illustrative, and Practical, of the Book of Job:* With New Translation and an Introductory Dissertation, by Albert Barnes (1845). The serious scholarship of the latter volume was evidenced by an introduction of 126 pages and notes that extended the text to 311 pages.

Books written by Jews were few and far between, the several thousand Jews in the country at the founding of the Republic boasting of neither scholars nor men of letters. Mordecai Manuel Noah was the first Jew to produce work of literary consequence. Born in Philadelphia in 1785, largely self-taught, he early became a prominent journalist and popular playwright. David Longworth of New York in 1808 brought out his play, *The Fortress of Sorrento;* eleven years later he published *She Would Be a Soldier,* or The Battle of Chippewa. Other of Noah's plays were *Paul and Alexis,* or The Orphans of the Rhine; *Marion,* or The Hero of Lake George; *The Siege of Tripoli;* and *The Grecian Captive,* or The Fall of Athens. These plays, catering to the current taste, attained wide popularity. He also wrote *Travels in England, France, Spain, and the Barbary States in the Years 1813–1815, Discourses on the Restoration of the Jews,* and *Gleanings from a Gathered Harvest.* A proud Jew, he became one of the first Zionists in America and conceived a fantastic plan to establish a temporary asylum for the persecuted European Jews on an island near Buffalo.

Isaac Harby, a Southern journalist and Jewish leader, was also a successful playwright. At the age of seventeen he wrote *Alexander Severus* (1805). Two years later he produced *The Grecian Knot;* and the popular *Alberti* came out in 1819. He also wrote *Letters on the Presidency* (1821). A scion of a prominent family, Harby actively participated in Jewish affairs and was one of the leaders of the Reformed Society of Israelites, which campaigned for a shorter liturgy and the use of English in prayer.

Another Jewish dramatist of the period, S. B. H. Judah, wrote *The Mountain Torrent,* A Grand Melo-Drama in Two acts (1822); *A Tale of Lexington,* A National Comedy (1823); and *The Maid of Midian,* A Tragedy (1833). Henry Hart Milman, a scholarly historian, published two books: *The Fall of Jerusalem* (1820) and *The History of the Jews* (1822). Penina Moise of Charlestown, South Carolina, was a locally admired poet grown blind in her late years. She is best known as the chief composer of *Hymns Written for Beth Elohim Congregation* (1843).

The foregoing writers were of Sephardic origin. Michael Heilperin was the first Jewish writer from Eastern Europe. Born in Poland in 1823, he came to the United States in 1856 and quickly established his reputation as a journalist. For twenty years he was a frequent contributor to *The Nation;* he was also an editor of Appleton's *New American Encyclopedia.* His chief literary work was *Historical Poetry of the Ancient Hebrews.* At his death in 1888 he was highly regarded as a freedom fighter.

Adah Isaacs Menken, known best as an actress, also wrote poetry on Jewish themes. Born in Louisiana in 1835, she studied Hebrew along with her other school subjects. In 1856 she married A. J. Menken, but soon separated from him. Her second marriage, to the heavyweight champion John C. Heenen, was equally unsuccessful. After 1857 she made her reputation as an actress. *The Israelite* printed a number of her verses, one with the title "Hear, O Israel"—all later included in *Infelicia.*

Although Grace Aguilar (1816–1847) was a European writer of a Sephardic family, her fiction was read widely by readers in

Europe and the United States. Among her published books in this country were *The Perez Family* (1847), *The Vale of Cedars* (1850), *The Women of Israel* (1864), and *Home Scenes and Heart Studies* (1871). The Jewish content of much of her writing and her highly readable style made her a favorite author among Jewish readers. Her popularity gave her name to the library serving the Jewish population on the lower East Side of New York when it was formed in 1886. It should be pointed out, incidentally, that all books on Jewish subjects were published by non-Jewish firms.

The most prominent Jewish writer in the nineteenth century was Emma Lazarus. She came of an assimilated Sephardic family. Although her father was still sensitive enough of his background to resent anti-Jewish slurs, one of his daughters, Annie Humphries Johnson, had become an ardent Catholic living in Rome and was later quite irritated by her younger sister's Jewish activity. Emma herself at first felt little Jewish awareness, and her early verses were general in content and in imitation of the distinguished poets she admired. When the critic E. C. Stedman suggested that she turn to Jewish subjects, she told him that they did not appeal to her. Her first volume of poetry, *Poems and Translations* (1866), was printed privately, but it brought her the first of a number of friends among writers of eminence, especially Emerson and Browning. Another volume of verse appeared in 1871. Three years later she published a novel, *Alide: An Episode of Goethe's Life*. Her play, *Spagnoletto,* appeared in 1876. During these years she enjoyed her literary friendships but had gained little general recognition.

The Russian pogroms in 1881 so aroused her indignation that she suddenly felt her kinship with the victims. It was as if she had experienced a revelation, as if the dead embers of her Jewishness had miraculously flared into a passionate and glowing awareness of her closeness to the tragic yet glorious Jewish people. The urge to embrace this truth caused her to study Hebrew and to delve into the Jewish past. The verse she now wrote was mostly Jewish in content and was expressed with a freshness of emotion and literary glow that brought her wide acclaim. Many of these

Emma Lazarus reached her deepest poetic expression in her Jewish writings, which predominated her work after 1881.

poems appeared in *The American Hebrew* and were later published in *Songs of a Semite* (1882), and included the play, *The Dance of Death,* based on a massacre during the Black Death period of the fourteenth century.

When Longfellow, after visiting the Jewish cemetery in Newport, Rhode Island, wrote his poem about it containing the quatrain:

> But ah! what once has been shall be no more.
> The groaning earth in travail and in pain
> Brings forth its races, but does not restore,
> And the dead nations never rise again.

Emma Lazarus rejected this assumption as far as the Jews were concerned. In an article on the subject she stated:

> The rapidly increasing influence of the Jews in Europe, the present universal agitation of the Jewish Question hotly discussed in almost every pamphlet, periodical, and newspaper of the day, the frightful wave of persecution directed against the race, sweeping over the whole civilized world, and reaching its height in Russia: the furious zeal with which they are defended and attacked, the suffering, privation and martyrdom in the name of Judaism, prove them to be very warmly and thoroughly alive, and not at all in need of miraculous resuscitation to establish their nationality.

A series of articles, entitled "An Epistle to the Hebrews" and printed in *The American Hebrew,* gave strong emphasis to the pride in her Jewishness and her belief in the future grandeur of her currently persecuted people. It was in this spirit that she wrote her best-known sonnet, "The New Colossus," of which the following lines were graved at the base of the Statue of Liberty:

> . . . Give me your tired, your poor,
> Your huddled masses yearning to breathe free,
> The wretched refuse of your teeming shore,
> Send these, the homeless, tempest-tossed to me.
> I lift my lamp beside the golden door.

Her final work, *By the Waters of Babylon,* was completed in 1887, the year of her death.

2

The Jewish Publication Society

Until late in the nineteenth century Jewish scholarship in the United States was incidental and, compared with Jewish erudition in Europe, relatively unimportant. Much of the writing pertained to Judaic liturgy. Although the number of Jews continued to increase with the years, few devoted themselves to intellectual pursuits; the large majority were intent on acquiring material security and satisfied their spiritual needs with synagogue attendance. With rare exceptions the rabbis were too preoccupied with their efforts to affirm and standardize their particular brand of Judaism to delve deeply into the history of their people and the philosophy of their religion. And the few Jews who required intellectual sustenance obtained the works of scholarship being produced in Europe. Yet the urge toward cultural productivity was on the rise.

As early as the 1840s a small number of Jews in Philadelphia were interested enough in Judaic thought to encourage the publication of scholarly writing. Outstanding among them was Rabbi Isaac Leeser. Primarily devoted to the advancement of Judaism among his fellow Jews, but also eager to stimulate Jewish scholarship as well as book reading among them, he was helped to form a Jewish Publication Society for the purpose of bringing out books that would become the "proper weapons to defend it [the faith] against the assaults of proselyte-makers on the one side and of infidels on the other." Because the missionaries were then distributing their literature without charge, he hoped to place "a mass of good reading within the reach of even the poorest of families." With the cooperation of Solomon Solis and Abraham Hart—the latter a prominent publisher—Leeser established the Society in 1845 and planned to issue four inexpensive volumes annually in a series entitled The Jewish Miscellany.

The Society quickly found itself faced with the fact that there were not enough Jewish writers and scholars to provide it with the needed manuscripts. Leeser thereupon turned to England for books, by both Jews and Gentiles. Among the volumes he issued were two reprints from the writings of Grace Aguilar as well as works of a religious content. Although it was an uphill struggle from the first, Leeser managed to bring out 14 books by 1850. By that time the small membership had dwindled to a point that forced Leeser to postpone the publication of books that year. Then a fire in 1851 destroyed the Society's plates and printed books, thereby putting an end to its existence.

For the next two decades very little scholarly publishing was done within the Jewish community. By 1870 the intellectual climate had improved, owing largely to the newcomers after 1848, who were both better educated and more liberal than the earlier immigrants from Germany. This stimulated a second Jewish Publication Society in 1871. Among the founders in New York were Leopold Bamberger, B. J. Hart, Myer Stern, and Simon Wolf. They and others, still relatively few in number, were eager to further the writing and reading of books among their fellow Jews, and it was their hope to attract a large enough membership to make it possible for the Society to publish books on a self-sustaining basis. The five volumes it actually published are indicative of the kind of intellectual fare with which they expected to attract a hopefully growing membership: Heinrich Graetz's *History of the Jews,* volume four, translated by J. K. Gutheim; Wilhelm Herzberg's *Jewish Family Papers,* or Letters of a Missionary, translated by F. De Sola Mendes; *Hebrew Characteristics,* a selection of essays by William Lewis; Leopold Zunz's *Extracts from Jewish*

Moralists; Joseph Perles' *Jewish Marriage in Post-Biblical Times* and *On Interment of the Dead in Post-Biblical Judaism.*

The time for such an organization had not yet come, however. The hoped-for membership did not materialize. Then came the economic depression of 1873 and the Society was compelled to disband two years later.

From ancient times the Jews were rightly known as "the people of the book." A portion of them were always inherently motivated by a yearning for intellectual and spiritual stimulation. This stimulation had manifested itself more in the long-established Jewish communities of Europe, but was also beginning to appear to an increasing degree in the newer settlements of the United States. It was not surprising, therefore, that both the producers and consumers of learning, despite the failure of the first two efforts, should make a third attempt to establish a Jewish Publication Society.

On December 11, 1887, Rabbi Joseph Krauskopf of the Philadelphia Kneseth Israel Congregation preached a sermon in which he urged the formation of a publication society. The call was readily heeded by a number of public-spirited individuals. Several meetings were held, and a number of local Jewish organizations expressed interest in the project. The leaders thereupon issued a call for a national organizational meeting. Interested Jews from various cities answered the appeal, and the group met in Philadelphia on June 3, 1888. Morris Newberger was elected president, Rabbi Krauskopf secretary, and an executive committee of twenty from every part of the country was chosen to establish the third Jewish Publication Society, with meetings to take place biennially.

Two factors indicated that the time for such an organization had come. By the end of the 1880s Jewish learning had become firmly established, both in the rabbinical schools of Cincinnati and New York. Moreover, young American Jews and recent arrivals were by then dedicating themselves to intellectual pursuits within and without American universities. One example, remarkable but not atypical, will indicate how close Jewish learning in

America had come to that of Europe. In 1903 Rabbi Marcus Jastrow, who came to Philadelphia in 1866, completed his *Dictionary of the Targumim, the Talmud Babli, and the Midrashic Literature*. The work was printed in Leipzig in two large volumes totaling 1736 pages, and was published by Laizac in London and by Putnam in New York. The immense scope and tremendous erudition of the work may be gathered from the following quotation from the preface:

> The subjects of this literature are as unlimited as are the interests of the human mind. Religion and ethics, exegesis and homiletics, jurisprudence and ceremonial laws, ritual and liturgy, philosophy and science, medicine and magics, astronomy and astrology, history and geography, commerce and trade, politics and social problems, all are represented there, and reflect the mental condition of the Jewish world in the seclusion from the outer world, as well as in its contact with the same whether in agreement or in opposition.

The second factor was the increasing availability of Jewish men of wealth interested in cultural matters and ready to support them financially. Thus Jacob H. Schiff, the most generous of Jewish philanthropists, and Meyer Guggenheim, head of the affluent family distinguished by its cultural benevolence, each contributed $5000 to launch the work of the Society. Subsequently they and others assured the realization of editorial projects by providing financial assistance when needed.

The purpose of the Jewish Publication Society was made manifest at the outset: "The publication and dissemination of literature, scientific and religious works, and also the giving of instruction in practices of the Jewish religion, history and literature." The published books were to be distributed to members of the Society in accord with their annual fees. Others interested, individuals and organizations, could obtain the literature at specified prices. The editors sought to encourage scholars to undertake studies which they would not have been able to do without this stimulus. The Society also aimed to bring out in English translation old and new works of European origin which would not have become available otherwise—commercial publishing being what it is. And at first, also, the editors looked to Jewish scholars in England for guidance and cooperation.

By January 1889 the Society had 882 members from every part of the country. The membership grew steadily thereafter, receding and advancing in the manner of most cultural organizations, so that the number reached 2442 in 1890, 4501 seven years later, around 11,000 at its twenty-fifth anniversary in 1913, and achieved a record high sixty years later. By that time it had published over 700 books and distributed nearly 8,000,000 volumes to every part of the world, with most of them going to its American members.

Intent on producing books on Jewish religion and history and thought by the best-qualified scholars regardless of their origin or the language they wrote in, the Society has over the years brought out distinguished works of erudition and belles-lettres by writers from every part of Europe as well as from the United States. Significantly, its first book, issued on May 1, 1890, was Lady Magnes's *Outlines of Jewish History*, revised by M. Friedlander. A third edition was brought out in 1929, with additional chapters written by Solomon Grayzel. The book was long used as a text in Jewish schools.

The Society's first major project was the publication of an English edition of Heinrich Graetz's monumental eleven-volume *Geschichte der Juden*. Such an edition was already under way in London, with the rights to the translation controlled by F. D. Morcatta, the British philanthropist. The translators, working under the editorship of Bella Lowy, were using a specially prepared version by Professor Graetz. The Jewish Publication Society obtained the American rights, and Henrietta Szold adapted the English manuscript to American needs. By omitting the numerous footnotes and appendices of the German edition and by increasing the length of each volume, the American edition included about two thirds of the original work into five volumes. The first was published in 1891 and the fifth four years later. A sixth volume, prepared by Henrietta Szold and Philip Bloch, and published in 1898, contained a memoir of Professor Graetz, a chronological table of Jewish history, and a comprehensive index. In 1944 the Society published Ismar Elbogen's volume which brought the Graetz history up to date. Jewish readers found the work highly rewarding, so that it had to have numerous printings.

An estimate of its prestige and popularity is given by Joshua Bloch in *Of Making Many Books:*

> Graetz's *History of the Jews* is still the leading work on the subject in the English language. By the comprehensiveness of its scope, by the exhaustiveness with which it treats the pilgrimage of Israel through the nations and ages, by its rare combination of sound scholarship and critical acumen and by the perfect fusion of solidity of learning with popularity of style, it still remains unsurpassed by any work of its kind. Though not always objective, it is written with a spirit of enthusiasm and a tone of warmth that are contagious. It has become a classic in the literature of Jewish historiography.

Although this outstanding history made Jews aware and proud of their remarkable past, it was considered too detailed and erudite for many members. In time, therefore, the Society published several briefer histories. The first was *A History of the Jewish People,* by Alexander Marx and Max Margolis. This conjoint labor of two authors was written with the layman and student in mind. Its popularity was attested by new editions in 1934 and 1947, by several reprintings, and by translations into French and Spanish.

In 1947 the Society issued Solomon Grayzel's *A History of the Jews from the Babylonian Exile to the End of World War II.* A work of 837 pages, its purport was well described in the preface by the author who was long the Society's editor-in-chief:

> One of my reasons for writing *A History of the Jews* has been my desire to fortify the spirit and strengthen the determination of my fellow Jews to persevere in the path of our ancestors, and patiently and hopefully to labor for the welfare of mankind. The struggle against injustice, oppression and tyranny, the cooperative effort to expand the human spirit and the hope of achieving a better world for all humanity have been, to my mind, the historic task of the Jews.

Five years later the Society arranged with Professor Salo W. Baron to reissue *A Social and Religious History of the Jews,* an erudite multivolume work, first published in 1937, completely rewritten and greatly enlarged. The first two volumes were brought out in 1952, and the 14th appeared in 1975. An index to volumes

HISTORY OF THE JEWS

BY

PROFESSOR H. GRAETZ

VOL. I

From the Earliest Period to the Death of Simon the Maccabee (135 B. C. E.)

PHILADELPHIA
The Jewish Publication Society of America

This book, translated in condensed and revised form from the German, was a work of superior scholarship in Jewish history.

1–8 was issued separately. In the preface to the first volume Professor Baron stated that in rewriting this work he had abandoned some of his earlier views. "Many others," he continued, "had to be amplified and newly documented in such a way as to make the present edition to all intents and purposes a new book." He also quoted more fully from primary works "in order to acquaint the reader with the nature of the available sources." Although the study is not intended for the casual reader, its intensive scholarship provides both students and scholars with a basic history of high distinction. The Society also published Baron's *History and Jewish Historians* (1964).

The trustees of the Society have from the first stressed historic scholarship as fundamental to an appreciation of Judaism by the average Jewish reader. They have therefore encouraged historians to produce books on every aspect of Jewish history. Among the early publications were Gustav Karpeles' *A Sketch of Jewish History* (1897) and *Jews and Judaism in the Nineteenth Century* (1905), David Philipson's *Old European Jewries* (1894), Israel Abrahams' *Jewish Life in the Middle Ages* (1896), and S. M. Dubnow's *Essay in Jewish History* (1903). Each of these volumes has, of course, the stamp of the author's personal interpretation in the light of his research and reflection. Some later additions were Dubnow's three-volume *History of the Jews in Russia and Poland* (1916–1920), Joseph Jacobs' *Jewish Contributions to Civilization* (1919), Max Radin's *The Jews Among the Greeks and Romans* (1915), and Louis Finkelstein's *The Jews:* Their History, Culture, and Religion (1949), a work consisting of three volumes, with eminent contributors to every aspect of the subject. A trade edition was issued by Harper & Brothers.

Over the years the Society also published a number of books on specialized phases of Jewish history, each the work of an eminent writer on a subject that added fresh light on the variegated Jewish past. Among these books, selected at random, are Norman Bentwich's *Philo-Judeus* (1910), *Josephus* (1914), and *Hellenism* (1919); Louis Finkelstein's *The Pharisees* (1938); A. A. Neuman's *The Jews in Spain* (1942); Marvin Lowenthal's *The Jews of Germany* (1936); and Cecil Roth's *Venice* (1930), *A History of the Marranos* (1932, 1947), and *A History of the Jews of Italy* (1946). The Society's list from year to year included numerous books on Israel, Eastern Europe, and the United States, with those on various aspects of Jewish life in America predominating.

One of the important contributions to American Jewish culture made by the Society was the publication of *The American Jewish Year-Book*. Conceived by Cyrus Adler, it was projected as an annual demographic and sociological appraisal of problems and progress within the Jewish community as they occurred from year to year. The first volume appeared in 1899, and it has been issued uninterruptedly since—76 volumes in all. Each contains accurate and essential information on the year's events in the Jewish community in this country and abroad. The articles treat current topics with an objectivity and specificity that shed light on them for readers wishing to obtain a clear understanding of the issues involved. Thus, when Jewish conditions in Europe began worsening in the 1930s, the articles dealt at length with the actual acts of persecution in Germany and elsewhere. Each volume also includes memoirs of departed leaders of the Jewish community. In addition it provides directories of national organizations, lists of published books and periodicals, population statistics, informational appendices, an annual calendar, and a summary review of the year's events. These Year-books are therefore highly useful tools of research for the student of Jewish life and culture. The first ten volumes were issued by the Society alone; thereafter the American Jewish Committee became joint publisher.

The trustees of the Society were early aware of the need of an adequate and updated English translation of the Old Testament. The available one by Isaac Leeser was still widely used, but scholars felt it needed considerable improvement in both accuracy and clarity. They also indicated that while the King James Version was excellent in its language, it was neither entirely accurate nor suited to Jewish requirements. As Israel Zangwill had aptly stated: "The English of the Bible may be magnificent, but it is not always truth. The Hebrew concept is too often distorted by ignorance or prejudice." At a meeting on June 5, 1892, therefore, the trustees declared:

> We look forward to the time when the Society shall furnish a new popular English rendition of the book which the Jews have given to the world, the Bible, that shall be the work of American Jewish Scholars. . . . Resolved, That the Executive Committee be requested to examine the feasibility of issuing an English translation of the Bible, at a low price, for general use.

The Society appointed Dr. Marcus Jastrow editor-in-chief, with Kaufmann Kohler and F. De Sola Mendes as co-editors. The plan was to have each of the books translated by a competent Biblical scholar. For years little progress was made. In 1903 the Society published Kohler's translation of *The Book of Psalms.* It was favorably received, and *The American Jewish Year-book* considered it "a product of the highest scholarship, both as to literalness of translation and as to style." No other work of translation, however, was ready for years thereafter. When Jastrow died in 1903 and was replaced by Solomon Schechter, more progress was expected, but the procedure, carried on by correspondence, remained slow and complicated.

In 1906 the Central Conference of American Rabbis joined the Society in furthering the project. Agreement was soon reached in favor of a new plan in which the actual work of translation would be done by a board of editors. This board consisted of Cyrus Adler as chairman, and Schechter, Kohler, Joseph Jacobs, David Philipson, Samuel Schulman, and Max L. Margolis. The latter was made editor-in-chief, and the aim became not so much a completely new translation as an improvement upon those already available, primarily by the removal of obsolete words, errors and inaccuracies, and the Christological emphasis. The work was greatly expedited by a gift of $50,000 from Jacob H. Schiff.

These seven scholars worked, on and off, for seven years before the translation was completed and ready for the press. The procedure was for Margolis to prepare the text and for the board to edit and approve it—which they did in sixteen sessions of several days each. Where possible, they followed the Revised Version. Questionable words and phrases and the actual organization were closely considered and decisions were reached by general consensus. Publication was achieved in 1917—25 years after the project was initiated—and its appearance was met with highly popular approval, both in this country and in England. The following excerpt from the preface summarizes its character and purpose:

> It aims to combine the spirit of Jewish tradition with the results of Biblical scholarship, ancient, medieval, and modern. It gives to the Jewish world a translation of the Scriptures done by men imbued with the Jewish consciousness, while the non-Jewish world, it is hoped, will welcome a translation that presents many passages from the Jewish traditional point of view.

The book was reprinted numerous times, totaling upward of a half million copies.

More recently the latest linguistic research and new archaeological discoveries made a new translation advisable. Professor Harry Orlinsky, heading a group of eminent scholars, proceeded to prepare the new translation of the Pentateuch, which was published under the title of *The Torah: Five Books of Moses*. Professor Orlinsky included an account of the undertaking and gave an insightful explanation of the changes made in the new edition.

In 1975 the Society announced plans for a new English commentary on the Old Testament. The work will be undertaken by scholars in the United States as well as in Israel and will be based on the Hebrew text as newly translated by the Society. Dr. Nahum M. Sarna of Brandeis University will serve as general editor and Chaim Potok will be the literary editor.

The Society also brought out a number of important works dealing with the Talmud and other branches of Judaic literature as well as biographies of the rabbis associated with these writings. One of the most significant of such contributions was Louis Ginzberg's seven-volume study entitled *The Legends of the Jews* (1909–1938), most of it translated from the German by Henrietta

Szold. This is a complete collection of Agadic lore, revealing the imaginative efflorescence of Judaism. It was at once recognized as an epoch-making work of Judaic scholarship; a first attempt to gather from original sources all Jewish legends pertaining to Biblical persons and events, reproduced with erudite accuracy. The first four volumes dealt with the period from the Creation to Esther; volumes 5 and 6 contained notes and references for further study. A complete index was prepared by Boaz Cohen in volume 7. The originality of the work was stressed by *The American Jewish Year Book:*

> Written by one of the leading Talmudic scholars in the world, the work represents the first attempt to gather from original sources all the Jewish legends referring to Biblical personages and events, reproducing them completely and accurately. The work has been specially prepared for us, and though written in German, has never appeared in that or any other language.

Although these volumes were not written for the lay reader, their wide use necessitated reprintings from time to time, thereby making many Jews familiar with the imaginative literature of their ancestors.

The Society did not, of course, limit its publishing program to works of scholarship. From the first the trustees planned to bring out fiction, poetry, and biography—books that would entertain and inspire as well as instruct their membership. In 1890 the outstanding Jewish man of letters was Israel Zangwill. The editor communicated with him and arranged to publish *The Children of the Ghetto* in 1892. A portrayal of Jewish life in London's sordid slum of Whitechapel as well as the prosperous West End, the story includes an absorbing depiction of Jewish character, told with pathos and humor. The volume was widely read, and in 1895 The Macmillan Company brought out a trade edition. Years later Zangwill stated to the Society that he might never have written the novel if it had not encouraged him to do so:

> I do not speak merely of pecuniary stimulation. What was needed to draw this book from my subconsciousness was the wise and

DREAMERS OF THE GHETTO

BY I. ZANGWILL

PHILADELPHIA
THE JEWISH PUBLICATION SOCIETY OF AMERICA
1898

Israel Zangwill was the first Jewish writer in English to achieve world-wide prominence around the turn of the century.

understanding policy of your institution in giving the artist a free hand. It is the tragedy of the artist to supply what the public does not yet demand.

Zangwill's next book to be published by the Society was *Dreamers of the Ghetto* (1898). This volume consists of imaginary conversations and memories of prominent Jews who had rebelled against or had discarded Orthodox Judaism, men like Spinoza, Heine, and Disraeli. Here again Zangwill had manifested remarkable insight into Jewish characteristics. Of a less popular content than the novel, it was nevertheless highly regarded by many readers and required several reprintings.

The following year the Society issued a new edition of Zangwill's *Ghetto Tragedies* under the title *They That Walk in Darkness.* These tragedies, possessing flashes of fancy, irony, and humor, tend to arouse a compassion for the Jew.

In 1938, celebrating its Golden Anniversary, the Society issued a Golden Edition of Zangwill's works, which included the books which it had previously published plus *Ghetto Comedies,* which Macmillan had brought out in 1907.

The Society published fiction whenever it found it feasible, of which the following two are early examples: in 1892 it issued Louis Schnabel's *Vögele's Marriage,* containing sketches of European Jewish life. Eight yeras later it brought out Samuel Gordon's *Sons of the Covenant,* a story of two Jewish youths in England. It also arranged with Helena Frank, an Englishwoman who had become so interested in Yiddish writing that she learned the language well enough to translate some of it, to publish her translation of J. L. Peretz's *Stories and Pictures* (1906) and *Yiddish Tales* (1912), which served to introduce Yiddish fiction to the non-Yiddish reader. As Yiddish writing in the United States reached its wide popularity before World War II, the Society brought out translations of Sholem Asch's *Kiddush Ha-Shem* (Salvation, 1926) and *Shabbatai Zevi* (1930). When Joseph Opatoshu's *The Polish Woods* gained acclaim in both Europe and in this country, the Society issued a translation in 1938; fourteen years later it also published a translation of his fine historic novel,

The Last Revolt, which depicted life in Palestine in the time of Rabbi Akiba and Bar Kochba.

The Society published additional fiction and poetry from time to time. Among them were Ludwig Lewisohn's *Renegade* (1922); Charles Resnikoff's *The Lionhearted* (1944), a story about the Jews living in medieval England; Martin Buber's *For the Sake of Heaven* (1945), which deals with the life of Polish Jews in the time of Napoleon; Richard Beer Hoffmann's *Jacob's Dream* (1946); Selma Stern's *The Spirit Perturbeth* (1946); Soma Morgenstern's *The Son of the Lost Son* (1946), *In My Father's Pastures* (1947), and *The Testament of the Lost Son* (1949). In recent years the Society brought out other novels as well as stories for children. One of the latest publications was Moshe Spiegel's translation of Yoel Linetsky's classic story, *The Polish Lad,* an anti-Hassidic novel of more than a century ago.

Nor was Hebrew writing neglected. In 1915 the Society published a translation of Jehudah Steinberg's *In Those Days,* a story of Jewish life at the time of Nicholas I; Ch. N. Bialik's *Aftergrowth* (1939) contains a number of the great Hebrew poet's verses. In 1944 the Society also brought out A. M. Klein's *Poems,* thus giving due recognition to Canada's fine Jewish poet.

The Society's list of publications includes a good many biographies and autobiographies. An early example was Henry Zirndorf's *Some Jewish Women* (1892), containing sketches of notable women in post-Biblical history. Louis Ginzberg's *Students, Scholars and Saints* (1928) and Alexander Marx's *Essays in Jewish Biography* (1947) present evaluations of men who had contributed significantly to the enhancement of Jewish life and learning. Leo W. Schwarz's *Memoirs of My People* (1943) includes autobiographical selections of prominent Jews over a millennium. Among the fine biographies of eminent Jews are David Yellen and Israel Abrahams' *Maimonides* (1903), Maurice Liber's *Rashi* (1906), A. B. Rhine's *Leon Gordon* (1910), Henry Malter's *Saadia Gaon* (1921), Paul Goodman's *Moses Montefiore* (1925), Cecil Roth's *A Life of Menasseh Ben Israel* (1934) and *House of Nasi* (1948), Norman Bentwich's *Solomon Schechter* (1938), S. Posner's *Adolphe Cremieux* (1940), A. A. Neuman's *Cyrus Adler*

(1946), and Leon Huener's *The Life of Judah Touro* (1946). In recent years about ten additional biographies were added to the list, including such dissimilar notable figures as Don Isaac Abravanel, Abraham Cahan, Bernard Revel, and Leon Trotsky.

The Society continues to publish a number of books annually. In addition to *The American Jewish Year-book* it has recently brought out volumes on a variety of subjects, among them Eliyahu Ashtor's *The Jews of Moslem Spain,* Haim Hazaz's novel, *Gates of Bronze,* Simon Ravidowicz's *Studies in Jewish Thought,* Louis Harap's *The Image of the Jew in American Literature,* and Donald J. Moore's *Martin Buber.* It also continues to reissue some of the older books in paperback editions.

In 1912 Morris Loeb contributed $10,000 to the Society with the provision that "the income of which alone shall, from time to time, be utilized for and applied to the preparation and publication of a scholarly work devoted to the interests of Judaism." This income made possible the publication of such books as Louis Finkelstein's *The Pharisees and the Sociological Background of Their Faith* (1938) in two volumes, Salo W. Baron's *The Jewish Community—Its History and Structure to the American Revolution* (1942) in three volumes, and A. A. Neuman's *The Jews of Spain—Their Social, Political and Cultural Life During the Middle Ages* (1942) in two volumes.

James Loeb's gift to Harvard University for the publication of the Loeb Classics under its imprint very likely stimulated Jacob H. Schiff to endow The Schiff Library of Jewish Classics, to be published by the Jewish Publication Society. With $50,000 thus contributed in 1914, the Society was able to bring out a number of books, among them such works as Solomon Ibn Gabirol's *Selected Religious Poems* (1923), Jehudah Halevi's *Selected Poems* (1924), Joseph Albo's *Sefer Ha-Ikkarim* (1929–1930), Moses Ibn Ezra's *Selected Poems* (1934), *Ma-aseh Book* (1934), and Moses Hayyim Luzzatto's *Messilat Yesharim* (1936).

In the 1920s the trustees decided to start a Jewish Community Series in order to record the histories of various old centers of Jewish life. The first volume to appear was Ann Freimann's *Frankfort* (1929). Subsequent volumes were E. N. Adler's *Lon-*

don (1930), Cecil Roth's *Venice* (1930), Max Grunwald's *Vienna* (1936), Adolf Kober's *Cologne* (1940), Hermann Vogelstein's *Rome* (1940), and Israel Cohen's *Vilna* (1943).

An important phase of the Society's publishing activity was the establishment of a Hebrew Press. As early as 1914 Cyrus Adler, one of the Society's most energetic leaders, began to advocate the desirability of bringing out prayer books and other liturgic works in Hebrew. At the time the Society lacked the means to organize such a printing plant. Adler's persistence, however, soon enabled him to interest certain wealthy Jews in his proposal. In 1920 Schiff agreed to contribute $50,000, Louis Marshall gave $25,000, and another $25,000 was obtained in smaller donations. This capital made possible the establishment of the Hebrew Press. In time, enough Hebrew typefaces and printing machinery were acquired to make the press eminent in this language. One of its major achievements was to set by machine vowel points with consonants and Biblical texts with musical accents. It was thus able to produce various religious books in Hebrew to meet a growing need. Before long it also obtained types in various Oriental, Slavic and other foreign languages as well as five attractive faces in English—thereby becoming one of the best specialized printing presses in the country, with ten keyboard machines and five casting machines. In addition to printing the Society's books it also printed *The Jewish Quarterly Review, The Journal of Biblical Literature,* and various materials for scholarly organizations. In 1950 the Maurice Jacobs Press purchased the Hebrew press from the Society and has greatly improved its types and plant, so that it has come to be considered the finest Hebrew and foreign-language press in the world.

In the foregoing discussion mention was made of those books which best indicate the Society's scope and importance in the dissemination of Jewish literature. This listing was of course only a sampling of the upward of 700 books published by the Society. Among these works are studies of high scholarly content and literary merit, thus contributing mightily to the instruction and pleasure of Jewish readers everywhere.

In view of this publishing activity over eighty-five years, one must conclude that more than any other Jewish organization the Jewish Publication Society has fulfilled its aim of bringing the results of Jewish scholarly and literary writing to the Jewish community of America, broadening and deepening the cultural development of the Jewish reader. Again to quote Joshua Bloch:

> In spreading a knowledge of Jewish life and literature and in making that knowledge available in attractive literary form the Society is constantly endeavoring to satisfy a great need: it provided a strong bulwark against disintegrating forces in Jewish life in English-speaking Jewry which finds itself in the midst of an attractive culture and which comprises Jewish settlements in several lands. The work of the Society has exerted a most wholesome influence in these settlements. Indeed, it has contributed much to the raising of the intellectual level of English-speaking Jewry everywhere.

The current officers of the Society are A. Leo Levin, president; Bernard I. Levinson, executive vice-president; Maier Deshell, editor; and Chaim Potok, special projects editor.

3

Other Organizational Publishers

The intellectual atmosphere that prompted the formation of Jewish Publication Society also stimulated a number of Jewish scholars, in an unexpressed effort to establish their independence from European domination, to organize the American Jewish Historical Society. Its active proponents, aware of the rapid growth and increasing importance of the Jewish community in the United States, felt both a need and a curiosity to learn more about the early Jewish settlers and to establish a positive relationship between Jews and Gentiles in America. On June 2, 1892, they gathered in New York to form the Society. They elected Oscar S. Straus president and Cyrus Adler secretary. Its declared aim was to collect and publish materials concerning Jewish life and activities in America from the first arrival of a group of Jews in 1654 to the present.

One of the Society's first acts was to establish *The American Jewish Historical Quarterly*, thereby opening a means of publication to scholars interested in undertaking research in the field of American Jewish history. Soon every issue included essays of original research on specific topics or individuals pertaining to Jewish history. Many forgotten or obscure events and persons were rescued from oblivion and given the prominence of the printed record. Every year the four quarterly issues were bound in a volume which made a valuable addition to recorded American Jewish history. Many of the articles were later also combined into historical volumes on particular subjects or periods. Indeed, year after year the bound articles of the *Quarterly* added to a body of scholarly material on American Jewish history generally recognized as of the highest quality.

The Society kept increasing its collection of historical materials, and in 1903 this literature was housed in the library of the Jewish Theological Seminary. Some years later Dr. Lee M. Freedman of Boston, a lifelong active participant in the activities of the Society, and its president during 1948–1953, provided a legacy that enabled it to establish its own quarters. In 1968 the Society moved to Waltham, Massachusetts, where it became associated with Brandeis University. By 1970 its library, housed in its own building, had 42,000 books and pamphlets as well as important papers and letters by Jewish families from the early years of settlement to more recent times.

At present the bound volumes of the *Quarterly* are of inestimable value to students of American Jewish history. The originality and scope of the studies give evidence of the vast amount of research done by Jewish scholars. And while this is not the place to discuss the contributions in any detail, their richness of information and their enormous variety of content add incalculably to the story of Jewish culture in America. The Society has also published larger studies of great value. In 1904, in commemoration of the 250th anniversary of Jewish settlement in America, it issued a volume of addresses made on the occasion. Of unique importance is A. S. W. Rosenbach's *An American Jewish Bibliography* (1926), "being a list of books and pamphlets by Jews or related to them, printed in the United States . . . until 1850." More recently the Society issued Moshe Davis and Isidore S. Meyers' edition of *The Writing of American Jewish History* (1957), and Meyers' edition of *The American Jew in the Civil War* (1961). It also brought out *The Jewish Experience in America* (5 volumes, 1969), edited by A. J. Karp, and Martin S. Cohen's *The Jewish Experience in Latin America* (2 volumes, 1972).

Among the other books published by the Society in the area of American Jewish history are Sidney M. Fish's *Aaron Levy: Founder of Aaronsburg* (1951), Leon L. Watters' *The Pioneers Jews of Utah* (1952), Leo M. Hershkowitz's edition of *Wills of Early New York Jews, 1704–1799* (1962), and Hershkowitz's and Meyers' edition of *The Lee M. Freedman Collection of American Jewish Correspondence:* Letters of the Franks Family, 1733–1768 (1968). The Society has also brought out communal histories of Rochester, Utica, Minnesota, and New Orleans. These and other studies have in combination made the American Jewish Historical Society a prominent contributor to the cultural history of American Jewry.

Other large cities have also formed groups to promote Jewish history, usually of a local nature. The Chicago organization, for instance, made a listing of books of Jewish content available in the city's five libraries for the benefit of Jewish teachers and readers. Simon Radowitz, of the Chicago College of Hebrew Studies, edited the local *Pinkas*, a work dealing with the history of Jews in the Chicago area And Spertus College of Judaica, which prepares teachers of Hebrew, has a large library of Judaica and Hebraica.

As already stated, until some years after the Civil War the Jewish community in America was considered by European Jews in the western countries as an obscure, backward colony. Rabbi Leon Fram wrote:

> All the great Jewish institutions of Jewish life were to be found in Europe. American Jewry had virtually no institutions of its own; for its spiritual needs it was completely dependent on Europe. All of its rabbis, teachers and other religious professionals were imported from Europe. All its books and ritual objects were also imported from abroad.

Rabbi Isaac M. Wise, as was previously shown, early sought to remedy this situation. In 1873, as leader of the Union of American Hebrew Congregations, he was primarily interested in establishing the Jewish community in America as an independent entity. He knew, however, that this could not be brought about without a functioning rabbinical seminary, and in 1875 he founded Hebrew Union College. Equally essential to his thinking was the teaching of Judaic elements to children. This project was less simple of achievement. The available teachers, trained in Europe and not always having a mastery of English, seldom were able to appeal to the curiosity and interest of American-born children. Moreover, Rabbi Wise perceived the need of elementary textbooks adapted to the needs of children and youths attending American public schools. This required years of experiment and practice. The task was gradually undertaken by the faculty and graduates of Hebrew Union College, and in time they wrote books, hymnals, and texts that sought to attract and instruct Jewish children. One of the publications was the first four parts of *Junior Bible Stories* (1910).

In 1922 the Union of American Hebrew Congregations and the Central Conference of American Rabbis established a Joint Commission on Jewish Education, with Emanuel Gamoran, author of *Changing Concepts in Jewish Education,* as director. He was not long in preparing a complete curriculum for Jewish religious schools, with a program for books and equipment for class use from nursery through high school as well as courses and texts for adult education. He found gifted writers and encouraged them to prepare the needed texts, teacher's guides, and student workbooks. He also arranged with artists and illustrators to make the teaching materials esthetically appealing to the different-graded students. So successful was Gamoran in this undertaking that a number of the books were also used in Conservative and Orthodox schools. Subsequently, his successors have advanced the curriculum and study materials along the principles he had established. In addition texts were prepared for the study of Hebrew; also books on worship, ceremonies, holidays, social services, the Old Testament, and Judaic literature. At present this published material comprises around 400 books and film strips, the largest list of this kind in the country.

The value and applicability of this list may be gathered from a sampling of some of the popular juvenile texts: Lee L. Levinger's History of the Jews in the United States (1930) had 24 printings by 1971 and sold nearly 110,000 copies; Rose G. Lurie's *The Great March* (1931) has sold over 100,000 copies, and her *How the Jewish People Lives Today* (1936) 62,650 copies; M. Soloff's *When the Jewish People Were Young* (1936) sold 145,000 copies; Lenore Cohen's *Bible Tales for Very Young Children* (1936) 94,000 copies; Mamie G. Gamoran's *Hillel's Happy Holidays* (1939) 107,000 copies.

Among the books for youths and adults are the *Mah Tov* texts for teaching Hebrew, which were so well done that they are also used in Israel; Harry Essrig and Abraham Segal's *Israel Today* (1964), profusely illustrated and written with flair and enthusiasm, is one of the most attractive books on Israel and has sold around 82,000 copies; M. G. Miller's and Sylvan Schwartzman's *Our Religion and Our Neighbors* (1959), another highly popular work, has sold over 65,000 copies; Maurice Samuels' translation of Ch. N. Bialik's *Selected Poems* is a beautifully made book. These and other well-edited and attractive books make the publications of the Union of American Hebrew Congregations a valuable part of the literature of American Jewry.

The latest additions to its list, intended for the mature reader, enhance the Union's contribution. In January 1974 it published the first volume of a new commentary on the Torah by Rabbi W. Gunther Plaut. The purpose of this and succeeding volumes in the series is to help Reform Jews obtain a better understanding of their heritage. Rabbi Plaut will prepare the volumes on Numbers, Exodus, and Deuteronomy; Rabbi Bernard Bamberger will write the volume on Leviticus. Each volume will contain the Hebrew text and an English translation as well as commentaries and "gleanings" from earlier interpretations.

The Central Conference of American Rabbis, an integral part of Reform Judaism, began publishing its *Yearbook* in 1891. It is devoted mainly to the annual conference proceedings, and provides a valuable overview of the activities of the proponents of Reform Judaism. Among its contents are monographs, articles, and various appendices, all dealing with aspects of Jewish life and culture in every part of the world, thus becoming a valuable depository of modern Jewish history.

The Hebrew Union College began in 1875 with two students. It grew steadily in importance as the anchor of Reform Judaism. Some of its graduates became highly prominent rabbis and scholars, and their published writings went far to broaden and strengthen Jewish consciousness within the increasingly expanding American Jewish community. Its library in Cincinnati became the repository of many invaluable manuscripts and incunabula as well as tens of thousands of books on Judaism and Jewish philosophy. In the 1940s, when the College became united with the Jewish Institute of Religion, founded by Rabbi Stephen S. Wise, the library in New York added considerably to the Biblical resources of the combined seminaries.

The Hebrew Union College Press publishes the seminary's *Annual,* which is devoted to Biblical exegesis, Talmudic principles, Jewish art, Hebrew poetry, and other phases of Jewish learning. The Press's other publications are mostly the work of the faculty and graduates. In 1949, for instance, it brought out *Reform Judaism:* Essays by Hebrew Union College Alumni; *American Jewry, Documents, Eighteenth Century:* Primarily Hitherto Unpublished Manuscripts (1959), edited by the College's distinguished librarian Jacob R. Marcus; M. H. Stern's *Americans of Jewish Descent* (1960), a number of highly detailed genealogies of prominent early Jewish families.

The American Jewish Archives was from the first associated with and housed by the Hebrew Union College. Its founders aimed to collect, preserve, and make available for research miscellaneous material on the history of the Jews in the Americas. In its relatively brief existence it has accumulated much valuable original materials—its collection having become the largest of its kind. In 1948 it began to issue a semiannual publication devoted to the history of American Jewry. Each volume, in addition to various learned articles, gives a list of newly acquired manuscript accessions. From time to time it brings out books pertaining to its special field of interest. Among them have been B. W. Korn's *Eventful Years and Experiences* (1954), a series of documented research studies of American Jewish life in the nineteenth century; *The American Reaction to the Mortara Case: 1858–1859*

(1957), which discusses the forced conversion of a Jewish child in Papal Italy; and A. E. Levine's *An American Jewish Bibliography* (1959), a highly useful listing of books and pamphlets by and about Jews printed in the United States from 1851 to 1875, all in possession of the Cincinnati library.

The Jewish Theological Seminary of America, the stronghold of Conservative Judaism, was founded by Rabbi Sabato Morais in 1886. A year earlier, reacting critically to the Pittsburgh Platform of the Reform rabbis, he had issued a call for the establishment of a seminary in opposition to the teachings of Hebrew Union College. His energetic advocacy persuaded a number of Conservative rabbis to cooperate with him in the establishment of a more traditional seminary. At its formation he was elected president, and he headed it until his death in 1897. For the next five years the seminary functioned under an acting president. Then the eminent scholar Solomon Schechter was persuaded to leave his prestigious post at Cambridge University and assume the presidency. His prominence soon brought to the board of trustees several interested wealthy Jews, leaders in business and the professions, and their generosity enabled the Seminary to expand and to add to its faculty a number of eminent Jewish scholars. Its library was also greatly expanded and enhanced for research purposes by many valuable gifts. Judge Mayer Sulzberger, for instance, gave it a large collection of Judaica. In 1908 Jacob H. Schiff presented it with the library of Baron Ginsburg. In time, therefore, the library contained around 120,000 volumes and about 8000 manuscripts. In April 1966 a disastrous fire destroyed almost a third of its contents. Friends, neighboring institutions, and others helped to restore and replace much of the lost materials, and a new library and cataloguing system has made the library even more highly useful to numerous scholars.

The prestige of the Seminary inhered in the eminence of its faculty. Among the early scholars and theologians were Max Margolis, Cyrus Adler, Israel Friedlander, Alexander Marx, Israel Davidson, and Joseph Jacobs. Their writings over the years have been among the glories of Jewish erudition. Of interest is the fact that with the passing of time more and more of the additions to the faculty began to be selected from the Seminary's graduates—among them Boaz Cohen, Robert Gordis, H. Louis Ginsberg, and Hillel Bavli. The successors to the presidency, after Schechter's death in 1915, have been Cyrus Adler, Louis Finkelstein and Gerson Cohen. The Seminary's annual conferences, recorded in *Proceedings of the Rabbinical Assembly of the Jewish Theological Seminary of America*, throw light on the principles and practices of Conservative Judaism and add importantly to the religious history of American Jewry.

Although most of the writings of the faculty were published elsewhere, a number of highly erudite works were brought out by the Seminary. A listing of some of the books makes evident the high scholarship associated with the Seminary: Louis Finkelstein's *Jewish Self-Government in the Middle Ages* (1924) and *Social Responsibility in an Age of Revolution* (1971), L. M. Epstein's *The Jewish Marriage Contract:* A Study of the Status of the Woman in Jewish Law (1927), Max Kadushin's *Organic Thinking:* A Study of Rabbinic Thought (1938), Boas Cohen's *Law and Tradition in Judaism* (1939), Louis Ginzberg's *The Palestinian Talmud* (1941), Saul Lieberman's *Greek in Jewish Palestine* (1942), Alexander Marx's *Studies in Jewish History and Booklore* (1944), Abraham Heschel's eminent writings, and Gershom G. Sholem's *Jewish Gnosticism, Markabah Mysticism, and Talmudic Tradition* (1965).

United Synagogue of America is an organization inspired by and associated with the Jewish Theological Seminary. Formed in 1913, stimulated and advanced first by Schechter and after him by Adler, it aimed to further traditional Judaism by reviving and revitalizing Jewish learning and religious observance. From the first it concentrated on the religious education of Jewish youth. To make the tenets of Judaism palatable to American children, its leaders devoted their energies to developing an acceptable and effective curriculum. They also arranged for the training of teachers, the preparation of competent textbooks and supplementary materials, and they sought to inculcate in both parents and children an active desire for this education.

Solomon Schechter was the most eminent Jewish scholar of his time.

A COMMENTARY

ON THE

PALESTINIAN TALMUD

A Study of the Development of the Halakah
and Haggadah in Palestine and Babylonia

by

LOUIS GINZBERG

I

BERAKOT I AND II

NEW YORK
THE JEWISH THEOLOGICAL SEMINARY OF AMERICA
1941

An outstanding work of scholarship, brought out by the Jewish Theological Seminary.

In 1917, with World War I in progress and with Jews in Eastern Europe suffering grievously, many Conservative Jews were strongly moved toward the idea of Zionism by news of the Balfour Declaration of a Jewish homeland in Palestine. Cyrus Adler, president of the Seminary, remained strongly opposed to Zionism—as were most of the Reform Jews at the time—and resigned from the United Synagogue in protest. That did not, however, deter the other leaders of the organization from furthering the idea of a Jewish homeland in Ancient Israel. Their educational program subsequently included many books and text materials on Israel.

By 1920 there appeared a strong need for a prayer book "arranged for congregational participation and responsive reading." At the same time progress was also being made toward the further development of a curriculum that would serve the requirements of schools that met daily, thrice weekly, or only on Sundays. Among the numerous books the organization made available for these purposes were Shulamith Ish Kishor's *Primer in Biblical History*, Alexander Marx's *A Festival Prayer Book*, and Eugene Kohn's *Manual for Teaching Biblical History*. These and numerous other texts formed a body of teaching materials for the increasing number of Conservative schools.

The devastation of Jewish communities during World War II gave American Jews a strong sense of responsibility for the survival of Judaism. Members of the United Synagogue were acutely aware of this obligation. Many of them belonged to the third generation in America, and the Holocaust aroused their Jewishness—culturally more than religiously—to a greater extent than that felt by their parents. In this connection the historian Marcus L. Hansen stated what he considered a sociological law: "What the son wishes to forget, the grandson wishes to remember."

Will Herberg applied this thesis to his fellow Jews: "The third generation of American Jews, instead of somehow finally getting rid of their Jewishness, as the Italians were getting rid of their 'Italianness' and the Poles their 'Polishness,' actually began to *reassert* their Jewish identification and to *return* to their Jewishness."

This Jewishness was not, however, a return to the European ways of their grandparents, but rather to an Americanized version of Judaism. Conservative Jews began to develop synagogue centers, thereby transforming the synagogue, hitherto used solely for prayer, into spiritual, social, and cultural meeting places. The United Synagogue began to produce books, pamphlets, and periodicals which offered specific suggestions for programs that included activities in education and the arts. These synagogue-centers were soon functioning in every part of the country and attracted more and more Jews to their activities.

Concurrently, A. E. Millgram, the educational director, made use of previous experimentation in launching a series of textbooks which considerably improved the character of Jewish education. At his direction experienced writers produced teaching materials based on the latest pedagogical research. Some of the books, simple in style and attractively illustrated, made clear the origin and purpose of each of the holidays; others treated the history of the Jews and the lives of their leaders. Prayer books for every occasion and for various age groups were also made available. In addition the organization issued numerous volumes in music and dramatics. Harry Coopersmith's *The Songs We Sing*, for instance, is one of the most ambitious books of its kind, both in content and design, and has been deservedly popular. The study of Hebrew likewise occupies a prominent place in the curriculum—from flash cards for the beginner to advanced students. Nor is parent education neglected, and pamphlets indicate how they may best inform and interest their children in Jewish education and in the joys of the holidays.

The Burning Bush Press, sponsored by the National Academy for Adult Education Studies, is a division of United Synagogue. The thirty-odd books issued under its imprint were written by competent scholars on a variety of subjects pertaining to Jewish life and culture. The following volumes, selected at random, indicate the quality and scope of these publications: *Anthology of Medieval Hebrew Literature*, edited by A. E. Millgram; Israel Friedlander's *Past and Present;* Norman Bentwich's *Solomon Schechter;* Robert Gordis's *The Ladder of Prayer;* Moshe Silberg's *Talmudic Law and the Modern State;* Ben Zion Bokser's *Zionism and the Christian Predicament;* Cyrus Adler's *I Have Considered the Days;* and Boas Cohen's *Jewish and Roman Law.*

The United Synagogue and the Melton Research Center have joined forces to bring out a series of texts, student's manuals, teacher's guides, adult guides, and supplementary materials for use in the study of the Bible. United Synagogue has issued a Jewish Tract Series, edited by M. S. Wiener; also pamphlets on basic values, ideas, and practices of Judaism, written in a popular style by prominent authors. In addition it has developed a film library of 16 mm sound films of programs produced on television by the Jewish Theological Seminary in cooperation with the National Broadcasting Company for the Eternal Light program. All told, the educational and cultural activities of the United Synagogues add greatly to the scope and quality of Jewish education.

For a number of years it has been issuing the *United Synagogue Review* for distribution to its members. The quarterly contains in each issue a number of articles on subjects of direct and immediate interest to its readers, most of them written by rabbis out of first-hand knowledge, and several pages of news about members as well as about national events.

The Women's League for Conservative Judaism was founded in 1918 as an adjunct of United Synagogue. It now has around 200,000 members and 800 sisterhoods. *Women's League Outlook,* its magazine, is in many respects similar to the *Review,* except that the emphasis is on the woman's role in Conservative Judaism. The League also brings out books and pamphlets dealing with organizational aids, parliamentary procedures, administration of education—all aimed to train members for administrative and humanitarian services. Among the latest publications are Shonie B. Levi's and Sylvia R. Caplan's *Across the Threshold:* A Guide for the Jewish Homemaker, Rose Goldstein's *A Time to Pray,* Charles and Bertie Schwartz's *Faith Through Reason,* and Ruth and Milton Perry's *Kosher Cooking Unlimited.*

Dropsie College is another rabbinical seminary that added its share to the development of Jewish learning in America. Moses

Aaron Dropsie, a wealthy Philadelphian, in 1907 endowed a college, to bear his name, "for the promotion of and instruction in the Hebrew cognate languages and their respective literatures and in the Rabbinical learning and literature." Cyrus Adler accepted the office of president, and his successor was A. A. Neuman. From the first its faculty and students set a high academic level, and among them were a number who later produced serious works of Jewish scholarship. Mortimer J. Cohen wrote of them in 1957:

> They represent the building blocks out of which the Jewish historians of the future will some day create a universal Jewish history—a history composed not of legends, vague speculations and the idiosyncrasies of individuals, but of factual information weighed and evaluated in accord with the best standards of critical judgment and set down as authoritative knowledge.

Like teachers and graduates of the other Jewish seminaries, those of Dropsie University have produced books on the Bible, philosophy, theology, and Jewish law. In 1910 the college, located in Philadelphia, took over the English *Jewish Quarterly Review*, which had ceased publication two years earlier, and its issues have since mirrored the scholarly aspects of primarily American Jewish life and learning. Studies too long for the *Quarterly* were issued in a monograph series, open to scholars without regard to party or origin. Among the books issued under its auspices are A. A. Neuman's *The Jews of Spain*, in two volumes; Solomon Zeitlin's *Josephus on Jesus;* M. M. Zarchin's *Jews in the Province of Posen;* Cyrus H. Gordon's *Lands of the Cross and the Crescent;* Harry M. Orlinsky's *Ancient Israel;* and Judah Kaufman's *Rabbi Yom Tov Lippman Muhlhausen.*

Dropsie has also published new editions of *Apocrypha and Pseudepigrapha*. These writings have come down through the ages replete with misunderstandings. Written originally in Hebrew or Aramaic, they have been preserved in Greek and other translations, which resulted in misreadings and in misrendering of the original versions. The Dropsie editions were therefore an attempt to return to the original writings. Among the volumes made available were *The First Book of Maccabees, The Second Book of*

Maccabees, The Third Book of Maccabees, and *The Fourth Book of Maccabees,* in both Greek and English, and *Aritias to Philocratus.*

Although *The Jewish Encyclopedia* was brought out by Funk and Wagnalls, a non-Jewish commercial publishing house, it was in fact originated and largely financed by Jews as a work of scholarship. It was the brainchild of Isidore Singer (1859–1939), who came into prominence as an ardent defender of Captain Alfred Dreyfus, and who envisioned a world in which the ideals of the Hebrew prophets prevailed. When he conceived the idea of a Jewish encyclopedia as a means of providing generally accessable knowledge about Jews and Judaism, he at first vainly sought support from wealthy European Jews. In the United States he succeeded in arousing the interest of Isaac K. Funk, a pious Protestant minister whose reputation as a publisher was not of the highest but who earnestly sought to make available books of religious merit. Backed by the publisher, Singer proceeded to solicit financial assistance from Schiff and other wealthy Jews, and their contributions assured Funk against financial loss. Singer then began to enlist the cooperation of prominent scholars, Jewish and Gentile, as contributors. The grandeur and uniqueness of the project brought 600 of them to his aid. Among them were Cyrus Adler, Gotthard Deutsch, Louis Ginzberg, Richard Gottheil, Marcus Jastrow, Kaufmann Kohler, F. De Sola Mendes, Joseph Jacobs, and Crawford H. Toy. Jacobs, indeed, came from England to work with Singer on the editing and to translate articles written in foreign languages; he also wrote nearly 400 of the articles. Adler also assisted, and wrote 83 articles. The first volume was ready in 1901 and the twelfth five years later.

The Jewish Encyclopedia was at once hailed as a work of excellent scholarship and all-encompassing scope. It provided a record of the part played by Jews in the development of their religion and literature as well as in the expression of human thought and social progress. To quote from the preface:

> It endeavors to give in systemized, comprehensive, and yet succinct form, a full and accurate account of the history and literature, the

social and intellectual life, of the Jewish people—of their ethical and religious views, their customs, rites, and traditions in all ages and in all lands. It also offers detailed biographical information concerning representatives of the Jewish race who have achieved distinction in any of the walks of life. It will accordingly cast light upon the successive phases of Judaism, furnish precise information concerning the activities of the Jews in all branches of human endeavor, register their influence upon the manifold development of human intelligence, and describe their mutual relations to surrounding creeds and peoples.

Thus, when completely available in 1906, the *Encyclopedia* became the most important single depository of Jewish scholarship in the world. Its vast store of information tended to inspire scholars to complete planned projects or begin new ones, especially those men whose contributions had gained them a measure of eminence. Its appearance, moreover, furthered work on similar projects in other countries.

In the 1930s Isaac Landman, editor of *The American Hebrew,* began to plan an encyclopedia that would update and thus supplant the older one, then out of print. A man of great energy and drive, he soon interested many scholars in both the United States and Europe and obtained the support of Jewish organizations and wealthy individuals. With their cooperation and generosity, respectively, he was able in 1939 to publish the first volume of the *Universal Jewish Encyclopedia,* and the tenth appeared five years later. Although the numerous contributions were generally by scholars of established reputation, the new work did not receive the commendation and popularity of its predecessor. In 1948 a new edition was started, with Louis Rittenberg as editor-in-chief. Scholars from fifty countries contributed articles, and the finished project was fully informative—containing 12,500 articles, extending to 7000 pages, and including 4200 illustrations.

Encyclopaedia Judaica is the latest achievement in this field. Prepared in Israel, with Cecil Roth as editor-in-chief, it is a work of distinction, more comprehensive than the previous encyclopedias, and a definite contribution to Jewish scholarship. The work, in 16 volumes, was for a time distributed in the United States by the Macmillan Company. Keter Publishing Company, which brought it out in Jerusalem, has also prepared a one-volume updated edition, *Encyclopedic Dictionary of Judaica,* which is now marketed in this country by Leon Amiel. It is amply illustrated, contains maps and charts to clarify the 15,000 condensed items of international scope and basic information.

Yeshiva University, the citadel of intellectual Orthodoxy in America, grew around the nucleus of the Rabbi Isaac Elchanan Rabbinical Seminary, which was started in 1897 as the first Orthodox yeshiva in New York, primarily for immigrant youths eager to study for the rabbinate. As it developed its curriculum it increased the scope of its educational activity. In 1915 Rabbi Bernard Revel assumed the presidency, and under his aegis the institution began a process of expansion. Teachers Institute, founded by the Mizrachi Organization in 1917, became a part of Yeshiva College in 1922. Six years later the College consisted of a high school, the Teachers Institute, a secular college, and the seminary.

In the course of time Yeshiva College acquired a fine faculty, with Rabbi Joseph B. Soloveitchik as its most distinguished member. Rabbi Revel died in 1940, and three years later Rabbi Samuel Belkin was chosen as his successor, and dominated the activities of the university until his retirement in 1975, when he became its first chancellor. With its secular divisions expanded considerably, the College attained university status in 1945. It now includes the Ferkauf Graduate School of Humanities and Social Sciences, the Belfer Graduate School of Sciences, the Wurzweiler School of Social Work, the Albert Einstein College of Medicine with its affiliated hospital, and the Stern College for Women. Its latest addition, the Benjamin N. Cardozo School of Law, will be organized by Monrad G. Paulsen, formerly dean of the University of Virginia Law School, as vice-president for legal education.

Yeshiva University sponsors seven periodicals and a number of books. Among the latter publications are Belkin's *Philosophy of Purpose* and *Essays in Traditional Jewish Thought,* E. Berkovits's *A Jewish Critique of the Philosophy of Martin Buber,* M. Luban's *Kaddish,* N. Rosenbloom's *Luzzatto's Ethico-Psychological Interpretation of Judaism,* I. Jakobovits's *Jewish Law Faces*

Modern Problems, S. Roth's *Science and Religion*, D. S. Shapiro's *Studies in Jewish Thought*, and Fred Rosner's *Modern Medicine and Jewish Law*. Although these and other similar studies are obviously for the scholar rather than the lay reader, they definitely contribute in good measure to the pool of Jewish scholarship produced in America during the past half century.

Ephraim Deinhard belonged to no organization or school of learning, yet he contributed greatly to the cultural wealth of Judaica. Born in Russia in 1846, he early became an ardent bibliophile with a consuming ambition to bring to light the early Jewish writings. As a young man he managed to visit every part of Europe, and particularly the Eastern and Southern parts, in search of books and manuscripts. Without means of his own, he paid his way as a middleman, selling some of his discoveries in order to have the money for further searches. His hope was to interest wealthy Jews to purchase his discovered treasures for placement in established libraries. To assure the success of his efforts, he had prominent scholars certify the authenticity of his findings. In the process he wrote three books of travel in which he related where and how he came upon his rare discoveries.

In 1888 he migrated to the United States. Finding few Jewish libraries and very few of the older books anywhere, he resolved to enrich the existing libraries of his adopted land with rare books and old manuscripts of a Jewish content and to stimulate the establishment of new libraries. "It is my hope," he stated, "that in the course of time I shall succeed in disseminating Jewish literature in this barren country. . . . If a Jewish scholar needs an ancient text, he must go to Europe, to the British Museum or to the Bodleyan Library in Oxford." Having brought with him a large collection of his rare findings, he began to look for interested wealthy Jews willing to purchase them for one of the newly established Jewish libraries. He soon found an ideal patron in Judge Mayer Sulzberger, a lover of books who had long been interested in bringing to Jewish libraries part of the bibliographical wealth of Europe. Once satisfied with Deinhard's probity and ingenuity, he began to purchase old books and manuscripts from him. In the first few years of their association he bought over 600 manuscripts and thousands of books. In 1901 he was able to donate to the library of the Jewish Theological Seminary 2400 rare books and over 700 manuscripts plus the J. S. Halberstamm library of 5000 volumes which Deinhard had bought for him. Eight years later Deinhard enabled him to present the Seminary library with 364 Ladino volumes printed in Hebrew characters, 185 American imprints, and another 500 manuscripts.

Deinhard had for some time wanted the Library of Congress to possess a Judaica division. In 1912 he succeeded in interesting Herbert Putnam, director of the Library, in the idea of such an addition. At an early opportunity Putnam discussed the project with Jacob H. Schiff, and the philanthropist agreed to purchase Deinhard's collection of 10,000 volumes for presentation to the Library. He also set aside a sum of money for the maintenance and servicing of this collection, with a Jewish scholar in charge. Two years later Schiff added 4200 volumes to this collection, all bought by Deinhard. Not long after, the indefatigable Deinhard enabled Schiff to add another 2300 items, thus making the Judaica division of the Library of Congress one of the largest in the country.

Deinhard continued his wordwide search for Jewish bibliographical material to the end of his long life. He made his home in New Orleans, and the house he occupied was bursting with books in every available space. Now and then he sold a part of his treasure to an interested benefactor. A year before his death in 1930 Professor Harry A. Wolfson, the occupant of the Hebrew Professorship at Harvard University endowed by Lucius N. Littauer, persuaded his benefactor to purchase Deinhard's collection for presentation to the Harvard University library, thus enriching it by 12,000 books of Judaica plus 29 manuscripts and 16 incunabula (11 in Hebrew and five in Latin). This collection was later augmented by the Felix Friedmann library of 15,000 volumes of Hebraica and Judaica, in the acquisition of which Lee M. Freedman had assisted. Subsequently Freedman presented his own large collection to the library, as did Professor Leo Wiener and Dr. A. A. Roback—thus providing the Judaica division of Harvard with over 100,000 volumes.

More than any one individual, therefore, Deinhard succeeded

in enriching American libraries with many thousands of rare books and ancient manuscripts of Judaica. An acutely conscious Jew, he took an active interest in current affairs. The emergent idea of Zionism in the early 1880s caused him to write in Yiddish *America oder Palestiner Eretz Isroel.* While in the United States he followed Jewish events with keen attention and expressed himself on them in Yiddish journals. His importance as a bibliographer of Judaica was well indicated by Professor Alexander Marx:

> Deinhard was a curious personality. A great lover of books, he traveled all over the world, particularly in the Near East, in the quest of rarities. How he managed to obtain some of these unique rarities I do not know, but undoubtedly a considerable number would have perished in the disorder of the last decades if Deinhard had not found them a safe resting place in the great Jewish and general libraries, both here and abroad.

Although Deinhard did not contribute directly to the Jewish Division of the New York Public Library, its Judaica collection is among the largest in the country. It was started in 1897 by grouping the books of Jewish content in the Lennox and Astor libraries into a separate unit. A. S. Freidus, a graduate librarian, was placed in charge. The division was greatly enriched by the accession of the Leon Mandelstaum library of St. Petersburg bought by Jacob H. Schiff. He also provided the division with funds for later acquisitions. Other additions, among them around 500 volumes of rabbinical responsa from the Meyer Learen library and the Judaica collection of the Aguilar Free Library, brought the total number to about 110,000 volumes. Freidus and his successors Joshua Bloch and Abraham Berger helped to enlarge the division and to make it a research center for the largest number of active scholars and writers.

The American Jewish Committee was organized in 1906 by a group of prominent wealthy Jews of German origin with the following aim:

> To prevent the infraction of the civil and religious rights of Jews, in any part of the world; to render all lawful assistance and to take appropriate remedial action in the event of threatened or actual

invasion or restriction of such rights, or of unfavorable discrimination with respect thereto; to secure for Jews equality of economic, social and educational opportunities; to alleviate the consequences of persecution and to afford relief from calamities affecting Jews, wherever they may occur.

In 1910 the Committee joined the Jewish Publication Society, as already mentioned, in sponsoring research work and publication of the *American Jewish Year Book,* which has since been appearing annually and providing valuable information on interpretation of Jewish events the world over. After World War II the Committee subsidized the publication of *Commentary,* a successor to *Contemporary Jewish Record,* a monthly which has become one of the leading cultural periodicals in the United States. In addition it has recently started *Present Tense* and has sponsored such works as the multivolumed *Studies in Prejudice and other Sociological Studies* (1910), *The Communal Organization of the Jews in the United States* (1930), which contains many useful tables and figures on communities, organizations, religions, as well as educational and cultural data. Nathan Schachner's *The Price of Liberty* contains a history of the Committee.

The American Academy for Jewish Research was formed in 1919 to foster and promote the cause of Jewish learning and research. It was incorporated in 1929 with Louis Ginzberg as president, and consists of around thirty Fellows, some of them of great prominence. It holds, in addition to special meetings of the Fellows, periodic public meetings at which learned papers are read and discussed—with the first gathering taking place on December 27, 1928, at the Jewish Theological Seminary. Its annual *Proceedings* began to be published in 1930, and they have included a number of essays on scholarly subjects of Jewish interest. The diversity and depth of these studies have been especially notable in the medieval field, of which fifteen articles were recently included in a volume edited by Robert Chasan. Among the publications which the Academy has financed and sponsored are Guido Kirsch's *Jewry-Law in Medieval Germany,* critical editions of such classical texts as *Midrash Leviticus Rabbah* and the tractate Ta'anit of the Babylonian Talmud. The erudite character of the

Academy is reflected in the scholarly stature of the men who have headed it: Salo W. Baron, Louis Finkelstein, Alexander Marx, and Saul Lieberman. It is maintained by contributions from members and institutions in every part of the United States.

In 1925 Fanny Goldstein (1886–1961), a branch librarian in a Boston Jewish neighborhood, initiated the idea of a Jewish Book Week by preparing a modest exhibit of Judaica during the week of Hannukah. This exhibit she repeated from year to year, attracting more attention each time. In 1927 Rabbi S. Felix Mendelsohn published an article in the Chicago *Jewish Sentinel* urging a country-wide observance of an annual Book Week, thus giving the idea widespread attention. Hannukah was suggested as the appropriate time because it was a holiday of gift-giving, and the hope was that books would become the preferred presents. In the 1930s the National Jewish Welfare Board, an organization formed in 1917 to care for Jewish service men but later expanding its activities to include cultural affairs, became active in furthering the program of an annual Jewish book month.

The destruction of Jewish communities in Europe during World War II, with Jewish scholars killed and libraries demolished, a number of Jewish bibliophiles in the United States in 1942 formed the Jewish Book Council with the aim of starting "a Jewish renaissance in America." One of their objectives was to further the spread of Jewish books. To this end they sought:

> To infuse in both young and old the traditional ardent zeal for Jewish knowledge through reading the Jewish classics as well as contemporary works.
>
> To encourage the establishment of Jewish book shelves as an integral part of the home environment.
>
> To help augment Jewish book collections in libraries and synagogues, schools, centers, and other institutions, and to stimulate their utilization for enriching club programs, study circles, discussion groups, and the like.
>
> To make available books of Jewish interest for promoting reciprocal interfaith understanding and cooperation.

One of the first actions of the Council was to invite Yiddish and Hebrew organizations to participate in its program. In 1943, with the Jewish Welfare Board agreeing to support it, the Council decided to extend the Book Week to a month and greatly to energize its promotion on a national scale. With the cooperation of affiliated organizations and most rabbis, it publicized its program in synagogues and community centers. In discussing this activity in an article entitled "Literary Self-Education," Solomon Grayzel stated:

> The idea of devoting a period of time to the dramatization of Jewish book-reading has met with general acclaim and numerous achievements beyond the hopes of its originators. The idea acquired permanency through the foundation of the Jewish Book Council which has the adherence of every Jewish organization in the country. It gained nationwide sponsorship by becoming an integral part of the National Jewish Welfare Board. It won a place for itself in every Jewish community. The youngest among Jewish observances in the country, Jewish Book Month may yet become one of the most popular. The only explanation for the enthusiasm with which it has been received is that the idea of encouraging the reading of Jewish books answers to a deep-felt need in American Jewish life.

Sponsored by the Jewish Book Council, *The Jewish Book Annual* became, with its appearance in 1942, a major source of information concerning the year's publication of all books of Jewish interest in English, Yiddish, and Hebrew. Experienced librarians prepared bibliographic lists of books in each of those languages. In addition the *Annual* includes articles on Jewish writers in every part of the world, especially in celebration of an anniversary or in commemoration of a recent death. Certain articles also deal with various aspects of and activities in the tri-lingual literatures. The unique value of the *Annual* was indicated by Mortimer J. Cohen: "They bring together, under the skillful guidance of experts in various literary fields, a plethora of facts, ideas, tendencies and interpretations that help to understand better the creative Jewish spirit and the creators of Jewish values." And the American Library Association declared in its *Subscription Book Bulletin:*

> All in all, the Jewish person has in the Jewish Book Annual an excellent guide to the year's reading on Jewish interests. The non-Jewish reader is given an insight into the program and activities of

the Jewish Book Council as well as an acquaintance with the current Jewish book production.

The activities of the Jewish Book Month include exhibits, lectures, and author-autograph parties. Special events, like the Jewish Tercentenary in 1954, the tenth and twenty-fifth anniversaries of the establishment of Israel, were made the occasions of special exhibits and programs. The council arranges annual meetings at which certain writers are given awards and a number of libraries receive citations of merit. The Council also holds exhibits of Jewish books at meetings of public libraries and publishers associations in order to promote the availability of Jewish books.

In 1945 the Council began to publish *Jewish Bookland,* which provides brief reviews of new books in English, Yiddish, and Hebrew. In the beginning these reviews were written by Mortimer J. Cohen and Solomon Grayzel in a four-page issue. As the demand for it grew, other reviewers were invited to contribute. In time it became a supplement to the *Jewish Welfare Board Circle,* with a circulation of 20,000 copies. The number of pages was increased, and prominent scholars now provide essay reviews of one or more books of special interest. Rabbi Philip Goodman, the associate editor, who has for many years been the dedicated and highly competent director of Council activities, has well described the work of the organization: "Born in the dark, dismal days of the European *Hurban,* the Jewish Book Council of America has been mindful of the value of Jewish books as a source of strength and understanding for our struggles, our martyrdom and our hopes."

One reason for the success of the Jewish Book Council has been the support it received from the Jewish Welfare Board. The officers of the Board perceived that with the tragic Holocaust in Europe, Jewish world leadership had shifted from the old Jewish centers to the new. It was therefore incumbent upon them to accept the responsibility to the extent that they could. Originally formed to serve the cultural interests of the Jewish armed forces in World War I, it had prepared a prayer book acceptable to all Jewish creeds, a condensed Bible, a book of Psalms, and J. H.

Hertz's *Book of Jewish Thought*—all for use by soldiers. In 1921 the Board had reorganized itself as a permanent cultural institution to assist old centers and develop new ones. It became affiliated with the Young Men's Hebrew Associations and began in 1922 to publish *The Jewish Center*, a quarterly.

In the 1940's, faced with the shift of responsible Jewish leadership, the Board commissioned Professor Salo W. Baron to prepare a study of the altered situation in Jewish life. In his report Professor Baron stated that the shift has of necessity taken place "even in those areas of Jewish culture which had long been entrusted to the older centers of Jewish life in central Europe." He further indicated that American Jews were readily assuming their new responsibility. "There are incontestable signs not only of a general cultural awakening, but of a certain eagerness of the Jewish public to pioneer in the unexploited realms of a modern culture, which would be both Jewish and American." In the light of this evaluation, the Board assumed its share of the new responsibility. In colleges and Jewish centers, its main area of activity, it sought to stimulate and further the study and development of Jewish American culture. In 1948 it took over the sponsorship of the American Jewish Historical Society and its annual publications, the aim of which, as indicated earlier, was "to collect and publish material bearing upon the history of America, and to promote the study of Jewish history in general, preferably so far as it is related to American Jewish history." The Board continued, of course, to give its full support to the Jewish Book Council, as well as the Jewish Music Council.

Although the adult Jewish Education Division of the Fraternal Order B'nai B'rith was established relatively recently, B'nai B'rith itself, as previously stated, is the oldest Jewish organization in America. It was started in New York in 1843 with several members and with the grandiloquent motto: "Benevolence, Brotherly Love, and Harmony." With the passing of the years it grew to be the largest and most influential Jewish fraternal organization in the United States. Although it always paid lip service to cultural interests, it was only in 1923 that it began to sponsor Hillel chapters in colleges. Inspired by Edward Chauncey Baldwin and started by Benjamin Frankel after the earlier Menorah Society lost its appeal to students, the Hillel Foundation has formed branches in scores of colleges and disseminates a knowledge of Judaism to their members.

The education division of the B'nai B'rith published several series of popular books for the purpose of familiarizing Jewish readers with the classics of Jewish literature as well as with the principles of Judaism. The Jewish Heritage Classics Series, for instance, consists of ten volumes and includes such works as Norman Lamm's *The Good Society; The Hunter and Hunted,* edited by Gerd Korman; *The Sephardic Tradition,* edited by Moshe Lanzar; Hermann Cohen's *Reason and Hope,* edited by Avraham Holtz; *The Mishnah,* edited and translated by E. J. Lipman; *Rashi,* edited and translated by Chaim Pearl; and *Judaism and Human Rights,* edited by Milton R. Konvitz. The series was first distributed by Norton and is now marketed by Viking Press. Its Great Books Series contains three volumes on the outstanding Jewish personalities from ancient times to the present, a reader in contemporary Jewish thought, and a discussion of the great Jewish ideas. Other of its publications are A. J. Wolf's *What Is Man?* an Anthology of excerpts from Jewish traditional thinking on human existence; Simcha Kling's *A Sense of Duty,* replete with classical advice on realistic problems. The adult education division also produces study packets in paperbacks on problems of Jewish interest and two records from the writings of Isaac Babel and Maurice Samuel. All of these publications are prepared for the general reader and add positively to the cultural development of B'nai B'rith members.

Torah Umesorah, the National Society for Hebrew Day Schools, publishes a large number of textbooks, workbooks, pamphlets, supplementary readings, film strips, and other materials for use in Jewish day schools. These publications range from the elementary Hebrew primer to the study of the Torah, Rashi, and other advanced elements of Judaic study and ritual. Many of the texts are in English, and a number of the books and manuals, film strips and cassettes, teach the meaning and procedures of such observances as the making and use of Tefillin and Mezuzahs, the baking of Matzohs, and the like. The publication division of Torah Umesorah is active in the promotion of Hebrew education, and its materials are used in almost every part of America.

The Jewish Reconstructionist Foundation was established in 1940, and its Reconstructionist Press was started soon after. Rabbi Mordecai M. Kaplan was its founder and has been the moving spirit until recently. Rabbi Ira Eisenstein is now its president and active leader. An offshoot of Conservative Judaism, the Foundation seeks in its publication program, as do the foregoing organizations, to "further enrich American Jewish culture." It is of interest to note that of the books published by the Reconstructionist Press, twelve are by Rabbi Kaplan—works of erudite thought from his own particular point of view on Judaism in America. Other books are by Eli Ginzberg, Meir Ben-Horan, W. J. Cahnman, Stanley Rabinowitz, Ira Eisenstein, Eugene Kohn, and Arthur Gilbert. The Press also publishes *The Reconstructionist,* a monthly, which presents the ideas and events of the group as well as articles of a more general nature. Over the years the Press has brought out a half dozen books on education, seven on the arts, five cantatas, and nine volumes on Jewish liturgy. All this material is of solid distinction and furthers a knowledge of Jewish thought and religion from Rabbi Kaplan's Reconstructionist point of view.

The American Zionist Federation has been for many years active in its promotion of the Zionist idea. During these years it has published a number of books and pamphlets as well as periodicals in English, Yiddish, and Hebrew—with the latter language predominating, and with *Midstream* its most important magazine. To facilitate its publication program, the Zionists established the Herzl Press in 1958. The education department has brought out works on the Holocaust, Hebrew literature, texts on the Torah, the Talmud, and the arts. It also participated in the publication of the recently published *Encyclopaedia Judaica,* prepared and printed in Israel.

Among the books issued by the Herzl Press are James T.

Farrell's *It Has Come to Pass,* a Gentile's reactions and observations while on a visit to Israel; *The Herzl Press Year Book,* edited by Raphael Patai; A. Hertzberg's *The Zionist Idea;* F. Zweig's *The Israeli Society and the Israeli Worker; Zion in Jewish Thought,* edited by A. S. Halkin; E. Rosenberger's *Herzl as I Remember Him;* Ben Halpern's *The American Jew:* An American Analysis; a new edition of Mordecai M. Kaplan's *A New Zionism;* and Leon Simon's *Ahad Ha'am.*

The establishment of Israel in 1948 has in a sense fulfilled the goal of the Zionists, but it has also stimulated them to greater effort furthering Israel's cause and associating Israel with cultural Jewishness in the United States.

Soon after World War II The Leo Baeck Institute was founded by the Council of Jews from Germany for the purpose of collecting material on and sponsoring research into the history of the Jewish community in German-speaking lands from the time of the Emancipation in the eighteenth century to its decline and dispersion and destruction under the Nazis. The Institute was named in honor of the rabbi who was the last representative leader of German Jewry in the Hitler period. Born in 1873 in Lissa and the son of a rabbi, Baeck rose to prominence as a Reform rabbi and communal leader. When Hitler came into power and intensified his anti-Jewish crusade, Rabbi Baeck refused to leave Germany while Jews remained there. During the war years he suffered the horrors of a concentration camp, but somehow he managed to survive. After 1945 he left for England, where he devoted himself to Jewish scholarship and writing until his death in 1956. Branches of the Institute were established in London, New York, and Jerusalem.

The library of the New York branch has become the largest center of documentation of German Jewish history. The early periodicals in its possession were discovered at the end of the war in a German railroad car. The Nazis had filled it with Jewish printed materials and left it somewhere between Bavaria and Czechoslovakia. The periodicals date from 1837, and the National Endowment for the Humanities has given the Institute a grant of

$60,000 to microfilm these historically valuable magazines. The library also contains nearly a hundred collections entrusted to it by German Jews. At present the library has about 50,000 volumes, 700 periodicals, 550 unpublished memoirs by German Jews from 1790 to 1945, and letters and manuscripts from 150 literary estates. Its archives contain important collections of photographs, paintings, and engravings of documentary and artistic value. Numerous students and scholars use it regularly.

The Institute frequently holds seminars on subjects of interest to its members. In 1958 it began the Leo Baeck Memorial Lectures, each delivered annually by an eminent Jewish scholar and published in New York. It also has periodic exhibits of the life and work of prominent German Jews, among them Kafka, Einstein, Heine, Nellie Sachs, Max Liebermann, and Lesser Ury. Its *Bulletin,* a quarterly in German from 1957 to 1969, included essays on German Jewish life essential to an understanding of its complex history. In 1960 it began publishing *News* for its members.

The Institute's *Yearbook* was started in London in 1956 and was of course available in New York. The essays in it emphasize the Institute's ethical and scholarly orientation and are the work of notable contributors. Each annual volume is devoted to a main theme, such as The Legacy of German Jewry (1957), Men and Ethics (1958), Profiles of 20th-Century Jews (1960), Jewish Fighters for Equal Rights (1962), Jews Amidst Political Turmoil (1968), and Focus on Weimar Jewry (1971).

The American University Presses are of course not Jewish, but they have been publishing numerous books of Jewish content, many sponsored and subsidized by Jews. Yale University Press, for example, has been publishing a Judaica Series of scholarly importance, most of them by Maimonides. Yale has also brought out Louis Greenberg's *The Jews of Russia,* a two-volume history, and numerous other individual works.

The Harvard University Press publishes The Loeb Classics, endowed by James Loeb, and some of the volumes are on Jewish subjects. It also publishes, via Philip B. Lown's Institute of Advanced Jewish Studies, four volumes edited by Alexander Altman.

Among the other Jewish books with the Harvard imprint are the important works of Professor Harry Wolfson, Ben Halpern's *The Idea of a Jewish State,* Hugo Mantel's *Judaism in the First Century of the Christian Era,* and V. A. Tcherikover's *Corpus Papyronim Judaicorum.* More recently it brought out R. J. Clifford's *The Cosmic Mountain and the Old Testament,* George Nickelberg's *Resurrection, Immortality, and Eternal Life in Intertestamental Judaism,* and Yonina Talmon's *Family and Community in the Kibbutz*—to list a few books at random.

Princeton University Press has brought out the 13-volume work of Professor E. R. Goodenough's *Jewish Symbolism in the Greco-Roman Period,* three volumes on the Old Testament, and numerous other studies of Jewish content.

Wayne University Press in Detroit was given the Morris and Emma Shaver Publication Fund to bring out noteworthy Jewish studies, and eight volumes have already appeared. The University of Chicago Press has published many books on Jewish subjects, among them G. E. Wright's *The Challenge of Israel's Faith,* Nathan Glazer's *American Judaism,* Robert Gordis's *The Root and the Branch,* Shlomo Pines's edition of Maimonides' *Guide to the Perplexed,* and Jerome Mintz's *Legends of the Hasidim.* Columbia University Press has also issued a good many books on Judaica: Salo W. Baron's *A Social and Religious History of the Jews* (in cooperation with the Jewish Publication Society), Moses Hadas' translation of Joseph Ben Meir Zabara's *The Book of Delight,* W. R. Farmer's *Maalus, Zealots and Josephus,* Eli Ginzberg's *Agenda for American Jews,* and various other works of a similar content.

It is of interest that the relatively small Case Western Reserve University Press sought to bring out an English translation by Bernard Martin of Israel Zinberg's monumental 12-volume *History of Jewish Literature;* after the fourth volume, however, it had to be taken over by Ktav under a subsidy. Equally significant is the fact that the University of Alabama Press is issuing a Judaic Study Series with Professor Leon J. Weinberger as general editor. Five books have already been published and additional works are under contract or consideration.

The foregoing listing is only a sampling of the books published by these and other university presses which add importantly to Jewish literature in the United States.

When the nature and extent of the books, pamphlets, and periodicals mentioned in the last two chapters are considered as a whole, one cannot but be impressed by the tremendous effort made by American Jews over the past century to expand and enrich their cultural heritage. Nor must one overlook the fact that as part of the literature and scholarship produced in this country, it is a major contribution to American multi-ethnic culture.

4

Commercial Publishers

In 1854, when Rabbi Isaac Mayer Wise was eager to start *The Israelite* and had difficulty finding a cooperative printer in Cincinnati, he helped his young brother-in-law, Edward Bloch, who had worked for a printer, to set up shop for himself with the new weekly as a customer. This was the beginning of the Bloch Publishing Company. For years thereafter Bloch was busy printing, in addition to *The Israelite,* prayer and other liturgical books for the growing Jewish community of the Middle West. Many of these books were printed in German, along with Wise's *Die Deborah,* for use by Jews who still did not know English. Bloch of course published all of Wise's own writings, among them *Minhag America* in 1857 and *The Essence of Judaism* four years later.

Bloch published liturgical books for Orthodox as well as for Reform Jews, but he also brought out works by lay writers. Thus when the Mortara case was news in 1860, he issued H. M. Moos's drama, *Mortara,* or The Pope and His Inquisition. Soon after that he brought out a little play about Queen Esther by Julius Ochs, father of the future owner of the New York *Times.* In 1873 he began publishing *The Sabbath Visitor,* a periodical for children edited by Isidor Wise and later by Bloch's son Charles. He also brought out *The Hebrew Review,* a Reform magazine for rabbis. These and other printing activities made the Bloch firm a dominant publishing factor in Middle Western Jewish activities.

Charles Bloch entered the business in 1878, and three years later he assumed its management. Ambitious to expand his activities, he in 1888 opened a branch office and bookstore in Chicago under the name of Bloch Publishing and Printing Company. He described it at the time as the "publishers of, importers and dealers in Hebrew books and Jewish publications." He also announced his ability to sell "Jewish supplies of every description." In 1891 he began to print *The Reform Advocate,* edited by Emil Hirsch, a leading Chicago rabbi.

Although Bloch's business grew with the increase of the Jewish population in Chicago, he realized at the end of the 1890s that he had miscalculated in assuming that Chicago would become the largest center of Jewish residents. With his father having completely retired by then, he decided in 1901 to move the Cincinnati and Chicago branches of the firm to New York, which then and later had the largest Jewish population. Enterprising and energetic, he opened a large bookstore, filled with available Jewish books, texts, and various religious articles. He also increased his publishing program. Although other Jewish publishing companies were being formed then and later, the Bloch firm long remained the largest and most comprehensive producer and seller of Jewish writings, both in English and in Hebrew. It brought out such classics as Leopold Zunz's *The Suffering of the Jews During the Middle Ages,* edited by G. A. Kohut (1907), various juveniles, and pietistic volumes. The firm also became the agent for various European Jewish publishers, importing the more specialized works and reprinting books that had commercial appeal.

In the late 1920s the Bloch firm began to issue its *Book Bulletin,* a promotional bimonthly which featured news items pertaining to Jewish books, literary information, obituaries of writers, and similar material. It included advertisements of its own books as well as of books by other publishers. Another of its features was the listing and description of books on Jewish music, both religious and secular, which the store had for sale; these works were highly popular and provided about a third of the firm's sales. The *Bulletin* was issued for many years and was read by a large clientele.

Charles Bloch was naturally closely connected with Reform rabbis, and published many of their writings, but as a publisher he of course considered favorably any manuscript which in his judgment would yield him a profit. Among the books appearing under his imprint were Joseph Leiser's *American Judaism* (1925), Lee J. Levinger's *Anti-Semitism in the United States* (1925), Rabbi H. G. Enelow's *Menorat Ha-Maor* in four volumes (1929–1932), P. Masserman and M. Baker's *Jews Come to America* (1932), Max J. Kohler's *Immigration and Aliens in the United States* (1936), M. A. Gutstein's *The Story of the Jews of Newport* (1936), and Horace M. Kallen's *Of Them That Say They Are Jews* (1939). These are of course only a sampling of the firm's publications, and some of them were no doubt subsidized, but they give an idea of the firm's activities.

When Charles Bloch died in 1940, his son Edward, who had been assisting him for some time, continued the business along the lines established years ago. Among the books he published were S. Broches' *Jews of New England* (1942), Lewis Browne's *The Wisdom of Israel* (1945), M. A. Gutstein's *Priceless Heritage:* The Epic Growth of Nineteenth-Century Chicago Jewry (1953), Isaac Zaar's *Rescue and Liberation:* America's Part in the Birth of Israel (1954), A. J. Feldman's *The American Jew:* A Study in Backgrounds (1959), H. U. Ribalow's *The Jews in American Sports* (1959). To celebrate the firm's centenary in 1954, Bloch published thirteen books—their merit indicated by the following random examples: Albert Weisser's *The Modern Renaissance in Jewish Music,* Sol Liptzin's *The English Legend of Heinrich Heine,* J. B. Agus's *Guideposts in Modern Judaism,* and B. D. Cohen's *Judaism in Theory and Practice.*

Edward Bloch retired in 1968 and was succeeded by his son Charles. By this time the firm's large and crowded bookstore had become an increasing liability owing to the changing conditions of its location and of its clientele. More than ever the business was depending on its mail order sales. Charles Bloch therefore gave up the store and moved to a loft on Broadway, which housed his book stock as well as his publishing office. In 1970 he began to bring out a list of paperbacks, most of them taken from his backlist.

Although the Bloch Publishing Company had by then to meet keen competition from several active competitors, and although its more recent annual lists have not maintained the importance of earlier ones, the company's prestige and popularity as the literary commissary for the Jewish community has served to keep it in its primary position in Jewish publishing. Some of its latest publications are: J. B. Agus's *High Priest of Rebirth;* a biography of Rabbi A. I. Kuk; B. Laiken's *Memoirs of a Practical Dreamer;* Fred Rosner's *Modern Medicine and Jewish Law;* Max Kadushin's *The Rabbinic Mind;* Arthur Holde's and Irene Heskes' *Jews in Music;* Jacob Katzman's *Jewish Influence on Civilization;* and a new edition of Edmond Fleg's *Why I Am A Jew.*

Of approximately 2000 titles the firm has issued during its 120 years of existence, 350 remain on its active list. Its place in Jewish publishing was well stated by the Jewish Book Council on the occasion of its centenary:

> The Bloch Publishing Company has, for a century, been a source of instruction and inspiration for American Jewry. Periodicals, prayer books, Bibles, and about one thousand titles on every aspect of Jewish life and literature, in Hebrew and in English, for children and adults, have carried its imprint into every Jewishly conscious home. [It] won for itself a distinctive place among Jewish publishers both in the books which it accepted and those which it initiated. For there have always been authors whose books did not appeal to commercial publishers because they did not give promise of immediate success or to idealistic publishers because they did not correspond to their planned program. Such authors went to Bloch, and for half a century the Bloch Publishing Company has acted as literary midwife for scholarly, semi-scholarly and popular books which ended by exercising a considerable influence on the development of Jewish life in the United States.

In 1901 Joseph L. Werbelowsky was operating what he called the "oldest and largest Hebrew book establishment of America." Ambitious and aggressive, he was tempted by the idea of publishing books as well as selling them. He therefore persuaded three other booksellers to join him in forming the Hebrew American Publishing Company, with himself as president, H. Dogin as vice-president, M. Chinsky as treasurer, and David Werbelowsky as

Joseph L. Werbelowsky founded the Hebrew Publishing Company in 1901, which from the first dominated the publication of Hebrew and Yiddish books. Most of its current books are now in English.

secretary. They combined their book stores into one and began to plan the publication and importation of books. Much of what they had for sale were pamphlets, a variety of religious articles, liturgical books imported from Europe, and some Yiddish fiction. At this time almost all of it was in Hebrew or Yiddish. The 1902 catalogue, for instance, lists 1314 items, with prices ranging from 1½ cents for a book of *Kinoth* to $96 for a Torah with jeweled ornaments. The second half of the catalogue lists 451 items of a general content, from all types of Yiddish fiction to texts in elementary English. An undated catalogue of about that time was devoted to "Jewish music for piano and song," with items extending to 81 pages and giving evidence of the eagerness with which immigrant parents sought to inculcate a love of music in their children.

In the 1900s publishing and bookselling were still a combined enterprise in this country. Firms like Scribner, Putnam, and Dutton continued to maintain both functions for many years, and Scribner still does. Among the few Jewish publishers this practice was even more general. Thus the store operated by Hebrew Publishing Company catered to its largely immigrant and Orthodox clientele by placing on sale every type of book and religious article for which there was a likely demand. Thus, in addition to books and pamphlets it sold *etrogim, lulavim, taleitim,* Torahs, New Year cards, and the like. Cards were very popular at the time because newcomers felt a need to communicate with relatives and friends in the old country, and sent cards to them at the time of Rosh Hashanah and other occasions. To meet this demand, the store had an assortment of as many as 500 cards. When David Werbelowsky was sent to Europe on a buying trip soon after the company was organized—with a total expense account of $200—he was instructed to buy "New Year cards, candlesticks, mortars, slaughter knife stones, etc." Orders for Yiddish books were sent to the Romm firm in Vilna. An order for 1200 *etrogim* was cabled to Trieste.

As the store's business grew, it had for sale every kind of Judaic book for prayer, study and amusement. On its shelves were, for instance, several editions of the Pentateuch, each with the Hebrew text and with commentaries in Yiddish, English, or German. A similar diversity obtained for prayer books. It also sold volumes of popular science, humor, and drama. Yiddish ("Jargonic") romances, adapted and translated from world fiction or original stories by hack writers, were highly popular at the time. Dictionaries and songbooks were likewise in great demand. Sheets of music for the piano and the violin were featured in the firm's catalogue, which said in 1902:

> We, the publishers of "Jewish music," feel fully rewarded in having catered to Jewish taste, Jewish spirit and feeling, and we are getting ready to publish many more popular Jewish operas, which will appear soon; also new operas as they are staged in the Jewish theater.
>
> We hope that Jewish music will occupy a much larger place in the Jewish world than Christian music, since the Jew loves everything that is beautiful and Jewish.

Although the company began with limited capital and relatively modest salaries for its officers, it soon prospered enough to make possible a doubling of salaries—with the president receiving $4224 for the year. In 1907 Werbelowsky arranged with Alexander Harkavy, the lexicographer, to prepare a dictionary of Yiddish-English by paying him a thousand dollars for the publishing rights. The work proved highly popular and was subsequently reissued in several revisions. Fourteen years later Harkavy was paid $600 to prepare a Russian-English pocket dictionary.

The sale of New Year cards continued to increase annually, exceeding $30,000 in 1907—or one fifth of that year's sales. Prosperity emboldened Werbelowsky to expand his publishing program. He was aware of the hunger for cultural advancement on the part of a good many recent immigrants and believed that books by prominent authors would meet this need. He therefore brought out, in addition to works by Yiddish writers, translations from the writings of world-renowned authors. One of his projects, for example, was to publish the work of Goethe in "Jewish [Yiddish] in a volume of 1000 pages"; subsequently he published it in four volumes extending to 1200 pages. The translation, needless to say, was not of the best. Another project was recorded in the minutes of the directors' meeting in 1911: "Resolved, to publish a History of the World in Jewish, Graetz History of the Jews in English, and Bible in Jewish." These enterprises took time to materialize; before too long, however, Graetz's history was translated by A. B. Rhine and edited by Harkavy, with a supplementary volume by Max Raisen—all in six volumes. Years later the Old Testament was translated beautifully into Yiddish by the distinguished poet Yehoash (Solomon Bloomgarten).

In his eagerness to increase his business by bringing out the books of popular authors, Werbelowsky occasionally resorted to what many considered unethical practices. Like the earlier American "pirates" prior to the copyright law of 1890, he took advantage of the provision that a foreign book must be printed in America to be eligible for copyright. Since most of the Yiddish writers in the 1900s were still living in Eastern Europe and had no way of printing their work in the United States, Werbelowsky published their books without permission or royalty. For this action he was criticized in the Yiddish press and was even sued by at least one writer. But Werbelowsky rejected these accusations, stating that he was following a common practice and that, in fact, he was rendering the reading public a service by making these books available in the United States.

Death claimed the leading officers of the company during the years 1919–1923, and the following year David Werbelowsky assumed the presidency and Moe Werbelowsky became vice-president. Even earlier the scope of the firm's publishing program had greatly expanded in the area of general literature. In its 1914 catalogue, for instance, only 22 pages are taken up by religious items, while literary works, textbooks, dictionaries, and grammars occupy 72 pages, and 19 pages are devoted to music. Among the selected editions, in Yiddish translation, of the works of non-Jewish writers were those of Andreyev, Dumas, Goethe, Chekhov, Tolstoy, and Jules Verne. The writings of the most prominent Yiddish writers were of course included. In addition, seeking to meet an obvious need, the company brought out books in popular science which, in effect, offered a liberal education to Jewish readers who had not yet acquired a knowledge of English.

Special features are to be found in later catalogues. In the one for 1921 the company offered a twelve-volume edition of a world history in Yiddish, with the trade edition priced at $30 and the deluxe one at $50—large sums for Jewish workers in those days. Again, the 1929 catalogue lists an English translation of the Bible by Harkavy. The Hebrew and English versions appear on facing pages for the convenience of comparison, and the entire text was printed on a large format and fully illustrated. It was available in a four-volume edition at four different prices and in a two-volume edition at still lower prices. Also featured are the Torahs imported from Poland and written by men of unquestionable piety and learning. The holy articles of adornment that went with them were described in detail. Another prominent item was Harkavy's new dictionary which defined words in English, Hebrew, and Yiddish; it also contained listings of old and new proverbs and literary phrases in all three languages.

The company continued its annual active program of publishing, with most of its books in Yiddish, but more and more in English. A sampling of its 1936 catalogue indicates a trend to accommodate its publications to the increased Americanization of the Jews: Israel Friedlander's *The Jews of Russia and Poland,* originally published in 1916; H. A. Goldin's *Illustrated Bible Stories for Children;* Samuel Birenbaum's *The Life and Sayings of the Baal Shem;* M. M. Glenn's *Jewish Tales and Legends;* Shulamith Ish Kishor's *Children's History of Israel;* and various English editions of Hagadahs and prayer books.

When David Werbelowsky died in 1937, he was succeeded to the presidency by his son Isidor, who had shortened his name to Werbel. An energetic businessman, he was able to operate the firm on a part-time basis and devoted the rest of his energies to the development of The Montauk Press, which did a good deal of bookbinding for various publishers. He moved the Hebrew Publishing Company to Delancey Street on the lower East Side, where he used the ground floor to house a large and attractive bookstore and the second floor for the publishing offices.

Bridal Bibles had been a popular item for years, and in the 1954 catalogue one edition was described thus: "This English version of the 24 books of the Bible contains 1280 pages. It has pages for family records and autographs and is printed on fine Bible paper with an exceptionally clear and easily readable type." Among the new additions to the list were Betty Dean's *The New Jewish Cook Book,* its popularity attesting to its appeal to the new American-born generation; Daniel Persky's *Speak Hebrew; Seder Ritual for Passover Eve,* in Hebrew and in English, illustrated by Lola, with annotations by Rabbi J. D. Eisenstein; *Modern Hebrew Literature,* edited by G. L. Epstein and Max Zeldner; H. E. Goldin's *Hamadrich:* A Guide for Rabbis, Reverends and Cantors; Rabbi Joseph Marcus's *The Complete Bar Mitzvah Book;* and numerous additions to the music list. Of interest in this connection is the obvious adaptability of the list to the firm's more Americanized clientele.

A more recent catalogue featured many books in English,— the use of which increased with the slackening of the need for Yiddish. This is illustrated more and more in the ensuing lists. Thus, among the new books were *A Treasury of Tradition,* edited by Norman Lamm and W. S. Wurzburger; Walter Orenstein and Hertz Frankel's *Torah as Our Guide;* Solomon Ganzfried's *Code of Jewish Law;* H. E. Goldin's *Ethics of the Fathers;* Sol Liptzin's edition of *Stories from Peretz;* Howard Fast's *My Glorious Brothers;* Ben Zion Bokser's translation of the *Prayer Book* and the *High Holiday Prayer Book;* Maurice Samuel's translation of *Haggadah for Passover,* with music notations by Moshe Nathanson and an introduction by Louis Finkelstein. A special catalogue, entirely in English, provided a "revised comprehensive list of Anglo-Judaica which it sincerely hopes will meet the spiritual and cultural needs of English-speaking Jews of all ages." Upward of 150 titles were listed, most of which had been published in previous years and were now offered in new editions and in English translation.

Dr. Philip Birnbaum has been the firm's most productive author. One of his first publications, now in its eighth edition, was an abridged version of Maimonides' *Mishneh Torah,* designed for use by students and laymen; the Hebrew text is accompanied by brief English comments and glossaries. His other works which have been very favorably received are *A Treasury of Judaism,* containing the essential Jewish ideals and ethics; *A Book of Jewish Concepts,* providing Jewish teachings in encyclopedic form; prayer books for every occasion, including a large type edition for those with vision problems; and *Fluent Hebrew,* a novel approach to the study of the ancient-modern language.

By virtue of the fact that Dr. Birnbaum's prayer books (for daily use, Sabbath and festivals, and High Holy Days) have been purchased in tremendous quantities over the years, it would be fair to state that hundreds of thousands of Jews have developed a better appreciation of Jewish liturgy through his translations and commentaries.

In 1974 Isidor Werbel died and the Montauk Press ceased operations. Lawrence Werbel, Isidor's son, who had for some years been associated with the firm, succeeded him as president. Fully cognizant of the current situation in Jewish publishing, he undertook the expansion of the company's program while continuing with the religious books which had from the first been the mainstay of the business. Thus out of fifteen books scheduled for publication in 1976, eight were of a religious nature, in either new or revised editions. The others, appearing under the new imprint, Sanhedrin Press, included Azriel Eisenberg's *Earth, Be Not Silent* and *Israel's Momentous Century,* and Eliezer Berkovits' *Crisis and Faith.* Another new imprint, Bonim Books, was created for an innovative list of children's books, with five titles scheduled for publication in 1976. Werbel has also made arrangements with foreign firms to bring out some of their books in American editions, and a first work was Yaacov Herzog's *A People that Dwells Alone.* His plan to modernize the firm's activities is being carried out gradually with the help of his editor, David Olivestone, in an effort to adapt its program of publishing to the changing needs of the Jewish reader.

Louis Behrman was brought up by Edward Bloch in Cincinnati. When Charles Bloch moved his company to New York, young Behrman went with him. During the next twenty years he had made himself an important part of the firm. In 1921 he decided to leave the Bloch firm in order to go into business for himself. Fully knowledgeable of Jewish book needs, he formed Behrman House and specialized in the production and promotion of textbooks for Jewish schools. Over the years he published a number of successful texts, together with student workbooks and teacher's guides, each adapted to a grade ranging from the primary to the advanced. For beginners he brought out such titles as *Let's Talk about Right and Wrong, Let's Talk About God, A Child's Introduction to the Torah,* and *Lessons from the Living Past.*

For the intermediate grades he published the Jewish Heritage Series, which consisted of volumes on Judaism, the Synagogue, the Jewish way of life, and the beginning of Jewish philosophy. His Jewish Values Series dealt with Jewish celebrations and prayer along with workbooks and teacher's guides. The firm also issued a four-volume edition of *The Story of the Jewish People,* and books on the Holocaust, an introduction to the Bible, and stories of Jewish leaders.

The Junior High Schools Series included Frances Botwin's *The Jews of America,* Meyer Levin's text in *Jewish Philosophy,* W. B. Silverman's *The Still, Small Voice,* Hannah G. Goodman's *The Story of Prophecy,* and Joseph Rosner's *The Story of the Writings.* For young adults the firm published four volumes on Jewish tradition, E. L. Fackenheim's *Paths to Jewish Belief,* J. H. Hertz's *Pirke Aboth,* and a number of volumes relating to various other aspects of Judaism.

More recently the firm started, for the adult reader, the Library of Jewish Studies with Neal Kozodoy as general editor. The following volumes are already available or under contract: *A Shtetl and other Yiddish Novellas,* edited by Ruth R. Wisse; *A Maimonides Reader,* edited by Isidore Twersky; *Ideas of Jewish History,* edited by M. A. Meyer; *The Jew in American Society* and *The Jewish Community in America,* both edited by Marshall Sklare; Louis Jacobs' *A Jewish Theology;* Robert Chazan's *The Political Status of the Jew in the Middle Ages;* Joseph Dan's *Readings in Hasidism;* Lucy A. Dawidowicz's *A Holocaust Reader;* and S. Z. Leiman's *Jewish Moral Philosophy.*

Louis Behrman was 92 years old when he died in 1962. He was a man of small build but enormous energy and had developed a large and efficiently operated business. He was especially successful in gaining friendships with rabbis who impressed him as potential authors, and he catered to them to his considerable advantage. His son Jacob had entered the business on his discharge from the armed forces in 1946 and succeeded his father as the head of the firm. He has advanced the company's activities in various directions, accepting books of advanced scholarship, some probably with a subvention, and producing texts of modern curricular innovation together with his executive editor, Seymour Rossel. Among his more recent publications are *The Collected Articles of Jacob Mann* (three volumes), David Rudavsky's *Modern Jewish Religious Movements,* Robert Alter's *Modern Hebrew Literature,* and Joseph Heineman's and J. J. Petuchowski's *Readings in Jewish Liturgy.*

Zevi Scharfstein specialized in curricular reform while a teacher in his native Russia. Shortly after his arrival in New York in 1914, he became an instructor at the Teachers Institute of the Jewish Theological Seminary. In the course of time he became well known as a Hebrew scholar and served as a full professor until his retirement in 1960. A prolific Hebrew writer, he contributed a weekly column to *Hadoar* on political and literary events. Having as early as 1907 written on the teaching of Hebrew according to the latest pedagogical methods, he also introduced these methods into the study of traditional Jewish subjects in America. He wrote on Hebrew literature, on the Bible, and an autobiography of his forty years in the United States. To bring out his own writings and to promote his pedagogical reforms, he formed a publishing company, with his brother Asher assisting him.

In the early 1920s Asher and Fanny Scharfstein decided to open their own book business, which they named Ktav Publishing House. In addition to books on religion they stocked their store with articles used by Orthodox Jews in connection with ritual observance. Among the items they displayed were not only symbolic and novelty ornaments but also *draydels, graggers,* menorahs, and photographs of prominent Jewish figures. As their business increased, they concentrated on the stocking and production of books that were out of print and for which there seemed to be a demand. They also bought the stock of bankrupt firms.

At the end of World War II their two sons, both college graduates, entered the business and took control after their father's retirement. Sol, the elder son, joined in 1945, and Bernard did so four years later. Both young men, able, enterprising, and fully familiar with conditions in the Jewish book market, were not long in initiating a course of expansion and aggressive marketing that in time made Ktav one of the largest and most successful publishing houses in the Jewish field. At first they limited their publishing to important, standard classics for which they believed a demand was fairly obvious or could be stimulated. A significant example of their enterprise in reprinting was their reissuing of the classic ten volume *Jewish Encyclopedia,* then out of print. With no other similar work then available—they discounted the appeal of the *Universal Jewish Encyclopedia*—they were confident of its salability, but the cost of the undertaking gave them pause. On investigation, however, they learned that the plates were still in storage, along with about 400 sets of sheets. They managed to purchase both plates and sheets at a low price. On binding the sheets they had little difficulty in selling the sets. Thereupon they were encouraged to order a new printing. Thus, while the transaction proved profitable to the firm, it also benefited libraries and scholars who were in need of the work.

As their business increased, the brothers made arrangements with leading Jewish, and some non-Jewish, scholarly organizations to co-publish their works then out of print. They also brought out new books of merit under their own imprint. By these arrangements, and by reprinting books that had gone out of copyright, they were in time able to include in their catalogue books that comprised the most important scholarly works written in or translated into English.

Ktav's latest catalogue lists twenty different categories of books—from specialized bibliographies to *festschriften* and Hebrew literature. A sampling of the books listed indicates their wide range and scholarly content: Bernard Gronfeld's *Bibliography of Targum Literature,* the Hebrew Union College *Annuals,* the bound volumes of the *Jewish Quarterly Review,* the *Universal Jewish Encyclopedia,* 13 volumes of the *YIVO Annual of Jewish Social Science, Sefer Ha-Yashar,* translated and edited by S. J. Cohen, Eliezer Berkovits's *Faith After the Holocaust,* Sidney Jellicoe's *Studies in the Septuagint,* H. M. Orlinsky's *Understanding the Bible Through History and Archaeology* and *Essays in Biblical and Jewish Culture and Bible Translation, Encyclopedia of Biblical Interpretation,* edited by M. M. Kasher, Solomon Zeitlin's *Studies in the Early History of Judaism,* Louis Finkelstein's *Pharisaism in the Making,* an updated edition of Simon Dubnow's *History of the Jews in Russia and Poland,* Rudolf Glantz's *The Jew in the Old American Folklore,* a series of volumes on *Studies in Sephardica,* edited by J. H. Yerushalmi, and R. T. Herford's *Christianity in Talmud and Midrash.* Although the Ktav firm was commercially motivated in making available these and scores of other books, it has nevertheless performed a genuine service to the serious student of Judaica.

Another important part of the Ktav Publishing House is their list of educational books and supplementary materials. Influenced by their uncle Zevi Scharfstein and furthered by Sol Scharfstein's special interest in advancing modern pedagogical methods in the teaching of Hebrew and Judaism, the firm has developed up-to-date curricular plans and materials. While not alone in this respect, as previously discussed, the Scharfsteins have taken full advantage of the latest ideas in pedagogy and have arranged their curriculum materials into four parts: *Sidur,* History, *Humash,* and Language. Each of these categories is adapted to the various types of Jewish schools, with a total of eleven plans adapted to accord with time and age specifications of each school. Thus the *Sidur* plan "consists of a graduated series of texts and workbooks organized into a complete five year study program." Along with prayer skills are taught ethical and moral concepts. The language program is varied according to the overall objectives of a particular school, yet integrated with the other programs. *Humash* texts aim to "humanize" the content to provide for the student's gradual deepening of his understanding of the "Book of Books."

The supplementary materials from kindergarten to adult study are prepared with a view to stimulate the student's interest and to intensify his comprehension of the nature of Judaism. The firm promotes alphabet blocks, spelling games, coloring books, flip charts, film strips, fun books, cassettes, workbooks, and notebooks along with graduated texts. A good part of this material was prepared by Sol Scharfstein, either alone or with collaborators. Aware of the available competition, the firm has exerted itself aggressively to obtain the largest possible share of the business with Jewish schools.

In 1919 Simcha Goldman, an Orthodox Jew and follower of the Gerer Rebbe, opened a bookstore on the lower East Side for the sale of religious books. At first he imported his books from Europe. Later, when he was no longer able to obtain them from abroad, he began to reprint them in this country. He thus pioneered in the dissemination of Hasidic editions of Judaica and Hebraica. His bookstore became the center for the recently increased number of Hasidim, and his business grew accordingly.

In 1950 his son Jacob took over the management of the firm and began to enlarge its activities to include a greater variety of publications. Ten years later he started to issue a number of classics in Hasidic literature in English translation. At the same time he expanded his sales efforts to other parts of the world where pious Jews have need of books they could no longer obtain from Eastern Europe. The book store, crowded with books on shelves reaching the ceiling, remains a central gathering place for interested Hasidim.

The firm's current catalogue lists hundreds of books in Judaica and Hebraica. Among them, for example, are a number of editions of the Old Testament, both without commentary and with different kinds of commentary. Books of commentaries by eminent rabbis are available separately. The *Mishnah* is offered in six different editions. The *Pirkeh Aboth* is available in Hebrew, Yiddish, and English editions. The firm has, of course, a large assortment of prayer books, Haggadahs, *Mahzorim*, and the like. In addition, the store is crammed with books on ethics, religious philosophy, sermons, mysticism, legends, and folklore, as well as encyclopedias and dictionaries. Hasidim, in particular, know they can obtain any book they want from the Goldman firm and act accordingly.

In 1939 Phillip Feldheim came to New York from Austria to escape from the Nazis. In Vienna he was a printer of textiles. In need of earning a living in his new home, he opened a small book store on Hester Street on the lower East Side, stocked largely with the numerous books he had brought with him—the one item Jews were permitted by the Nazis to take with them. With the war in Europe making it impossible to import Hebrew books from that continent, Feldheim began to buy up the books owned by other refugees in order to fill a growing demand for them. This stock was nearly exhausted by 1945. By then, with Jewish printing presses in Poland and Germany destroyed, Feldheim was ready to reprint the books for which there seemed to be an urgent need.

A pious Jew, primarily interested in religious books, he first brought out Torah literature in Hebrew. As his sales expanded, and numerous inquiries came for other books in Hebraica, he started publishing different types of books. Later he also found it desirable to issue English translations of the classics. Adhering to his Orthodox program, he arranged with the Rabbi Samson Raphael Hirsch Publication Society to publish the rabbi's texts and commentaries for English-reading Orthodox Jews. His bookstore is stocked with works on history, philosophy, religion, art, music, and mysticism, many in English translation. He also collects and sells German Judaica in the original and in translation. With his large stock of specialized books, he is able to supply individuals and institutions with rare editions of works in Judaica. As the *National Jewish Monthly* wrote of his book store: "If someone wants a Jewish book he can't find anywhere, he comes here."

One of Feldheim's outstanding projects was to make available a series of Great Books of Judaism. Thus he has published an edition of *Penateuch with Rashi, Ahavath Chesed, Orchoth Tzadikim, The Hafetz Hayyim on the Sidur,* Kafia's *The Illuminated Haggadah,* Paul Forchheimer's *Living Judaism,* Rabbi Alexander Safran's *The Kabbalah,* J. M. Bunim's *Ethics from Sinai,* Meir Meiseles' *Judaism, Thought and Legend,* P. Biberfeld's three-volume *Universal Jewish History,* Charles Wengrow's *Baal Shem Tov on Pirkei Avot,* and Jacob Singer and Chaim D. Ackerman's *The Vilna Gaon Views Life.*

Feldheim's son, Yaakov, established a branch of the firm in Jerusalem and has published additions to the Torah Classics Library. Two of these works, both translated into English by Shraga Silberstein, but also available in Hebrew, are Luzzatto's *Messilat Yesharim* (The Path of the Just) and Yonah of Gerona's *Sha'arei Teshuvah* (Gates of Repentance).

Salman Schocken, born in 1877, was a successful businessman in Germany, the head of several moderate-priced department stores. A man of strong beliefs and intellectual interests, he was assimilated enough not to concern himself with Jewish affairs. In the early years of this century, however, a reading of Martin Buber's Hasidic stories turned him into "an active Jew." His subsequent friendship with Buber made him perceive the fallacy of assimilation in the midst of racial prejudice, and he began to interest himself in Zionism. In 1912 he organized a Zionist branch in Zwickau, where he resided. Ever a man of action, he sought to interest his fellow Jews in Jewish scholarship and in Hebrew as a means of national resurgence. "The reconstruction of our *wissenschaft,*" he declared, "will have to be accompanied by the publication of scholarly works for a wide audience. Our effort will be effective only if we can put into the hands of every Jewish reader a good presentation of our people's past and of its present persistence." With little Jewish publishing being done in Germany at that time, he was ready to underwrite the cost of making this material available for general distribution.

He outlined his publishing plan in 1916 at a Zionist meeting, and a committee was appointed to develop this plan. The war and subsequent conditions kept the committee inactive—much to Schocken's disappointment. In 1927 he undertook the project of bringing out a volume of Jewish material drawn from German literature. He also considered a similar volume from Hebrew and Yiddish sources. To publish these and other books he in 1931 formed the Schocken Verlag. Too involved in his business affairs to give careful attention to his publishing project, he engaged as managing editor Lambert Schneider, an impoverished German publisher who was keenly interested in Jewish literature and who had published some Judaica.

When the Nazis, after 1933, excluded Jews from German life, Schocken realized that his fellow Jews, both the committed and the assimilated, needed to learn more about their religious and cultural backgrounds in order better to cope with their new, restricted status. One of his projects was a German translation of the Bible, which Schneider had earlier initiated with Martin Buber and Franz Rosenzweig. Schocken also considered it a privilege to publish Buber's books, and as many as 27 of them had the Schocken imprint. Another of his undertakings was to publish the works of S. Y. Agnon, the Hebrew novelist whom he had met in 1914 and whom he had encouraged financially in the form of advances against the rights to his fiction. In 1931 he brought out four of Agnon's books as part of a collected edition, and two more in 1935.

The Schocken Verlag in 1933 began to issue an annual *Almanach,* which continued to appear until 1938 when the company was closed by the Nazis. It also started the Schocken *Bücherei,* a series of small volumes on early and modern Hebraic literature; some of them appeared in bilingual editions, and the contemporary editions included both prose and poetry. By 1938 the firm had published a total of over 200 volumes.

One of Schocken's aims was to bring out the work of Jews who had contributed to German literature but who were rejected by the Nazis—writers like Heine, Kafka, Werfel, Alfred Mombert, Freud, and Karl Kraus, and he managed to issue some of them by 1938. Early that year he also succeeded in printing the Palestine Royal Commission Report in record time in order to have copies for distribution at the opening of the Zionist Congress.

With Hitler's rise to power in 1933, Schocken made his home in Palestine. From there he continued to supervise the publishing activities in Berlin for the next five years, with Schreiber and Moritz Spitzer doing the actual publishing. The firm remained subsidized by the Schocken department stores, thereby reducing the taxes they paid to the Government.

Shortly after settling in Palestine, Schocken established a Hebrew language publishing branch in Tel Aviv. In 1938 he combined it with the confiscated Berlin branch and placed it under the direction of his eldest son, Gershom. Shocken himself took an active part in Zionist affairs. In 1935 he bought the newspaper *Haaretz* and made it a serious voice in support of a Jewish homeland. He also served as chairman of the executive committee of Hebrew University. Later he gave the university library the largest and most valuable collection of Hebrew incunabula ever gathered by an individual.

When World War II broke out in 1939, Schocken went to the United States to solicit aid for the university and remained for the duration. At the end of the war he became interested in opening a branch of his publishing firm in New York. In 1946 he had his son Theodore publish English translations of books by eminent scholars such as Baeck, Gortein, Simon Halkin, Franz Rosenzweig, and Scholem. The firm also started a popular price Schocken Library with about twenty volumes, which later became the initial part of Schocken paperbacks.

Franz Kafka was the first author of non-Jewish content to be brought out by the firm. Schocken had published him in Germany because his writings were proscribed by the Nazis. In 1946 an English translation of his *The Great Wall of China* was issued in New York. The book sold very slowly, but in 1948 *The Penal Colony* had a sale of over 30,000 copies in the trade edition and nearly 200,000 in paperback. Subsequently Schocken Books brought out a total of twelve of Kafka's books with increasing success. One of the firm's early publications, Bella and Marc Chagall's *Burning Lights,* issued in 1946 in an attractive format, sold very little until Chagall's growing popularity attracted readers to the book. Thereafter a paperback edition had several printings. The firm had a similar experience with Buber's books. His early volumes had very limited appeal, as he was hardly known to the general Jewish reader; now eight of his books require frequent reprinting. Another rewarding author with a poor beginning was Agnon. The first English translation of his novels sold very slowly until he was awarded the Nobel Prize.

In 1949 Theodore Schocken yielded the presidency of Schocken Books to his brother-in-law, Herzl Rome. For several years thereafter reduced sales forced the company to limit its publishing activities. In 1959, Salman Schocken having died, Rome sought to expand the scope of his activities and managed to place the firm on a solid business footing. Among his innovations was a paperback list, taken mostly from the firm's backlist, which he promoted vigorously in colleges. He also expanded the publishing program to non-Jewish subjects and increased the list of Judaica. Unfortunately he died in 1965, and Theodore again took over the presidency and proceeded to carry out the projects and plans initiated by his brother-in-law. During the past decade the firm grew considerably, issuing around 75 books a year and increasing its general list to a point where it now amounts to about two thirds of the list. In 1974 Theodore Schocken became ill and died in March 1975.

The Hermon Press, now renamed Sepher-Hermon Press, is the latest Jewish publishing house of a sizable nature, having been started by Samuel Gross in 1964. Born and educated in Hungary, Gross came to the United States after World War II and began to work for the Bloch Publishing Company. Thoroughly knowledgeable in both Hebrew and Judaism, he advanced himself rapidly and was for many years the firm's book editor.

In 1964 he decided to start his own publishing house as a part-time venture. As he stated it, his expressed aim was "to rescue from oblivion through reprinting books of Judaica that have gone out of print in the course of time and especially in the wake of the Holocaust." Although most Jewish commercial publishers whose activity dated after 1945 were primarily reprinters and have combed the field quite thoroughly, Gross considered himself the most knowledgeable and the most dedicated, asserting that he was "reissuing these rare gems of Judaica and Hebraica scholarship . . . in a spirit of public service." In 1973 he left Bloch and devoted himself completely to his own company.

Among the first of his publications were Gerald Friedlander's translation of *The Chapters of Rabbi Eliezer the Great,* W. M. Feldman's *Rabbinical Mathematics and Astronomy,* M. Steinschneider's *Jewish Literature,* and several books in Hebrew. To make these scholarly works available to students of Hebraica was of course highly commendable. Equally welcome were Gross's subsequent publications, most of them new editions of books no longer obtainable or new collections of old materials. Thus he brought back into print three volumes of Genizah documents, Solomon Schechter's epochal discovery in Cairo, edited by Louis Ginzberg and Israel Davidson. Equally significant was the reprinting of Ginzberg's two volumes on *Geonica.* Other reprints of particular importance were Moses Gaster's *The Ketubah,* with nine new plates and notes by Gross. The latter's interest in art is also evident in a new edition of Jacob Leveen's *The Hebrew Bible in Art.* Indeed, all the books on the firm's current list—upward of fifty items—are works of unusual merit and highly useful to scholars and librarians. Especially welcome are the new editions, with introductions and additions, of Menasseh Ben Israel's *The Conciliator,* Leo Wiener's *The History of Yiddish Literature in the Nineteenth Century,* and Bernard Grossfield's *The Targum to the Five Megiloth.* One of the latest additions to the list is *Studies in Jewish Jurisprudence,* "a collection of the important monographs on various aspects of Jewish law and its relationship to other legal systems, particularly the Anglo-Saxon."

The Judaica Press specializes in books of a religious character, although like larger firms it has also brought out works of general interest. One of its first publications was *The Book of Joshua,* the initial volume in a series on the Prophets. Edited by Sidney B. Hoenig, it had the collaboration of several other scholars. A feature of this as of other volumes is the collation of Hebrew commentaries, translated into English. One of the firm's important undertakings was the seven-volume *Pentateuch,* edited by Samson R. Hirsch and translated by Isaac Levi. Another major project was the six-volume *Mishnah,* edited by Phillip Blackman, with a separate volume for the index. Also available are the individual tractates for the convenience of separate study. Blackman has also edited *Ethics of the Fathers,* containing the text in both Hebrew and English. Another of the firm's publications is A. Z. Friedman's two-volume *Wellsprings of the Torah,* an anthology of Biblical commentaries by renowned scholars from the second century to the present. The author was a prominent Polish Hasid, killed in 1943, who prepared the book in Yiddish; all of it is now in English. Other books on its list are M. M. Kasher's *The Western Wall,* making clear its meaning in the thought of the Sages; Charles Raddock's *Portrait of a People,* a world history of the Jews in three volumes and also in one compact volume; and Abraham Rosenfeld's *Kinot for the Ninth of Ab* and *Slichot for the Whole Year.*

The firm of Shengold Publishers was started by Moshe Sheinbaum in 1955, and he named the firm after the man who loaned him the capital. Sheinbaum was born and educated in Warsaw, but came to the United States from Jerusalem in behalf of the *Encyclopedia Hebraica.* From the outset as a publisher he was interested primarily in issuing a few books annually—volumes which appealed to him as works both of merit and solid Jewish content. This has enabled him to take ten weeks off annually to visit Europe and Israel as an observer of Jewish activities in those parts of the world. He has thus been, in a sense, a one-man concern, a publisher who devoted himself personally to each book he brought out and who sought the kind of books that remain in demand indefinitely.

That he was largely successful in this regard is evidenced by the fact that a number of his publications have been reprinted in updated editions. Most successful, perhaps, was his first book, *Bar Mitzvah,* edited by Abraham I. Katsh, and containing contributions by such eminent writers as Ludwig Lewisohn, Cecil Roth, and Meyer Waxman. This book has been in steady demand since publication and is now in its seventh edition. Another highly popular work is the *Junior Jewish Encyclopedia,* edited by Naomi Ben-Asher and Hayim Leaf. Kept up to date and now in its eighth edition, this one-volume compendium of Jewish knowledge is of solid scholarship, written in a clear and simple style, and made vivid by hundreds of illustrations. A third book in wide demand is *Blessed Is the Daughter,* by Meyer Waxman, Shulamith Ish-Kishor, and Jacob Sloan; consisting of inspiring stories of Jewish heroines from Biblical times to the days of the Holocaust, the volume is simply illustrated and is now in its fifth edition.

Sheinbaum lavishly illustrated *Graphic History of the Jewish Heritage,* edited by P. Wollman-Tsamir. A unique feature is a master chart showing in detail the Jewish heritage and ramifications of all epochs and in all countries. Although the book was relatively popular, selling 15,000 copies, the increasingly high cost of printing compelled him to let it go out of print. Another sumptuous book which he had to stop publishing was *The Jewish People:* 4000 Years of Survival, by Max Wurmbrand and Cecil Roth. A very handsome book, illustrated with 600 photographs, graphs and charts, it makes clear how Jews have for millennia suffered the ravages of war, dispersion, and persecution without losing their identity and cultural heritage.

Although Sheinbaum has brought out relatively few books over the past two decades, each volume was prepared with a view to making evident the rich storehouse of Jewish history and culture. Many of the books treat the glories of Jewish holidays, Jewish heroes of the past and in our own time, works dealing with historic and current events, as well as studies of the various aspects of Judaism. Three late examples of these books are Lester Eckman's *The History of the Muser (Ethical) Movement: 1840–1945,* with emphasis on Rabbi Israel Salanter, the movement's founder; Louise D. Kayser's *Light from Our Past,* a description of the twelve stained windows in the Har Zion Temple in Philadelphia; Neil Rosenstein's *The Unbroken Chain,* containing biographical sketches and the genealogy of illustrious Jewish families from the 15th to the 20th centuries—all descended from Rabbi Meir Katzenelenbogen of Padua. At present Mr. Scheinbaum is planning to add a number of biographies to his small but distinguished list of books.

Although Keter Publishing House is a Jerusalem firm, it has an office in New York and a number of its books have been brought out in the United States by American companies. Keter was launched in 1959 as the Israel Program for Scientific Translations. Since then it has issued a total of over 1500 titles and has become recognized as a major contributor to the publication of books in the social and natural sciences. In 1973 the name was changed to Keter Publishing House. It is of interest to note that "Keter" is the Hebrew word for "crown," and the firm strives to live up to the connotation in the saying of a Talmudic sage: "There are three crowns: the crown of learning, the crown of priesthood, and the crown of royalty, but the crown of a good name excels them all."

The greatest achievement of Keter has been the 16-volume *Encyclopaedia Judaica*, which it published in 1972 under the editorship of Cecil Roth and Geoffrey Wigoder. The work has 25,000 entries by 2,000 contributors, and extends to 12,500 pages with 8000 illustrations. Updated annually by a Yearbook, it is widely regarded as a monumental work of popular scholarship.

Keter prints and publishes upward of a hundred books annually, and its Judaica book department includes, in English, the Israel Pocket Library, the Popular Judaica Library, the Library of Jewish Knowledge, and *My Jewish World* (a juvenile encyclopedia). Another of Keter's important enterprises is the Israel Universities Press, established in 1965.

In the first decade it brought out over 100 titles in the natural and social sciences, with a number of the volumes issued in American editions by such houses as John Wiley and Sons and Quadrangle–New York Times Book Company. Of particular interest are the books dealing with the various aspects of the Middle East. Other titles of the firm deal with Islamic culture, art, English literature, and contemporary science. The impact of its publications on American Jewish culture is self-evident.

In recent years interested individuals and small firms have been publishing books of Jewish content. Some merely bring out one or more books for personal or other reasons and have no intention of becoming commercial publishers; others are eager to enlarge their activities but lack the capital for their enterprise;

still others prefer to do these books as a kind of sideline to their main business. It should be remembered, however, that the books of all these semi-professional publishers added together further the cultural output of American Jewry.

As the number of Jewish publishing houses increased, the need of an association became obvious to their executives. About thirteen years ago they formed the Association of Jewish Book Publishers for the purpose of discussing problems and conditions of mutual concern. It holds several meetings a year, and usually a guest speaker is invited to discuss a topic dealing with Jewish publishing. There are now about twenty members, and the officers are planning to broaden the membership to include other companies which issue books of Jewish interest. The current president is Jacob Steinberg, and Robert Garvey is secretary.

An entirely separate area of Jewish publishing in America has been the steady production of books in Hebrew, and these in turn are separated by their contents—the secular Hebrew books forming one branch and the religious another. In the former category, authors affiliated with the Hebrew weekly *Hadoar* and its sponsoring organization, *Histadruth Ivrith,* as well as with the monthly *Bitzaron,* have published critical studies of modern Hebrew literature, poetry, and a great number of scholarly Judaica studies.

A totally different field of Hebrew publishing is to be found in the religious area, however. In addition to large numbers of elementary, intermediate and advanced textbooks in Hebrew language, Bible and Jewish history—turned out primarily for the students of Jewish schools—there have appeared serious works of religious commentary, all of them in Hebrew and on a high level of scholarship.

These include works on Halachah, Talmud, Bible, Midrash, Jewish history, and Jewish thought, and works of Responsa. Solomon Braun published a four-volume commentary on the abridged *Shulchan Aruch,* entitled *Sha'arim Hametzunayim b'Halachah;* a Hebrew language 10-volume encyclopedia, *Otzar Yisrael,* appeared as early as 1907–13, while *Otzar Midrashim*—an anthology of 200 minor midrashim—was published in 1915. One of the outstanding Jewish religious scholars in the world, Rabbi Moses Feinstein, has published original Responsa (*Sefer Igrot Moshe*) in four volumes, and other works of commentary. All of this material appeared in Hebrew.

5

Early Yiddish Periodicals

East-European Jews began coming to America as early as the eighteenth century, with Haym Salomon being the most conspicuous of them before the Revolutionary period. He and others spoke Yiddish and used it in their correspondence. Their number increased slowly, but by 1870 it was estimated to have reached about 7,500. During the next decade, however, the number had risen to about 40,000. Most of them had come to escape army service, or local persecution, or were lured by the hope of material improvement. On the whole they were observant Orthodox Jews, neither highly learned nor untaught in Judaic lore. Once settled in their new environment, the exertion of making a living kept many of them from daily practicing the ancient ritual of their fathers. Eager, however, to refute the allegation among European Jews that those in America had ceased to adhere to the Orthodox faith, Rabbi J. D. Eisenstein declared:

> It is a lie they tell in the cities of Poland that the Jews here do not observe their religion. . . . In Bet ha-Midrash ha-godel, on 69 Ludlow Street, they will find Jews engaged in study and that it has many books, as in the great Houses of Study in Poland.

It was not surprising that the desire for news from Europe and for other information, especially about the progress and outcome of the Franco-Prussian War in 1870, stimulated the appearance of periodicals in Yiddish, the language these Jews knew best. In that year J. K. Buchner, a scholarly young man, undertook the publication of a weekly, which he named *Yuedishe Zeitung* (Jewish Times). Since he could not readily obtain Hebrew type from Europe, he produced the periodical by the lithographic process.

Buchner had been befriended by Horace Greeley, the famous editor, and had previously started the Jewish Workers Immigrant Institute with a series of popular lectures at Cooper Union. He was also active in the organization of the Jewish Handworkers Union, helped new immigrants find work and housing, and sought to keep them from undue exploitation. His weekly aimed to provide his readers with all the aspects of "politics, religion, history, science, and art."

Yet he was unable to establish it on a firm financial foundation. He continued to issue it intermittently, most often during political campaigns, but he finally had to suspend publication in 1877. It should be noted that his Yiddish was a mixture of Hebrew and German, then commonly employed. For years thereafter, indeed, Yiddish writers were egregiously careless in the use of this "jargon," and they considered a stilted Germanic Yiddish an elegant use of the tongue.

In August 1870 Z. H. Bernstein, an uncle of the prominent journalist, Herman Bernstein, began to publish *The Post* in New York. He imported Hebrew type and engaged Z. Gershuni, who knew how to set type, as his co-publisher. After the fifth issue the partnership was dissolved, and Bernstein proceeded to bring out the weekly by himself. For a time he did well enough to have gained a circulation of about 4000. To bring his readers news from Eastern Europe, he reprinted articles in translation from *Hamagid*, a Hebrew periodical published in Russia.

On April 1871 he was persuaded by Jacob Cohen, who was ambitious politically, to change the weekly's name to *Hebrew News* and to bring it out in four languages: Yiddish, Hebrew, German, and English. The periodical began promoting Cohen's candidacy for municipal supervisor during the campaign of that year. When he failed to win the election, Cohen backed out of the partnership, causing the demise of *Hebrew News.* Bernstein, who was also a Hebrew scholar, thereupon started the first Hebrew weekly in America, *Observer of the New Land,* with M. Jolamstein as editor. With too few readers to give it financial support, it appeared only irregularly and ceased to appear in 1876.

In the 1870s and even later Yiddish periodicals were still unable to establish themselves on a permanent basis because there were not as yet enough readers to assure them financial security. Yet one after another weekly was started with high hopes—only to founder for lack of funds. One of the most persistent and ultimately successful of these journalistic entrepreneurs was a young printer, Kasriel Z. Sarasohn. Born in Russia in 1835, he made his first trip to the United States in 1869, but did not remain long. He returned to America in 1871 and opened a printing shop. Soon he sought to become a publisher of a periodical, and in partnership with E. Shrengel he started *The New York Jewish Times,* which lasted five months. Not discouraged by failure, in 1874 he began to issue *The Jewish Gazette,* with Jolamstein as editor. Of interest is the fact that in 1876 it printed serially a long poem by J. Z. Sobel, a young Hebrew scholar, which appeared in book form a year later—the first Yiddish work to be published in the United States; also notable is that the 32-page poem was printed in Hebrew as well as in Yiddish.

In 1881 Sarasohn turned the weekly into a daily—the first Yiddish daily newspaper in the world—but he was soon forced to return to the weekly schedule. Two years later he again sought to make it a daily, but after three months he had to resort to its weekly appearance. Yet he persisted in his effort to publish a daily newspaper, and in 1885 he brought out the *Tageblatt,* which established itself as the only Yiddish daily in the United States for more than a decade. Six days a week Sarasohn's son and a number of newsboys peddled it successfully on the streets of the lower East Side.

A sizable Jewish settlement in Chicago made possible several efforts at the publication of Yiddish periodicals. In 1877 N. B. Etelson began to issue *Israelische Presse,* with a section in Hebrew. A year later M. Topolsky brought out the *Yiddishe Folk*

Zeitung and used a simpler Yiddish. Chaim Aliosoph also attempted to publish periodicals in both Yiddish and Hebrew. Gershuni, who went to Chicago after leaving *The Post,* in 1878 started *Jewish Advance,* which lasted three years. It is of interest to note that years earlier he had become converted to Christianity in order to marry a Russian girl and had gone to London, where he associated with missionaries. After some time, however, he repented his apostasy, resumed his observance of Judaism, and dedicated himself to the welfare of his fellow Jews.

In both New York and Chicago, the Mintz brothers were enterprising journalists of the period. In 1885 Moses Mintz and partners started the *New York Yiddish Folk Zeitung,* a socialist weekly that endured until 1889. In 1887 Michael Mintz founded the weekly *Courier* in Chicago, then returned to New York to start *The Folk Advocate,* a liberal weekly. In 1891 the Mintz brothers began to issue *The Daily Jewish Herald,* and made *The Folk Advocate* its Sunday edition. They sold the weekly for one cent, lowering the price from the going rate of three cents, and greatly increased its circulation by a series of articles on Moses Mintz's visit to Palestine, entitled "A Regard from Mother Zion." Lack of political patronage and the oncoming depression, however, forced its cessation after eighty issues.

During the last two decades of the nineteenth century a number of Yiddish periodicals were started, most of them as forums for various ideologies and "isms." In Chicago the *Jewish Courier* was long published as a daily, and weeklies appeared in Boston and other cities. In New York, where most Jews lived, a good many periodicals were started—among them *Der Neier Geist, Unser Wort, Die Freie Geselshaft, Dos Neie Leben, Der Haus Freint, Dos Yiddish Folk, Die Neie Welt*—most of them organs of radicals and idealists eager to present their views to a public not yet ready for an intellectual fare. Certain individuals of literary inclination also brought out short-lived magazines; one of them was Shomer (N. M. Shaikewitch), the popular concocter of romances, who issued *Der Mentchlicher Freint* and *Die Natzion.*

In those days political bounty in the form of advertising was a common support of periodicals, but the only one who had gained the continued favor of politicians was Sarasohn. Yet despite their precarious existence these magazines did much to inculcate ideas and aspirations in the minds of their readers. The editors of *75 Years of the Yiddish Press in America* have stated succinctly what these ephemeral weeklies had achieved: "The Yiddish periodicals organized the first wave of Jewish immigrants and molded it into a civilized form; they taught it manners and gave it a world orientation. They also Americanized it."

Perhaps the best of these journalistic efforts was *The New York Yiddish Folk Zeitung*, the socialist weekly. Of interest is the editor's attitude toward the Yiddish of the time:

> The Jewish jargon is composed of words of various languages. It is without rules and without grammar. We think it unnecessary to strive for only jargon. Therefore our worthy readers need not be surprised that the different articles are written in different jargons. We consider it only right to omit Russian words from our newspaper.

This weekly was the first to emphasize literary quality and to print the poems of Morris Rosenfeld and other writers. If its literary position was largely receptive, it was politically didactic and anti-capitalist.

In 1889 the anarchists started *The Truth*. Naively utopian, the editor asserted that it "will fight until slavery is abolished . . . fight against popes, rabbis, swindlers, laws, and chains." During its brief existence it printed current verse, polemical articles, and translations of radical world literature. The following year this group founded *Die Freie Arbeiter Shtimme* (The Free Worker's Voice), which after an insecure beginning has continued to the present.

The Americanized German Jews, feeling a real sense of responsibility for their immigrant co-religionists, strongly opposed the use of Yiddish among the newcomers. They regarded this "jargon" as a corrupt and vulgarized adaptation of German and maintained that writers employ a correct German or, preferably, good English, thereby expediting the process of Americanization. In 1900, angered by what they considered the *Tageblatt*'s betrayal of the Republicans during the campaign, Jacob H. Schiff and Louis Marshall decided to sponsor a Yiddish daily that would advance the Americanization process. They engaged Z. H. Masliansky, the highly popular lecturer, to launch *The Jewish World* in 1902. Although the staff of writers were competent journalists, the daily soon failed. Readers found it too didactic and too intellectual, so that it bored them by comparison with the *Tageblatt*'s sensational serials. The antagonism to Yiddish and to radicalism among German Jews nevertheless continued for years afterward. Shmuel Niger later commented on this situation:

> The Yiddish newspapers, despite their Germanized Yiddish, their purely utilitarian character and their expressed desire to cultivate not Yiddish but English, were met with the contempt and hatred of the English Language Jewish press and all who advocated rapid Americanization and opposed Orthodoxy.

Ironically, the opponents of Yiddish were joined by Orthodox spokesmen—their antagonism being based on the assumption that Jews should give their free time to the study of holy writ rather than to the perusal of Yiddish periodicals.

Russian pogroms in 1881 produced a mass migration from Czarist lands to the United States and elsewhere. The previous trickle of immigrants quickly became a steady stream of harassed and distressed refugees. Most of these escapees from Russian persecution were inured to the medieval strictures of the Orthodox faith. Their outlook on life was circumscribed by the synagogue and house of study. They functioned in the primitive ways of their fathers and had little or no inkling of the mechanical and scientific developments in the world outside their *shtetl*. Most of them were either petty merchants or tradespeople, and nearly all were stone poor.

The siren lure of the "golden land," which in one way or another had reached the remotest village, caused the bolder young men to set out on the long and hazardous journey westward. With little money, without travel experience, without any knowledge of the languages spoken in the countries they had to pass, they somehow managed to steal across the Russian border and traverse the European continent to one of the ports on the

Atlantic Ocean. Their strict observance of Kashruth led them to live mostly on bread and tea, with now and then some herring and potatoes. They boarded the steerage hold of an ocean vessel that was dank and depressing, and clung to their hope of survival by frequent prayer and sheer physical persistence.

On reaching New York, where most of them remained, they were helped by charitable Jewish organizations to find tenement apartments on the lower East Side and work in one of the sweatshops operated mostly by German Jews. Inured to the hardships of the *shtetl,* they sought to accustom themselves to their new adversities. With no knowledge of English, with many having no training in any craft, they had no choice but to do the work available to them at wages offered them.

Among the mass of immigrants were also a number of young men who were already emancipated from their medieval childhood environment. These youths had gone to cities to become workers or students, and a number were members of radical groups intent on freeing Russia from the grip of Czarist oppression. In danger of incarceration, or having already served time, they fled the country and, after sojourning in Germany or France, reached New York. Although many of them were relatively well educated, they were without means and little or no knowledge of English. Consequently most of them were also forced to work in sweatshops and live in dank tenements.

"Sweated" workers perforce, many remained ardent idealists dedicated to the glowing promises of socialism and anarchism. They refused to acquiesce in the drudgery of the sweatshop and the obsequious attitude of their fellow workers. Night after night they met to discuss and condemn the prevailing inequities. Expounding their utopian aims, they spoke enthusiastically of a social revolution that would abolish human exploitation and bring the blessings of freedom and equality to all men. They began to agitate among the workers in their shops for higher wages and better working conditions. Frequently they invited them to meetings at which speakers sought to inspire them to form unions. They also published periodicals to appeal to these workers.

Abraham Cahan, one of the most active of these radicals, was from the first realistic in attitude and specific in his objectives. Aware that most of the workers knew only Yiddish, he spoke to them in their own dialect. Later he stated:

> The Jewish artisan was even in the beginning of the 1890s an artisan in the old sense of the word. He spoke the artisan's dialect and hardly understood any other. Many of our workers could barely read unvocalized Yiddish texts. Not only did we have to teach them in our writings how to think, we also had to teach them how to read our writing.

In 1886 Cahan began to edit *Die Neie Zeit* (The New Times), the first radical weekly. He used a relatively simple Yiddish in his advocacy of socialist principles. After the fourth issue, however, he and his colleagues ran out of funds and had to suspend it. Two months later the *Yiddish Folk Zeitung* was started by them. The anarchist *Truth* and later *Die Freie Arbeiter Shtimme* also agitated against capitalist exploitation. Ephraim London, father of Meyer London, joined with fellow anarchists to start *The Morning Star,* a weekly still written in Germanized Yiddish. Nor were the socialists discouraged by early failures. They invited Philip Krantz to come from London to edit their new weekly, *Die Arbeiter Zeitung;* when Krantz did not see eye to eye with the active radicals, he was replaced by Cahan, who made it an effective propaganda medium and printed the writings of the better Yiddish authors, among them Peretz's famous story, "Bontche Shweig."

In 1894 the socialists launched a daily newspaper, *Die Abendblatt,* but the prevailing friction within the Socialist Labor Party gave it short shrift. It should be stated that all the Yiddish dailies then and later followed the practice of European newspapers in printing verse and fiction by writers from Eastern Europe as well as from those living in New York; the editors also arranged for translations from the work of prominent non-Jewish writers. Thus, however brief their existence, these early periodicals served to present political ideas and belles lettres to their readers. Shmuel Niger stated: "The socialist and near-socialist press which began to appear in the second half of the 1880s, was on the whole very important for the dissemination and fructification of Yiddish culture."

In the 1890s Jewish immigrants, becoming more acclimated to their new environment, began to form *landsmanshaften* and *farbanden,* the first uniting former residents of a town or area in their native lands and the second organizations of a more general nature. They also started to patronize the emerging Yiddish theater, to read humorous magazines, and to read trade periodicals. To stimulate their interest in these activities, various magazines came into existence. Among the theatrical periodicals were Jacob Gordin's *Theater Journal and Family News* (1901), *The Dramatic World* (1904), *The Yiddish Stage* (1909); *Puck* (1894), *Der Kibitzer* (1908), and *Der Groisser Kunds* (1909), supplied the humorous aspects of current life; the unions struggling for recognition issued periodicals for members; and Zionists also brought out several magazines. All this activity served both to educate and to entertain the constantly increasing community of East European Jews in the United States.

Morris R. Cohen, the incisive and perceptive philosopher who grew up in this environment, praised highly the Yiddish press which he read during his formative years. In *A Dreamer's Journey* he maintained that it was superior to the English newspapers of the time:

> Having no army of reporters to dig up news, the Yiddish press necessarily paid more attention to things of permanent interest. It tried to give its readers something of enduring and substantial value. . . . My intellectual life before I could read English books with understanding would have tapered off to nothing, had it not been for the stimulus of the little Yiddish literature I devoured at home. . . . For intellectual stimulus I turned to *Die Arbeiter Zeitung*, the Jewish organ of the Socialist Labor Party. In its columns I read Flaubert's *Salambo. . . . Die Arbeiter Zeitung,* in its incisive comments on politics and world affairs, always stressed the significance of the economic element. And to this day it seems to me that it had a more realistic understanding of public affairs than anything I could see for years afterwards in the English press. It was indeed almost a genera-

tion later that men like Lincoln Stekens began to appreciate what *Die Arbeiter Zeitung* was saying in 1892, that behind the "bosses" and the corruption of our politics were the economic interests that did the bribing, because it was cheaper to hire politicians than to enter politics directly. . . .

The Yiddish press has prepared millions of Jewish people to take their full place in American civilization while also promoting the national self-respect to which Jews are entitled because of their character and history.

K. Z. Sarasohn was an able and shrewd businessman. When he started the *Tageblatt* in 1885 he had the benefit of nearly fifteen years of experience in Yiddish journalism—the only one to survive the almost inevitable failure suffered by his competitors. By 1885 he was aware that the Yiddish-reading public had not only become sizable but was relatively little affected by the agitation of radical periodicals. He therefore adopted an Orthodox position, which was congenial to him, as his editorial policy. He also realized that most of his potential readers were hard-working people and little interested in intellectual stimulation; that what they appreciated most during the brief period before bedtime was the relaxation of light reading—an amusing story or a titillating romance. This Sarasohn gave them in full measure. Over the years his first editor, Jalomstein, and later the dynamic Johan Paley also engaged staff writers who were conservative in both religion and politics but who were able to hold the attention of readers with their persuasive discussions and assertive statements concerning current events.

As stated previously, Sarasohn was early successful in obtaining financial patronage from politicians, a factor contributing to his survival during his initial efforts. By 1900 he perceived that Tammany Hall support would be more useful to him than that of the Republican Party, which he had favored hitherto, and two weeks before the election he switched his loyalty to the Democratic candidates. One reason for this political independence was the fact that for the past fifteen years the *Tageblatt* had been the only Yiddish daily in New York. It was therefore read not only by religious and conservative Jews but also by numerous radicals who disdained its politics. After 1900, in competition with emerging rivals, Paley's use of "yellow journalism," then employed by popular English dailies, served to attract and retain readers who would normally not read his newspaper. His sensational headlines in large type served to arouse the curiosity of those who saw them; and the serials of intrigue and mystery often kept these readers for months on end.

An interesting side effect of these trashy serials was the sale of "parts"—a general publishing practice in the time of Charles Dickens. Serials in the *Tageblatt* such as *The Secrets of the Czar's Court* caused readers to wait daily for the appearance of the next installment. This interest started the sale of parts—usually 16-page forms printed on the cheapest paper and sold for five cents. This particular serial had 81 parts. Soon serials from other periodicals began to appear in separate parts, so that around 150 romances, mostly translations from popular fiction in other languages, were issued in this manner. It should be stated that this craving for exciting fiction arose from a yearning for relief and relaxation on the part of "sweated" workers who had not yet been influenced by the agitation of radical organizers. From a positive standpoint it should also be noted that these sentimental romances served to habituate their followers to reading, which in time brought them to literature of greater merit.

To the *Tageblatt*'s credit is the fact that most of its content was serious and solid. Jewish activities the world over were reported regularly; educational articles, adapted to the level of most readers, appeared frequently; various departments catered to the needs and interests of readers devoted to their religious practices as well as to their nostalgic yearning for news from their native lands. Also featured were stories and verse by Yiddish writers from both abroad and at home. One of its leading contributors from 1890 till his death in 1926, Professor Getzel Zelikowitch did much to remove the Germanisms from Yiddish. His weekly article entitled "Literature and Scholarship" was highly valued by many readers. Among the numerous other contributors was Rose Pastor, who later married the millionaire Stokes. Her column, appearing in the English section started by Paley, was called "Ethics of the Dust Pan," a title taken from one of John Ruskin's books.

As a conservative Orthodox newspaper, the *Tageblatt* ignored the labor turmoil agitating Jewish workers during the 1890s and later. It deliberately omitted news of strikes and lockouts, which were occurring almost daily in one industry or another. Occasionally, when it did comment editorially on some aspect of labor unrest, it did so critically of the workers rather than of the employers. This and other shortcomings notwithstanding, the *Tageblatt* served well the needs of the first-generation immigrants, and was a bridge leading its readers from their old-country nostalgia to the positive aspects of their American life.

Paley committed suicide in 1926. By that time the newspaper found itself unable to cope with the increasing competition from rival dailies. Succeeding editors failed to retain the loyalty of readers who had become more and more affected by the social and cultural changes which had come to prevail within the Jewish community. Its circulation, for some years on the decline, amounted to only 57,000 in 1920. Eight years later it was merged with the *Morning Journal.*

Jacob Sapirstein, founder of *The Jewish Morning Journal,* was thus described by a contemporary: "He was a publisher and businessman. Tall, well-built, with neatly combed brown hair over a tall forehead, and a brown Van Dyke beard, Sapirstein impressed people with his nimbleness and vivacity." As Orthodox and conservative as Sarasohn, he had started *The Evening Post* in 1899 in the hope of competing with the successful *Tageblatt.* He also featured popular fiction and religious news.

Unable to compete as an afternoon daily, he decided to make his newspaper a morning edition. When it appeared in 1901 as *The Jewish Morning Journal,* many Jews were in search of work and perused all available want ads. The advantage of time made them await the appearance of the *Morning Journal* in the early hours of the day. Before long its circulation rose notably. To attract more readers, Sapirstein ordered serials from well-known

Yiddish writers, among them the popular Shomer. He also sought to outdo the *Tageblatt* in his Orthodoxy and Americanism and, for a time, in opposition to Zionism. This enterprise gained his daily a sizable slice of Yiddish readership, so that it ultimately surpassed the *Tageblatt* in circulation.

Sapirstein did some book publishing for a while. At one time he arranged with Alexander Harkavy to prepare a textbook in English, for which he paid him $75. The work proved exceptionally successful, yielding Sapirstein a handsome profit—which he refused to share with Harkavy. On the whole, however, his main interest was with the success of the newspaper, and his activity as a book publisher ceased not too long after it had begun.

Much of the success of the *Morning Journal* resulted from the editorship of Peter Viernick, who was in control from 1914 until his death in 1926. He was not only an able journalist but a commendable historian, having written a history of the Jews in America among other works. Philip Rubin wrote of him in *The American Mercury* in 1927: "[He] is in love with everything American, sees all the virtues of the world embodied in Anglo-Saxonism and no good whatever in the Slavs, and never misses an opportunity to chastise the Jewish radical element for its romantic expectations from the erstwhile land of the Czars and pogroms."

As editor he wrote three editorials daily (except Saturdays and holidays) on Jewish and general subjects; also a weekly survey of Jewish literary activity. A free thinker personally, he adhered strictly to the newspaper's Orthodox policy, and made an effort to provide readers with the writings of prominent Yiddish authors. He also edited *The American*, a weekly started by Sapirstein in 1905. For years it added little to Yiddish journalism, and in 1925 Louis Gerson took it over and achieved a circulation of 30,000 by means of popular fiction serials.

Viernick's successor, Jacob Fishman, was more liberal in outlook. While adhering to the newspaper's established conservative position, he modified its policy toward Zionism and continued the effort to keep up the quality of its contributors. Over the years he published the writings of such men as B. Gorin, G. Bublick, A. Mukdoini, and later still Jacob Glatstein. He also serialized the diaries of Theodor Herzl, and the memoirs of Z. H. Masliansky, Madame Max Nordau, and Vladimir Jabotinsky. So popular did these works prove to be, that Cahan successfully obtained the autobiography of Shmaryahu Levin before Fishman was able to bid for it. Although Fishman retired as editor in 1938, he continued as a columnist to the end of his life.

The circulation of the *Morning Journal* increased from year to year, reaching 111,000 in 1916. Thereafter it began to decline slowly along with the other Yiddish dailies, and fell to 77,000 in 1921. In 1928 it rose somewhat after the absorption of the *Tageblatt,* but its readership continued to decline year after year and in 1953 it was merged with the *Day.*

Although most of the early Jewish immigrants were Orthodox and non-political, so that the *Tageblatt* well served their needs for news and reading matter, many of them were working in sweatshops and sufficiently dissatisfied to lend a willing ear to the talk of radicals working with them. Their continued exploitation by employers gradually caused them to heed the calls to strike in the attempt to improve their lot.

The educated and semi-educated radicals in the shops were united, regardless of their political complexion, in their condemnation of capitalism. Socialists, anarchists, and adherents to more abstruse "isms"—all were idealistically dedicated to the equality of men—continued to agitate their "unenlightened" fellow workers. Evening after evening the more energetic radicals called meetings, delivered impassioned speeches, urged unionization, and solicited subscriptions to periodicals they were issuing or hoped to issue. Abraham Cahan, the most articulate of them, worked hard to develop a radical consciousness among Jewish workers; although in his first years in New York he sometimes doubted the effectiveness of his oratory, he knew the effectiveness of his writing. Occasionally aware that he spoke with more passion than sense, he confided to a friend in a moment of candor: "It is a joke. I debate, I argue, I get excited, I shriek, and in the middle of all this, I remind myself that I am a vacant vessel, an empty man without a shred of knowledge, and I begin to blush. I am ashamed of myself."

As was inevitable under the circumstances, one after another of the early periodicals started by radicals failed for lack of funds and readers. The socialists were persistent, however, and when they had to stop bringing out *Die Neie Zeit,* they soon followed it with *Die Arbeiter Zeitung* and *Das Abendblatt,* and proceeded in 1897 to establish *The Jewish Daily Forward.* This newspaper, which in time became the most widely read and longest-lived Yiddish daily, has been so much the creation of Abraham Cahan, the most influential and dynamic of Yiddish editors, that its history is essentially the story of Cahan's own career.

Born in Russia in 1860, Cahan had just graduated from a teachers college when the police found his name on a list of student radicals, and he had to flee the country to avoid imprisonment. As so many other young radicals, he found his way to the United States. Unlike most of them, however, he at once determined to learn English and for several months he sat with ten-year-olds in an elementary school and learned every word uttered in the class. His simultaneous intensive study of Appleton's *Grammar* helped him to master the use of the language. To earn his living he soon began to teach English to immigrants. His free evenings he devoted to discussion and agitation among fellow intellectuals and interested workers. His first public speech in Yiddish was delivered at a workers meeting, where he expounded Marxian socialism for two hours. Aware of his shortcomings as an orator, he knew how to get the utmost effect from his talks. Writing about him years later, M. Epstein pointed out his characteristic traits: "Cahan knew what he wanted, and what he wanted he knew how to get, his indomitable will crushing all opposition. . . . he knew his people and possessed an uncanny intuition of their desires and moods, and these he gratified abundantly. Therein lay the secret of his achievement."

In 1884, eager to unionize the tailors, he spoke at their first organizational meeting. He helped them form the Cloakmakers Union, which became the strongest of the needle-trade organizations and struck frequently to improve their bargaining power. When he began editing *Die Neie Zeit* he realized that in order to reach the mass of workers, who knew only the limited Yiddish of common speech, he and his fellow writers had to teach them how to read and to apprehend what they read. It was a "going to the people" in simple Yiddish. To achieve this linguistic simplicity Cahan had to edit the writers who had been influenced by their reading of German socialist newspapers and wrote in a Germanized Yiddish. It should be added that in editing their material he tended to replace Germanisms with Americanisms.

During this period Cahan began to write for the New York English newspapers—having mastered English with relatively little difficulty. His first article dealt with the coronation of Russia's Alexander II for the New York *World*. He also wrote for the *Sun* and other dailies. For a time he was tempted to make his career as an American journalist, but in 1889 he had definitely decided that it was his duty to work for the Jewish socialist movement. The following year he undertook to edit the newly established *Arbeiter Zeitung*, succeeding Philip Krantz. In the course of time he wrote for it articles on political economy and American history, and also printed translations from currently prominent writers, among them Zola's *Germinal*. In 1894 he also assumed the editorship of *Die Zukunft*, and during the three years he was in control it appeared regularly every month—no mean achievement in the face of financial hardship.

For some time Cahan had promoted the idea of a daily socialist newspaper. When the inner struggle between the De Leon faction and its Jewish opponents resulted in a party split that forced the rebels out of the *Arbeiter Zeitung*, they started *The Jewish Daily Forward* in April 1897 with Cahan as editor. Although the newspaper was officially published by the Forward Association, Cahan was too domineering a personality to do its bidding. To attract readers among Jewish workers he printed popular articles, stories, serials, and catchy headlines. His doctrinaire colleagues disdained these enticing devices and argued for straight socialist propaganda. Unable to quiet them, he resigned after several months and did not return until nearly five years later.

Cahan now devoted his time to writing fiction in English. Even earlier one of his stories had brought him to the favorable attention of William Dean Howells, who encouraged him to write

Yekel, a novel which was published by D. Appleton and Company in 1896. Cahan also became friends with Lincoln Steffens and was employed by him as a police reporter on the *Commercial Advertiser.* In his free time he also wrote *The Imported Bridegroom and Other Stories* (1898). When Steffens subsequently resigned from the newspaper, Cahan also left it. By that time the appeal of the Jewish milieu was very strong, and he again began to contribute articles to the *Forward.* The newspaper was in decline, and members of the Forward Association began to urge him to return on his own terms.

One of the terms on which he accepted the editorship was that he leave the office at 2 o'clock in the afternoon in order to have time for his English writing. In his effort to build up the readership of the *Forward,* however, he seldom left early and often remained till late in the evening. Aware that many Jews had not yet become habituated to reading a daily newspaper, and eager to attract non-radical workers, he made many changes in his effort to achieve a liveliness of style and an appeal of curiosity—features he had learned from Arthur Brisbane and Steffens. Thus he used screaming headlines, sensational stories, and popular articles—very much like the *Tageblatt.* He stressed news having human interest as a means of both educating and titillating his readers.

To satisfy his doctrinaire colleagues he also preached socialist ideals and principles, denounced intolerance, and favored human brotherhood. An instance of his tolerance was his approval of a socialist freethinker saying *kaddish* for a deceased father to please his bereaved mother. He further insisted on the use of "plain Yiddish" without Germanisms or fancy vocabulary. "The *Forward,*" he maintained, "is not only an organ for socialists; it is a socialist daily for Yiddish-speaking readers." As a socialist he refused to accept advertisements from capitalist sources, and rejected those from the American Tobacco Company because it was anti-union. Soon, as a result of these innovations, the circulation of the *Forward* rose to 19,000 within four months after he had returned to it, or five times its previous number.

Critical members of the Forward Association remained dissatisfied with what they considered his low-level standards. To this accusation he replied: "If you wished to lift a child you must first bend down to the ground, for otherwise how would you reach it?" In his linguistic reform he stressed clarity above purity, and substituted common Americanisms for objectionable Germanisms. Thus he did not hesitate to use Yiddishized English words and phrases in his editorials and articles. Simultaneously, however, wishing to give the *Forward* a literary flavor, he began to print stories and poems by such Yiddish writers as Peretz, Z. Libin, Abraham Reisen, and Sholem Asch. He also published political articles by leading European socialists. His own articles of literary criticism gained in influence as the *Forward* grew in popularity, so that he in time became a leading popularizer of Yiddish literature.

Around 1903 Cahan began to encourage readers to send him written contributions concerned with their personal experiences, acting on the truism that truth was often stranger than fiction. The appeal soon brought numerous accounts of real-life stories. These communications were printed in a column entitled "From the People to the People."

One day three such letters came which did not quite fit the column, and Cahan decided to print them separately under the heading of "*A Bintel Brief*" (A Bundle of Letters). Since the epistles required a response, Cahan did so and asked for more such communications because of their intrinsic interest. "These letters," Epstein wrote, "touching upon delicate problems encountered in daily life by people from widely separated areas suddenly thrown together as next-door neighbors, roused wide interest; others were encouraged to open their hearts to the editor."

Indeed, for many of these correspondents the editor in effect replaced the *shtetl* rabbi as counsellor. Soon many letters began reaching Cahan's desk—letters dealing frankly with matters of love, jealousy, marital relations, parent-and-child difficulties. All these writers asked for advice, and Cahan responded sympathetically. Years later he stated: "Hundreds of thousands were torn from their homes, from those closest to them; they are lonely

Abraham Cahan, from early young manhood to his old age, was the most influential Yiddish journalist.

souls seeking an opportunity to open their hearts and arouse an interest in themselves, to get an opinion or advice about what concerns them."

As the number of the letters increased, Cahan's secretary, Leon Gottlieb, read them as they arrived, selected what seemed to him the most significant, and improved their grammar and clarity. Cahan wrote the responses. "I could do this with the greatest pleasure," he stated in his memoirs, "For in these letters one perceived a rare panorama of human souls. I had a literary interest in this work." To keep this popular column active in the early years, when letters were few or not interesting enough, staff members either wrote imaginary epistles or edited dull ones to make them more interesting. Later the number of letters increased to an extent that Cahan was unable to deal with all personally, and the replies were assigned to his associates.

Another of Cahan's innovations was "The Gallery of Vanished Husbands." The fluid, chaotic social conditions among the Jewish immigrants, especially after the large influx following the 1905 pogroms in Russia, created situations in which young husbands came alone, often with borrowed funds for expenses, with the understanding that they would bring over their wives and children at the first opportunity. A number of these men, relishing American freedom, and meeting young women who appealed to them, tended to relax their ties to the families they had left behind or had brought over. The result frequently was abandonment, with the rejected wife left in dire need. Some of these wives wrote to the *Forward* to express their misery and to appeal to their vanished husbands to return to them.

When four such letters came one day, together with photographs of the missing husbands, Cahan printed them in the hope that exposure would help the distressed wives. Soon other similar letters reached the office, along with photographs, and were printed once a week. In time the letters were brought to the attention of the United Hebrew Charities, which established the National Desertion Bureau under the direction of Charles Zunser, son of the popular poet. This feature continued to appear weekly for many years, with the letters investigated by the Bureau before they were printed. Many husbands were brought back to their families or compelled to provide for their support.

Cahan, assured of success as editor, brooked no opposition. He arrogated to himself the reviewing of plays and books, and his criticisms were sometimes highly laudatory or harshly unfavorable. When Jacob Gordin, at the time the leading Yiddish playwright, objected to Cahan's criticism of his dramas, the latter feuded with him for some years thereafter. Although Abraham Liessen was one of his editorial writers for a decade, he lost favor with him when he wrote poems in praise of the Jewish past at a time when Cahan was still anti-nationalist. Years later Cahan himself became interested in traditional Jewishness, and indeed approved the celebration of the Passover Seder, which many socialists continued to ignore.

In 1905, reacting to criticism that the *Forward* had little of literary content, Cahan started a weekly, *Spirit of the Times,* which published literary and political articles of a serious nature as well as stories and poems and humor by established writers. Although the weekly soon achieved a circulation of 28,000, Cahan had to suspend it because it proved too costly. Thereafter he expanded the literary section of the *Forward.*

In his effort to spurt the circulation of the newspaper, Cahan gave out as a premium 25,000 copies of Harkavy's *Dictionary.* He also disposed of a premium of 26,000 copies of volume one and 25,000 of volume two of *The History of the United States,* which he had written in Yiddish and which the *Forward* published. Many of the readers were members of various unions then struggling for recognition, and the *Forward* backed them in every strike and in their membership campaigns. In 1913, however, when Cahan urged compromise in a strike of tailors, some of the extremists broke windows in the *Forward* office.

One of Cahan's aims was for the *Forward* to have a home of its own. This ambition was realized when in 1911 the newspaper was housed in its own ten-story building on East Broadway. The following year the *Forward* celebrated its fifteenth anniversary with a gala affair at the Hippodrome. By that time its circulation had risen to 130,462—much the largest of any Yiddish or other foreign-language newspaper in America. Always eager to improve the usefulness of the daily, Cahan initiated a new feature which proved very popular: resumés of informative or interesting articles in the Sunday editions of the New York newspapers were provided every Monday.

Busy as Cahan was as editor and socialist leader, he in 1913 began writing fiction for *McClure's Magazine*. These stories later became the basis for *The Rise of David Levinsky* (1917), a novel that has stood the test of time as a work of fine realistic fiction.

Although Cahan would not take criticism of his editorial policies, he so enjoyed the humorous skits critical of the *Forward* which J. Adler wrote for *Der Groiser Kunds*, that he engaged him as a staff writer, having him use the pseudonym of B. Kovner. The latter's series of sketches under the title of "Yente Telebende" described with broad humor the foibles and experiences of Yente, her husband Mendel, and their son Pinne—to the great enjoyment of many readers.

In 1914 the *Forward* began to print "Folk College," a section on popular science which included simple expositions of physiology, astronomy, civics, and other natural and social sciences. Cahan wrote articles on the Spanish Inquisition, Spinoza, and Russian history. In the same year Zigmund Mogulesco, the leading Yiddish comedian, was interviewed at length by Cahan on his activities and experiences in the Yiddish theater, which Leon Gottlieb edited for publication in the *Forward*. Cahan also wrote in great detail about the Mendel Baylis case in Kiev as well as on the Leo M. Frank trial and lynching. At first he had assumed Frank was guilty, but a trip to Atlanta, where he investigated the accusation against the Jewish businessman from every angle, convinced him of the man's innocence. "The impressions with which I returned from Atlanta," he stated later, "were the deepest and most painful I have ever experienced." In addition to the series of articles in the *Forward* he also devoted much space to the case in his memoirs.

In 1914 the *Forward* reached its peak of popularity with a circulation of 206,000. When the war in Europe started that September, the *Forward* along with most other Jewish dailies sided with Germany because of their animosity to Czarist Russia. Not a few readers, well along in the process of Americanization, favored the Allies, however, and they began to boycott the newspapers. As a consequence their circulation fell off drastically from the peak total of 762,910, and the *Forward* along with the others, never regained their losses. In 1917 the entry of the United States into the war caused intensive anti-German hostility in the country, and the *Forward,* as a socialist organ, was in danger of suspension, but was saved by the intercession of Louis Marshall.

The *Forward* has remained the most widely read Yiddish daily to the present day. At the end of the war it took over *The Daily Workers World* of Chicago and turned it into its Midwestern edition, which was continued until 1951. In the 1920s it started an English section and had prominent liberal writers of the calibre of Sidney Webb and Bertrand Russell contribute to it; it was stopped, however, during the Depression of the 1930s. Another of its features was a week-end rotogravure section that proved very popular.

After the Bolshevik revolution, Cahan became extremely anticommunist and fought the communist section among the Jewish radicals without let-up. He also became more sensitive of his Jewishness and even approved of Zionism. When Sholem Asch submitted *The Nazarene* to him for serialization, as he had his previous books for many years, Cahan found it too pro-Christian in spirit and rejected it with a blast that broke up his long and intimate friendship with his featured novelist.

To the end of his long life, even when he was incapacitated for seven months by a stroke, Cahan retained full control of the *Forward's* editorial policy—or at least so he assumed. All the while after 1914, of course, the daily's circulation and influence were shrinking. On his death in 1951, the editorship was assumed by Hillel Rogoff, and he was followed by L. Fogelman and M. Kristol; and although it is now the only Yiddish daily newspaper in America—except for the communist *Freiheit*—its circulation is down to around 30,000 and its one-time strong financial position had become so attenuated that it has to depend on assistance from the Workmen's Circle. On its 75th anniversary its lead editorial proudly yet nostalgically restated its original position as a socialist organ:

> *To help the workingman and the Jewish immigrant in the new land were the main reasons for the forming of this paper.* The *Forward* has changed with the times but has never deviated from its real goal: to help improve the living conditions of the workingman and create a better world.

Louis E. Miller was one of the pioneering socialists on the lower East Side. For a time a practicing lawyer, he was too involved politically to stick to his professional work. A highly persuasive speaker, he strove energetically to organize Jewish workers. When the break with De Leon's Socialist Labor Party occurred in 1897, Miller became one of the founders of the *Forward* and was for a time one of Cahan's closest collaborators. They sometimes differed in their views and attacked each other viciously, much to the pleasure of their readers and to the benefit of the newspaper, but usually they soon composed their differences and remained friends. In 1903, however, they found themselves at loggerheads, and the final break came when Cahan attacked Jacob Gordin's stature as a dramatist and refused to print Miller's defense of the playwright.

Thereupon Miller left the *Forward*, took over the moribund *Daily Herald*, which was started in 1895, and transformed it into a new daily, *Die Warheit* (The Truth). He engaged a number of the better Yiddish writers as contributors, among them Chaim Zhitlowsky, N. Syrkin, Joel Entin, and aimed to compete with the *Forward*. He stated at the outset that he would pursue a socialist policy. A year later, however, he realized his inability to divert readers from the *Forward;* that his best chance of success was with the literary and liberal elements. In 1906 he indeed lost a number of his radical readers when he came out in favor of William Randolph Hearst's candidacy for governor of New York, but the move brought him revenue from Tammany Hall. His editorials, neither as incisive nor as forceful as Cahan's, tended toward bombast.

Having abandoned his socialist position, Miller began to stress

Louis Miller rivalled Cahan as a Jewish leader and journalist, but failed to attain his ambitious aims.

Jewish nationalism and to promote Jewish culture. In these aims he was fully supported by his leading contributors, and the *Warheit* became the standard bearer of liberal and literary readers. When Miller perceived the popularity of "*A Bintel Brief*," he initiated a section called "The Pigeon Post" and urged readers to send their letters to it. He also started a column of social and sentimental gossip, and ran fiction serials written by popular authors. All these attractions to gain readers resulted only in mild success. For nearly a decade, however, the more intelligent members of the Jewish middle class supported it loyally.

When the war started in 1914, Miller was the only Yiddish editor to favor the Allies. Most of his readers, still strongly opposed to Russia, were antagonized by Miller's position, and many stopped reading the *Warheit*. His financial backers became alarmed at the prospective loss of their investment and relieved Miller of his editorship. The damage was already done, however, and the daily failed to recover its readership. In 1919 it was merged with the *Day*.

Miller made a valiant effort to continue as editor of Yiddish newspapers, and in 1916 he started *The Leader*, but after several months he had to admit failure. The following year he began to publish *Miller's Weekly*, an illustrated periodical, but this too was stopped within a year. His final attempt as an editor was in 1926, when he started the abortive tabloid, *The New Truth*.

Der Tog (The Day) was founded in 1914 by a group headed by Judah Magnes, M. Weinberg, and Bernard Semel. Herman Bernstein of the New York *Times* was engaged as editor, and the policy of the sponsors was to make the daily non-partisan, politically liberal, and literary in the best sense of the term. Many of the leading Yiddish writers were invited as regular contributors. The aim of all concerned was to uplift the standard of Yiddish journalism and provide readers with the best available writing. In its first issue the daily declared its policy: "Impartial, clean in politics, adapted to the spirit of the time, accurate and rich in news, both of America and abroad, this newspaper will strive to become a creative and productive force in the life of the Jewish people." One hundred thousand copies of the first issue were printed and quickly sold, and thereafter the sale averaged 60,000 copies during the first year.

When Bernstein resigned to become a war correspondent in the European war, he was replaced by William Edlin. Written in a careful Yiddish and printed in an attractive format, featuring prominent writers, and free of political handicaps, *The Day* greatly benefited from Miller's pro-Allied position and attracted many of the *Warheit* readers, so that its circulation rose to 81,000 by the end of its second year. It should be stated that among its prominent features were Vladimir Grossman's reports of the war from his home base in Denmark. Syrkin's anti-German articles were complemented by Edlin's sympathy toward the Allies. With *The Day* prospering during and after the war, it was logical for it to absorb the *Warheit* in 1919. Nor did it suffer when Herman Bernstein, back in the United States, started *Haint* (Today) and made a strong effort to compete with *The Day;* after two months he had to suspend publication.

In 1919 Weinberg, a wealthy realtor and the biggest investor in *The Day,* gained complete control. By that time, however, the Yiddish readership had already begun its state of decline owing to reduced immigration and the natural process of Americanization. Weinberg strove to improve the efficiency of the staff and set a policy that combined those of the New York *Times* and the *Forward.* He also added such distinguished contributors as David Pinski, Shmuel Niger, and others—so that the newspaper was able to boast of a galaxy of the best writers. In the early 1920s its circulation was 86,000, with 118,000 on Sundays.

In an effort to stop the decline in circulation *The Day,* like the other dailies, started an English section. For years Samuel Margoshes, who became the editor not long after, wrote a column in English for the left-hand column on the front page. After 1945 the Sunday edition had an entire page in English. But the decline continued. In 1953 the merger with the *Morning Journal* helped somewhat temporarily, but the struggle for survival persisted, and in 1973 deep losses forced the management to stop publication, leaving the ailing *Forward* alone in the field.

Not entirely alone. For the political schism at the end of World War I caused the Socialist Party to split into three factions, with the two communist groups uniting soon after into the Communist Party. The Jewish section felt the need of a daily organ in order to propagate communist doctrine among the Jewish workers, and in 1922 it started *Die Freiheit* (Freedom), with M. Olgin as editor and P. Novick as his associate. From the first the *Freiheit* and the *Forward* attacked each other brutally, vulgarly, venomously. During the 1920s the new daily achieved a circulation of 23,000, but thereafter the number declined, especially after the editors, in line with communist policy, approved of Arab attacks in Palestine in 1929 and the Soviet-Nazi pact ten years later. The loyal supporters, however, have kept it going despite its unavoidable deficits. To the *Freiheit's* credit must be mentioned that in addition to its doctrinaire policy it provided its readers with a good amount of meritorious verse and fiction as well as articles of information.

In sum, the Yiddish newspapers have for nearly a century served the Jewish community in America—composed at first of hapless, provincial immigrants thrust upon a civilization completely alien to them—as guide, counselor, comforter, educator, and cultural mentor. Intellectuals learned to write for these dailies, and readers found them a source of much-needed information and entertainment. Time helped editors to cleanse Yiddish of Germanisms, and later also of Americanisms, and the better writers molded it into a flexible and imaginative means of literary expression, adapted to both poetry and science. And although relatively few Jews now depend on Yiddish for their reading, enough of them cling to it nostalgically, or out of a sense of ethnic appreciation, to keep it alive, perhaps indefinitely.

6

Later Yiddish Magazines

The urge to publish in order to give expression to ideas and ideals and doctrines caused various individuals and groups to continue to break into print. Most of the periodicals were short-lived, but they gave evidence of the cultural ferment within the bustling Jewish community. The Jewish unions, in the early years struggling to attract the "sweated" workers, sought to win their adherence by issuing periodicals which advocated unionization as a means of obtaining better working conditions. Thus the United Hebrew Trades began in 1899 to publish *The Daily Folk-Times* to inform members of the labor situation in their specific trades and to spur the unceasing effort at greater unionization. Other similar periodicals, started after 1900 and continued for years thereafter, were *Equality, The New Post, The Ladies Garment Worker, Justice,* etc.

Enterprising journalists outside of New York—in Chicago, Boston, Cleveland, Baltimore, and other cities—started Yiddish periodicals, mostly ephemeral, in emulation of their New York colleagues, In their effort to gain readers they provided educational and informational articles as well as verse and fiction. The majority of Jewish readers in those cities, however, continued to look to New York for their reading matter, and the local weeklies succumbed.

Many periodicals started in New York were equally short-lived, owing largely to the fact that the Yiddish newspapers took up most of the reading time available to many Jewish workers. But the effort to advocate ideas and ideals dear to them did not discourage a number of individuals and groups. For instance, the Labor Zionists, spurred by N. Syrkin, issued *The People* in 1906, first as a monthly, later as a weekly, but lack of funds stopped it after a brief struggle. In 1909 Chaim Zhitlowsky, the prestigious thinker and lecturer, brought out *Dos Neie Leben* (The New Life). He and other prominent writers, socialists with a nationalist bias, asserted in their well-written articles that Yiddish culture was a requisite of modern Jewish life and that the Yiddish language had become comprehensive and refined enough to serve speakers and writers as a fully competent means of expression. Although this magazine's circulation never exceeded 3,000, it was a positive influence in the Jewish community during its four years of existence. David Pinski and other writers started the literary weekly, *Yiddishe Wochenschrift* (Jewish Weekly News), and strove hard to attract readers, but after twenty months of effort they had to give it up. In 1921 the Jewish Socialist Farband began publishing *Der Wecker* (The Awakener), which appeared nine times a year; one of the few weeklies to persist, it is now edited by Elias Schulman. In 1925 Yosele Rosenblatt, the prominent cantor, began to issue *The Jewish Light*, but after keeping it up for a year and going into debt, had to give it up. Of a more permanent existence are *Die Yiddishe Kultur*, started by the Yiddish Kultur Farband in 1938, and *Kultur un Leben*, founded by the Workmen's Circle in 1967—both having a similar aim from different political positions.

Of the magazines currently in existence, several are of notable significance. The oldest Yiddish periodical still in existence is *Die Freie Arbeiter Shtimme.* It began to appear in July 1890 and has continued, with early interruptions, to the present. Sponsored by anarchists and edited by Philip Krantz, it was stopped after two years by the depression of the 1890s. An effort was made to revive it in 1893, but it had to suspend after a year and was not restored until 1899. In that year it began to be edited by Saul Yanowsky, an able and devoted anarchist journalist, and he made it an organ of free thought and literary expression. During his twenty years as editor he became the most hospitable publisher of new and experimental writing. His columns were opened to anyone who manifested a modicum of literary talent, so that the magazine became in a real sense a laboratory for Yiddish literature. Furthermore, he helped young authors by criticizing their work and encouraging them to keep writing. By this procedure he was instrumental in publishing the first efforts of most Yiddish writers in the first two decades of this century.

Yanowsky's own articles were polemic in content and cogent in reasoning. They introduced his readers to the basic problems of world politics, American democracy, and Jewish trade unionism. He improved the literary taste of thousands, and his tolerance toward those differing with him ideationally made possible greater responsibility in the expression of ideas. On occasion, of course, he was inconsistent in his editing—rejecting a poem or story and then accenting it when resubmitted under a pseudonym, but that spoke more for his heart than for his intellect. Although he left the weekly to edit *Justice* for the next six years, he continued to write for it to the end of his life in 1939. And his influence remained evident through the years that followed. At present the *Freie Arbeiter Shtimme* is issued as a monthly and edited by P. Konstan.

The most important Yiddish periodical to be published in this country is *Die Zukunft*. It was founded in 1892 by the United Hebrew Trades, which had started the *Arbeiter Zeitung* two years earlier but now needed a monthly in which to print substantive articles of a socialist and cultural content for the more serious-minded members. Philip Krantz was asked to edit it, and the opening statement made clear its intent:

> We are saying openly: We do not wish to hide the fact that we are starting a scientific journal in jargon—a new event in the poor jargon literature—*only as an experiment*. The Jewish workers movement is growing fast and is bringing forth workers who wish to learn fully

the social problems of our time as well as to educate themselves; yet they cannot achieve this because hitherto jargon only gave them old wives' tales and mere rhetoric, and they do not know other languages enough to be able to read a book or article in these languages. . . . Other than scientific articles in our pure mother-tongue on various important questions, we shall also provide stories, poems, and art criticism; for we maintain that art educates and ennobles man, and we wish to combine, as we said, the useful with the enjoyable.

The *Zukunft* started as an avowed socialist monthly. Yet Krantz and his sponsors felt the need to educate its readers not only in socialist doctrine but in the use of good Yiddish and in the appreciation of sound literature. The lack of money caused the monthly to appear irregularly at first, but when Abraham Cahan took over the editorship in 1894 he managed to stabilize its publication. From the outset Krantz and his successors welcomed Yiddish writers regardless of their political views, although their hospitality did not approach Yanowsky's. Among the early contributors were Jacob Gordin and Morris Rosenfeld. It also welcomed translated contributions from major non-Jewish writers, and an article by Ibsen appeared as early as 1894; subsequently it printed essays by Tolstoy, Gorki, Zola, de Maupassant, and Poe, as well as by radical leaders everywhere.

The writings of Yiddish authors published in the 1890s and later dealt with morals, ethics, linguistics, and philosophy in addition to belles lettres. The educational articles were written mainly from a socialist standpoint, but the editors were equally cognizant of the importance of literary merit and at times accepted contributions of quality despite their variance from the monthly's socialist position. Thus in 1897 it published Abraham Liessin's "Two Prayers," which had a definitely nationalistic content. Cahan felt apologetic about it but explained: "We publish this poem on the strength of its poetic quality, although its tendency is somewhat foreign to us."

The fact need not be labored that the *Zukunft* was for many years in a condition of financial precariousness. Its readership was never large enough to provide it with a sound economic base, so that it had to depend on subventions and contributions from radi-

Die Zukunft has been the leading literary and cultural monthly since its founding in 1892.

Abraham Liessin was a fine poet and the great editor of *Die Zukunft*.

cal organizations. Yet its journalistic quality always remained high and its editorial policy was immune to influence.

The *Zukunft's* golden period began in 1913 with Liessin's assumption of the editorship. He had been on the staff of the *Forward* up to that time. A dedicated socialist, he did not always see eye to eye with Cahan, much to the latter's annoyance. When the break between them was becoming obvious, leaders of the Forward Association, appreciating Liessin's worth as a writer and respectful of his independence, yet loath to antagonize Cahan, arranged to have Liessin become the editor of the *Zukunft* and to assume its financial support.

Liessin became a superior editor. Unlike other editors of the time, he respected the writings of contributors and did not tinker with the content of their articles, even as he had not permitted other editors to alter any of his writings. His attitude attracted the more talented Yiddish authors, and they were pleased to be published by him. Liessin, moreover, while respecting the socialist bias of the monthly, did not hesitate to accept contributions of merit by writers who were politically averse to radicalism. The advantages of his editorship were manifested by the end of the first year, when the circulation jumped from 3000 to 21,000.

He himself was deeply immersed in Jewish history and rabbinical writings. In poem after poem he enlivened the heroic martyrs of the Jewish past as well as of the more recent revolutionary period. "Rabbi Akiba" and "Hirsh Leckert" were among his best lyrical creations. With the same affection and respect he wrote about the pioneers of the Jewish workers movement. His editorial articles were written with the utmost literary care, and his views on the events of the month and on basic current problems were expressed with great clarity and profound thought. More than once he intimated that he cherished these journalistic essays more than he did his poetry.

An examination of the magazine's contents during 1916, a year chosen at random, will indicate its scope and character. The twelve issues included 99 writers, and they provided 30 stories and plays, 30 poems, 22 articles of literary criticism, 22 biographical sketches, 14 theoretical essays on nature and culture, 29 articles on socialism, 30 contributions on Jewish problems, 35 on current affairs, and 47 on a variety of American subjects. All this material was written specifically for the *Zukunft,* and all were carefully edited by Liessin.

If Liessin was critically rigorous with his own writing, he was sometimes less firm with the contributions of newcomers or of those in obvious need. He was the first editor able to pay for material he accepted—the honorarium was of course relatively small—and he at times agreed to publish a poem or article he was doubtful about in order to help the impoverished writer. It is also true that he had his preferences, but he was objective enough not to let that govern his acceptances. Nor did he, like many magazine editors, limit himself to relatively short pieces. When A. Glantz-Leyeles submitted his drama, *Shlomo Molkhu,* Liessin found it of such merit that he agreed to publish it serially in five installments. Some years later the distinguished poet Jacob Glatstein summed up Liessin's editorial career:

> There is not one great name in Yiddish literature that did not find an open door to the *Zukunft.* A. Liessin placed his stamp on the monthly but he was broadminded enough to print things which he considered too daring, too revolutionary artistically, so long as he saw they possessed merit.

When Liessin died in 1938, the editorial function of the *Zukunft* was assumed by Sh. Niger, D. Pinski, and H. Rogoff—three men of high literary repute. By that time the Forward Association had come upon hard times and was no longer able to assume the monthly deficits. Thereupon CYCO (Central Yiddish Cultural Organization), established that year, took over the task of sponsorship. It called a conference of writers and organization leaders for December 12, 1940. Workmen's Circle, The I. L. Peretz Writers Union, and other groups joined in the discussion, and after a lapse of nine months the *Zukunft* resumed publication. Emphasis on the part of the editors was modified from Socialism to culture, and this policy has been maintained to the present, although the editorship has changed several times. On the occasion of special anniversaries the monthly appeared in considerably enlarged editions—issues noted for their historic, reminiscent, and literary content.

As indicated previously, every political, labor, and cultural Jewish group, regardless of financial paucity, sought to give voice to its aims in a periodical. In most instances this journalistic effort was short-lived. One of the important groups to establish a permanent magazine for its members was the Labor Zionists. In March 1906 they started *Der Yiddisher Kemfer* (The Jewish Fighter) in Philadelphia. The following year it was moved to New York. The weekly expounded the aims and activities of the socialists who favored a Jewish homeland in Palestine. Its first prominent leader was N. Syrkin, a gifted serious thinker; somewhat later B. Borukhov assumed leadership in the organization. In the early years of its existence, with the sponsoring membership small, the weekly remained in financial difficulties and appeared irregularly into the 1920s. From the first, however, the editors were highly critical of the cheap journalistic devices of the daily newspapers. They also advocated Yiddish education of children and encouraged the serious writing of Yiddish. As a literary center for Labor Zionist thought, the weekly printed numerous articles on political and social topics. To further the education of Jewish children, its sponsors began to establish Peretz schools in which stress was laid on Jewish nationalism.

In 1924 the *Kemfer* became a biweekly and was renamed *Der Yiddisher Arbeiter* (The Jewish Worker). During the next several years it functioned with the assistance of K. Marmor, D. Pinski, Borukhov, J. Entin, and Chaim Greenberg. In 1932 it again became a weekly under its original name, and its editorial policy was directed by Greenberg. He was not long in taking the weekly out of its narrow party status and developing it into a prestigious literary periodical. His energy and ideological depth made him the spiritual leader of Labor Zionism. In 1934 he also assumed the editorship of *The Jewish Frontier* and made it a popular periodical for English-reading Jews. A passionate Zionist, he was also a strong exponent of Yiddish and was highly critical of the anti-Yiddish attitude of Zionists in Palestine.

An examination of its issues in 1942, again a random choice, gives a fair idea of the general content of the magazine. During this year it published numerous stories, poems, general articles, and war news. Greenberg's editorials and essays dominated each issue, and he was acutely critical of the national superiority assumed by certain Jews and non-Jews. The literary flavor of the weekly was evident in every issue, and books were given as premiums to new subscribers. B. Glazman's novel, *Bread* was serialized for over seven months; Kadia Molodowsky's long poem, "Brownsville," was also serialized. Literary criticism by Yiddish writers appeared frequently, and Greenberg himself wrote essays on William James and the Nietzsche. Each issue also had several serious book reviews. In May a Jubilee edition marked the tenth year of Greenberg's editorship and the 35th year of the weekly's founding. In its 224 pages there was a twelve-page section of M. Boraisho's long poem, *The Walker,* and the issue concluded with Shlomo Bickel's long critical essay on the basic tendencies and directions in Yiddish literature.

Greenberg died in 1953, but his influence remained evident in the character of the weekly in the years that followed. Special expanded issues were brought out twice a year in celebration of Rosh Hashanah and Passover. The establishment of Israel caused most space to be given to articles dealing with the problems of the new homeland, so that less fiction and poetry were printed, but the quality remained high.

In 1943 I. A. Weissman and L. Feinberg, both poets, started the monthly, *Epoch,* with the aim of providing a journal devoted to Yiddish verse. It also printed critical articles on poets as well as sections of reminiscences of older poets. For a couple of months the editorship was given to the well-known poet, Mani Layb, who quickly took issue with David Ignatov's self-serving recollections of his role as leader of the *Yunge*. This and other polemical articles took up more space than the printed poems. By 1948 Weissman, the monthly's editor, had to stop its publication for lack of funds.

In 1945, when Yiddish journalism reached its 75th anniversary, David Pinski's "Salute" to it in the *Zukunft* well summarized its nature and achievement:

> The Yiddish periodicals were not only bringers of news, information mongers, but also, and essentially, conveyors of ideas. . . . So-

cialism, Zionism, anarchism, free thought, conservatism—all the periodicals were fighting organs. And all were thoroughly Yiddish, always ready to protest and storm against repression and persecution. The Jew in Eastern Europe had never heard such bold language, and must have felt supported and encouraged. And best of all, they created Yiddish literature—their greatest achievement! They nursed Yiddish literature . . . the first steps and the later development of its creators. This cannot be found in newspapers of other languages . . . only the Yiddish press did this—and what a distance it had to go in its development of Yiddish . . . from its Germanism to its proud word-richness, which makes it one of the richest literary languages.

Hebrew has of course a much older history in this country than Yiddish. In addition to its study by Christians from the earliest settlement, it was part of the synagogue service and prayer by the Jewish immigrants since their first arrival in 1654. Prayer books in Hebrew as well as other religious tomes were printed, as previously indicated, by Jewish communities from the early decades of the nineteenth century. Nevertheless it was a weak transplant when compared to the efflorescence of Yiddish after 1900.

For years Hebrew writing was done mostly by scholars who were born in Europe and who maintained the traditional pedantic flavor of their early training. Among the early East European Jews who wrote in Hebrew were M. M. Dolitsky and N. H. Imber, who had come to this country in the 1890s. Some of the later Hebrew writers were Simon Halkin, Hillel Bavli, Israel Efros, I. Silberberg, Reuben Wallenrod, J. D. Eisenstein, J. Twersky, Meyer Waxman, Simon Bernstein, Shalom Spiegel, Zvi Scharfstein, M. Ribalow, Daniel Twersky, and H. Sackler—a random listing that makes evident the considerable richness of the Hebrew literature produced by them. What is significant is that these writers were learned men steeped in Jewish tradition and conveying an exotic flavor in their American setting. Their writings have been used mostly by teachers of Hebrew. It is also important to note that as early as 1903 there were four Hebrew translations of Harriet Beecher Stowe's *Uncle Tom's Cabin.* About that time and later there also appeared translations of Mark

Twain's books as well as works by Cooper, Irving, Whitman, Emerson, Thoreau, Henry James, and Hemingway. Several volumes of American verse, short stories, and novels were also translated. Most of this literature was of course used by students of Hebrew.

In 1913 Reuven Brainin, a prominent Hebrew writer who had migrated to the United States, started *The Mast,* a Hebrew monthly, but it failed to maintain itself. Three years later advocates of Hebrew formed the Histadruth Ivrith (Federation for Hebrew Culture) for the purpose of furthering the study and use of the Holy Tongue among their fellow Jews. To this end they started *Hadoar* (The Post) in 1921, and this weekly continues to the present. Edited by M. Ribalow, it had sought to enrich Hebrew literature and strengthen the position of Hebrew in the United States. In 1928 *Bitzaron,* a Hebrew monthly, was issued to further Hebrew scholarship and literature. It prints articles on philosophy, belles lettres, Zionism, and current events. Scholarly in content, it strives to be popular in style.

In 1942 Sefarim, a Hebrew publishing organization, was merged with Histadruth Ivrith for the purpose of publishing Israeli-American books in Hebrew. In its first year it managed to bring out six volumes. The organization has produced a number of books annually since then, and most of them are of a religious content.

In addition to Hebrew and Yiddish one might mention Ladino. Sephardic Jews employ the Ladino dialect as their mother-tongue. These Jews have come from the Mediterranean lands and continued to use the speech developed by their Spanish and Portuguese forefathers. Although their number in New York is not large, they publish a Ladino periodical, *La Vara,* and thus add their small share to Jewish publishing in America.

7

Early Yiddish Literature

As indicated previously, a number of young Jews who came to the United States in the 1880s and later were fairly well educated and free of religious dogma. Many had to flee from Russia because of their radicalism. Regardless of their early training, they were forced to join their fellow immigrants as workers in the expanding sweatshops in order to earn the means for their meager living. In Russia they had rebelled against Czarist oppression; in America they cried out against the evils of capitalism and the exploitation of which they were most unwilling victims. Young and idealistic, many naively utopian in attitude, they preached the tenets of socialism and anarchism to their fellow workers. Some of them had to learn Yiddish in order to do so. With many workers still steeped in the medieval piety of their fathers, cowed and insecure in their new environment, the effort to organize them was an uphill struggle. The very attempt, however, sharpened the minds and developed the gift of writing of a good many of the young propagandists.

There were other immigrants, mildly liberated religiously and with only a smattering of secular education, who were equally rebellious against sweatshop slavery. Having a latent literary potential, they cried out against this exploitation with an emotional intensity which resulted in "kettle-drum" verse. One of the better-educated and more sophisticated of this group, though no sweatshop worker, was Morris Winchevsky (Lippe Benzion Novakhovits), born near Kovno in 1856. At seventeen he began working in a bank and writing verse in his free time. Three years later he went to Germany, already a convinced radical, but government hostility forced him to leave the country for England. There he became intimately connected with the Jewish socialist movement and wrote Yiddish and Hebrew articles under the cognomen of "The Mad Philosopher." In 1885 he began editing *Der Arbeiter Freint* (The Worker's Friend), which soon extended its influence to New York. He also continued to write verse of considerable merit. In the words of M. Epstein, "His fighting poems ring with true pathos. Strikingly fresh and challenging, they awakened hope in working men and women on both sides of the Atlantic." His popularity caused New York socialists to invite him to work with them. His independence proved unacceptable to many, however, and he had to function as best he could as a journalist and editor. His verse and articles in time earned him the title of "Grandfather of Jewish Socialism." Liessin later stated that Winchevsky was "the first socialist writer of prose whose talented columns and precise polished short pieces have contributed to our press, grace, and style."

David Edelstadt was a sensitive romantic youth who grew up on radical literature and was traumatically affected by the Kiev pogrom of 1881. Sixteen years at the time, knowing no Yiddish and having no Jewish background, he nevertheless decided to leave Russia and soon reached Cincinnati, where he had some relatives. There he began to work in a clothing factory making button holes. Having soon learned Yiddish from his fellow workers, he expressed his antagonism to government and capitalism in impassioned polemic verse. His poems, he stated, "were not born in a flower garden [but] in the dark world of slavery. They were written by a slave whose enthusiasm derived from the struggle against slavery." He soon went to New York to be with kindred spirits, and before long he became an editor of the anarchist *Truth* and a founder of the *Freie Arbeiter Shtimme*. His poems became very popular among Jewish workers and were sung by them while at work. Tuberculosis, then endemic among sweatshop employees, soon caused Edelstadt's death at the age of 26.

Joseph Bovshover was twenty when he learned of Edelstadt's death. That day he wrote an elegy which mourning radicals hailed as a masterpiece. He had come from Russia the year before, and was also writing verse of protest against injustice and oppression. In addition he translated *The Merchant of Venice* and part of *Faust* in felicitous Yiddish. But unrelieved poverty preyed on his hypersensitive mind, and at the age of 26 he sank into a melancholia from which he never emerged.

Morris Rosenfeld was the most popular of the radical versifiers. His poetic gift, while limited and relatively short-lived, was genuine and suited his fierce, anguished cry against his sweatshop torment. In poem after poem he depicted the dire results of work in the oppressive clothing factories. Feeling himself doomed to a living hell, he sang with lyrical outbursts of deep anguish. The pathos and poignancy of the lines were fully appreciated by the workers who read them. The poems, moreover, were very different from those of Peretz and Frug, the two leading Yiddish poets in the 1890s, expressing emotion with the artless sadness of folksongs and with a fervent feeling that compensated for their tendency to sentimentality and unrefined diction.

In 1897 Professor Leo Wiener of Harvard University came upon these poems and reacted with the enthusiasm of a discoverer. In an article in *The Nation* he stated:

> His ballads and legends have all a painful charm about them, and even such sentiments as generally cause other unpleasant sensations make him smile through tears. The poet's technique is perfect, the melody of his rhythm and word grouping is remarkable in a dialect in which Hebrew elements seem to have corrupted its German base. Mr. Rosenfeld is the first one in his language to sing of youth and spring and love.

Wiener edited the poems in a prose translation which he called *Songs of the Ghetto,* and stated in the preface that in their intense poignancy they approached the vivid realism of Dante's "Inferno."

American reviewers echoed Wiener's praise, and before long the volume appeared in several languages in Europe. Thereupon life became easier for Rosenfeld. He was able to leave the sweatshop and soon wrote for Yiddish newspapers. But material easement did not stimulate the lyricism and anguish which had made him famous. His later verse verged on bombast and bathos, causing a decline in popularity which deeply wounded his vanity and aroused his irascibility. His poems on Judaism and current events possessed a contentiousness which irritated fellow writers, to which he responded with devastating satire. There is no gainsaying the fact, however, that his early verse remains a solid contribution to Yiddish poetry.

The early decades of Jewish settlement on the lower East Side thus brought forth a goodly number of Yiddish writers. Born and raised in Eastern Europe, many came here, in the 1890s and later, in their late teens or early twenties, afire with ideals and rebellion and hope. In time they began to express their dreams and feelings of disillusionment in the ephemeral periodicals. Older and more or less creative writers also settled in New York, among them Eliakum Zunzer, the popular bard, and Shomer, the even more popular concocter of exciting romances. Those men found it difficult to adjust to the new environment and ended their days as printers.

This period also saw the establishment and popularity of the Yiddish theater. Boris Tomashevsky, Jacob Adler, David Kessler, Zigmund Mogulesco, and other aspiring actors and actresses came to New York in the 1880s and later and began first to produce Abraham Goldfaden's operettas and soon the dramatic concoctions of Joseph Lateiner and Moshe Hurvitz, who tailored plays of sentiment and romance with little or no artistic content. Their audiences, consisting mostly of workers and their wives who had never before been to a theater and who sought the relief of amusement from their humdrum existence, accepted what they saw with unrestrained enjoyment.

In the early 1890s the Yiddish theater took a radical turn for the better with the arrival of Jacob Gordin. Born in 1850, he had begun adult life as a Russian writer. Attracted to the Evangelical Biblical Brotherhood, he formed the Spiritual Brotherhood as a means of weaning Jews from ancient dogma—urging them to cleave to the ethics of the Pentateuch. Making little progress and harassed by the government, he left for the United States in 1891. In New York he began to write for the *Arbeiter Zeitung*. In need of making a living for his large family, he was advised by Krantz, the editor, to write for the theater. This he did, and *Siberia* was produced by Jacob Adler. The play was not successful financially, but its dramatic integrity gained him much respect. Encouraged to continue writing plays, he was not long in becoming the most prestigious dramatist of the Yiddish theater.

When Gordin came to the theater, actors were ad-libbing for laughs and there was no respect for either play or audience. Gordin was repelled by this vulgarity and irresponsibility. Possessed of a keen sense of dramaturgy, he wrote plays vastly superior to the current productions. Before long, he was hailed by reviewers, and his plays began to attract large audiences. *The Jewish King Lear,* for example, brought into the open the increasingly troubling problem of the widening schism between immigrant parents and their Americanized children. *Mirele Efros* dealt with a similar problem from the point of view of a mother. *Kreutzer Sonata* was an effective adaptation of Tolstoy's drama; *God, Man, and the Devil* was a combination of the themes of *Job* and *Faust.* These and other of his plays—sixty in all—skillfully written, and many of them well-suited to Adler's histrionic talent, easily equalled the current productions on the English stage in both merit and interest. His aim was largely educational, and his plays, supplemented by his lectures, sought to uplift his audiences culturally. There was, moreover, a dignity and firmness about his person which made him an imposing figure. Epstein wrote:

> A handsome man, with dark flashing eyes, black Assyrian beard, a silver cane in hand, his Russian accent, proud bearing, and polished manners made him the most imposing figure on the East Side. He stood taller then those around him, he tore the masses away from trash, improved their taste, and unmasked falsehood, dishonesty, and irresponsibility.

He indeed revolutionized the Yiddish theater and greatly encouraged the more serious actors who found his dramas fine vehicles for their histrionic art. He also compelled actors in his plays to speak naturally and to adhere to his simple Yiddish and shun the Germanized jargon they had considered more elegant.

In 1903 Abraham Cahan started his feud with Gordin by an attack on his newest play. A man of strong conceit, Gordin was easily angered by criticism. Suspecting personal animus, he responded to Cahan's attack in kind, and the two remained enemies until Gordin's death six years later. Cahan's wide influence caused a decline in Gordin's popularity. At his death, however, Jews by the tens of thousands mourned their loss. And in 1938 Morris R. Cohen voiced this sentiment:

> I also wish to express my indebtedness to what Jacob Gordin did to educate me in whatever taste I have for dramatic literature. Gordin might have made a name for himself in Russian or English literature, but he preferred to stick to Yiddish and portray the life of his own people.

During Gordin's own lifetime and later, other playwrights began to write for the Yiddish theater, some of them definitely influenced by him. Among the better-known of his contemporaries were Z. Libin (Israel Hurwitz) and Leon Kobrin.

The latter came to the United States more familiar with Russian and French literature than with Yiddish writing. Finding manual labor irksome and having a strong urge to write, he began to improve his Yiddish and to write for the available journals. Following Gordin's example, he also wrote for the theater. Although he adapted his plays to the level of his unsophisticated audiences, he did not stoop to cheap intrigue or sentimental melodrama. Influenced by Russian and French models, he maintained a simple yet authentic literary standard. His first play, *Minna,* was completed with Gordin's assistance. He followed it with *Nature, Man, and Beast,* a work of character delineation and moral probing, and *Yankel Boileh,* the story of a simple fisherman whose love for a Christian girl ended tragically. In his prose writings he was the first to treat carnal passion naturalistically. Perhaps his best work of fiction, *Oreh the Beard,* serialized in 1913, discusses the circumstances which enabled a simple, energetic Jew to become wealthy during a real estate boom. Kobrin also did a good amount of translation from the French, and his two volumes of reminiscence are rich in information and reflection.

Libin also began to write plays under Gordin's aegis. Only superficially educated and for years a worker in a sweatshop, he wrote of the life he knew with bold realism and sentimental sympathy. His numerous plays dealt mostly with tense family problems relieved by comic effects. *Broken Hearts,* one of his most successful dramas, best illustrated his dramatic achievement. His short stories concern mostly the life and trials of workers, treated in a warm, personal manner. Largely influenced by Cahan, who was the first to encourage him to write, he sometimes marred his realistic style with anglicized words and expressions.

As already indicated, most of the writers who came to the United States before 1900 were social rebels. They sought to abolish the sweatshop system, to educate and to organize the Jewish worker in unions, and to enhance Jewish culture. While also radically inclined, Yehoash (Solomon Bloomgarden) and David Pinski, who came to New York in 1890 and 1899, respectively, took their writing too seriously to be dominated by efforts of reform or rebellion.

Yehoash (1870–1927) began to write poems while still in his teens in Russia. Although Peretz praised him highly and called him "our Byron," he was not deluded by his approbation—knowing how much he must work and experiment before reaching poetic maturity. Loath to be drafted into the Russian army, he migrated to the United States, where he found himself too harried to write. He taught Hebrew, he worked as a bookkeeper in a glass factory, and for a full decade he did very little writing. Then he became ill with tuberculosis and went to the Denver Jewish Sanitorium to recuperate. For the next nine years he remained there as a patient. Moved by the grandeur of the mountain scenery and the intensiveness of his spiritual solitude, he resumed his writing of verse. In 1907 he issued a volume of poetry with an imaginative range and prosodic felicity new to Yiddish literature.

Returning to New York in 1909, he began to contribute poems to Yiddish periodicals; these and others appeared in a collection entitled *Through Mist and Sunshine* (1913). Following a journey to Palestine the ensuing year, he recorded his impression in a sensitive travel book, *The Feet of the Messenger* (issued in English in 1923). All the while his late-blooming poetic talent was occupied with experiments in rhyme, rhythm, and meter. He maneuvered iambs and trochees, line lengths and stanzas with dazzling dexterity. In a cycle of 45 love poems, "Flowers and Thorns," he wrote not as the naive swain or the jaded sensualist but as the reflective yet sensual suitor. He wrote of "feelings, even the most beautiful, fading"; of the bruises of jealousy, of love as a mirage—all with a coldness of yesterday's fire. His nature poems are imbued with a free fancifulness. The poem, "Twilight," for instance, is an achievement of almost pure melody and intuition. *In the Weave* (volume 1, 1919; volume 2, 1923) possesses the mature beauty wrought consciously with the fine and firm feelings of the gifted poet. Yet color and sound, rhythm and metaphor, imaginatively conceived and beautifully expressed, would not make Yehoash and the distinctive poet he was were it not for his centripetal view of life.

One of his great achievements as a Yiddish writer was the translation of the Bible into Yiddish. He began to experiment with it as early as 1907; in time it became a labor of enduring and absorbing love and ended only with his last breath in 1927. In his effort to produce a work worthy of the original, he equipped himself with prodigious erudition. He went to endless trouble to find in old tomes, folklore, and folk speech the idiomatic Yiddish words and expressions that rendered exactly the original Hebrew meaning. Thus the printed translation renders clearly the spirit, poetry, color, and grandeur of the Book of Books. An interesting effect of the translation is that its vocabulary and diction have enriched Yiddish enormously without resorting to solecisms or obsolete words. He also completed two volumes of scholarly annotations to elucidate the obscure and confusing passages met with on almost every page of the Bible.

א גהעטטא־לעגענדע

צום גאון, א ריטטער מיט גאָלדענע שפּאָרען,
קוממט יעטוועדע נאַכט שטיללערהייד,
מיט פעדערן באַפוצט איז זיין גלאַנציגער קיווער,
זיין ברוסט איז מיט סאַמעט באַקליידט...

אין אָרעמען צימער, וואו ס'צאַנקט פון א לעמפּעל
דער מאַטטער און עלענדער שיין,
דער קריסטליכער פּרינץ זיצט און הערט צו די חכמה
פון אידישען גאון זיך איין...

דאָך אידער עס הויבען די גלאָקען אָן קלינגען
צום מאָרגענגעבעט, אין דער שטאדט,
זיך גנב'עט דער ריטטער ארויס פון דער גהעטטאָ,
און קיינער דערגעהט ניט זיין סוד...

דער רב זיצט און לערענט... זעהט קיינמאָל ביי טאָג ניט
דעם פּרינץ וואָס ביי נאַכט איהם באַזוכט,
אין תלמיד'ס געדאַנקען און עובדות נאָר ווייזט זיך
פון רב'ס קלוגע לעהרען די פרוכט...

דאָך רייט אָפט דער פּרינץ מיט זיין גלאַנצענדער סוויטע,
ביי טאָג דורך די גהעטטאָ און קוקט
פאַרטראַכט אויף דאָס הויז וואו זיין אידישער רבי
אין דחקות און שמוץ לעבט פאַררוקט...

Yehoash (Solomon Bloomgarden) was an early prominent Yiddish poet.

תורה
נביאים
וכתובים

עם יידיש
תרגום פון
יהואש

שנת: תש"א: לפ"ק
נו-יורק ניו-יארק

הוצאת
יהואש פארלאַג געזעלשאַפט

Yehoash's translation of the Old Testament was an enormous literary achievement, published by his family after his untimely death.

David Pinski (1872–1959) was the first Yiddish writer in Russia to produce short stories about the plight of Jewish urban workers. He too gained Peretz's blessing. In 1899, at the age of 27, he migrated to New York and for the ensuing half century, devoted himself to writing and to promote the cause of Labor Zionism. For years he composed mostly plays, and *The Treasure* (1906) was highly successful on the Yiddish stage and was produced in English and other languages. A number of his other dramas, beginning with *Isaac Sheftel* (1899) and continuing to *Shabbati Zevi and Sarah* (1952), suffer more or less from his inability to view his work self-critically—confusing content with artistic expression. Thus the fact that the action had for its motif the tragedy of motherhood (*Mother,* 1901), or the decline of religion (*The Family Tzvi* 1904), or the power of the beast in man (*Better Not to Be Born,* 1914), or the pathos of human cupidity (*The Last Reckoning,* 1918), gives them in his view inherent dramatic cogency; that dramatic ideas become banal without artistic truth seldom impinged upon his critical consciousness.

When his inner censor was actively in control of the dramatic development of his themes, Pinski was more successful. Among these plays are *Yankel the Blacksmith* (1901), *Gabri and the Women* (1908), *Professor Brenner* (1911), and *Alexander and Diogenes* (1930). His most successful play, *The Treasure,* was considered by Professor George Baker of Harvard the best comedy produced in America in the 1900s.

Pinski's composition of plays of disparate dramatic worth arose from his tendency to write with conscious ideation rather than with artistic authenticity. He thus illustrates the truism that a writer reveals himself more in the process of literary expression than in the originality or ingenuity of thematic conception. The discrepancy, for example, between *The Family Tzvi* and *The Treasure* was with him a matter of chance. Both plays are based on novel ideas and developed with dramatic skill. The first, based on an idea dear to him, became mangled when mated with dementic action; the other, conceived in a happy moment and developed with mature and sympathetic humor, became a play of high comedy. Again, the protagonists in *Better Not to Be Born* and *Isaac Sheftel* are alike seized by sudden frenzy. Yet in the first a psychological truth is marred by having an apparently normal young man commit a hideous crime without any other provocation than the heat of a summer's day; Isaac's act of destruction is provoked by circumstances so dire and a temperament so brooding that his outbreak seems almost inevitable.

Pinski wrote much fiction. His early stories treat with workers suffering from exploitation and yearning for their human rights. Much of his later writing deals with amorous themes. In "Awakening" and "The Earth Spirit" the shy but ardent youth loves with adolescent innocence. "Jonathan the High Priest," "Beruriah" and "The Temptation of Rabbi Akiba" are written in a polished, quasi-Biblical style and give the impression of having been composed with the intellect rather than with the imagination. Each of these stories is embellished with rhetorical brilliance, but with a conscious endeavor to demonstrate the infirmity of human flesh and the futility of resistance, thus resulting more in artifice than in art.

The three novels written by Pinski have their setting in the United States. *The House of Noah Eden* (1913) is a family saga based on the thesis that life in America is antithetical to Orthodoxy. *Arnold Levenberg* (1920) deals with wealthy German Jews in New York. Completely Americanized, the men and women remain Jews only because they are excluded from Gentile society. Some yield to debauchery, and Arnold is too habituated to his snobbish way of life to be won over by the idealistic Russian Jews with whom he has come in contact. *When the Roads Part* (1950) has its setting in 1931, when unemployment and hunger were agitating Jewish workers. Radical philosophies are examined by the protagonists, but they find them suffering from exaggerated motivation. Here, as in much of his writing, Pinski is more the moralist than the literary artist, and in yielding to his ethical nature he weakened much of his work.

In 1949 he left for Israel, made his home on Mount Carmel, and continued to write until his death in 1959. Much of his work appeared in English translation, and his place in Yiddish literature remains historically secure.

Of the numerous Jewish intellectuals who migrated to the United States around 1900, Chaim Zhitlowsky stands out as one of the most distinguished men of letters. Born in 1865 of a well-to-do family in Vitebsk, he was of a serious turn of mind and early joined the current revolutionary movement. As a youth of seventeen he became a "Narodnik" and went to Tula to work for the liberation of the Russian peasants. The increasing anti-Semitism of that time aroused his interest in Jewish nationalism. Considering himself as much a Russian as a Jew, he sought to develop Jewish national unity within Russia. The revolutionary leaders, however, disliked his separatist tendency—which caused him to delve further into the nature of Jewish nationalism. In time he developed the thesis that the Jews were essentially a national entity and would remain Jews even if they abandoned Judaism. As he stated later, it was "purely a literary experience that settled these doubts and sent me flying on a new road, not *assimilation,* not even *nationalism* in the old sense, but what appeared to me as the right and natural solution to the Jewish problem in full harmony with my socialist ideas." He also concluded that Yiddish was the Jewish mother tongue and therefore the national language of the Jews.

Eager to study the history of the Jews in order to learn the nature and causes of assimilation, he persuaded his father to send him to St. Petersburg. There he wrote his first book, *Thoughts on the Historical Destiny of Jewry,* which his father printed for him in 1887. He then went to Germany and Zurich for further study and gained his doctorate in Jewish philosophy. In 1903 his Russian wife and the mother of his six children became pregnant by a young lover, who subsequently shot himself. Deeply distressed, Zhitlowsky left for Amsterdam, and soon reached New York.

He became a contributor to Yiddish periodicals and presented his ideas with a philosophical depth and yet with a stylistic felicity that made his articles and later his books among the best serious writings in Yiddish. His lucidity of thought and homely expressions made his abstract ideas simple and concrete enough to be appreciated by many readers. His lectures also attracted large audiences and gained him the admiration of many thousands.

In 1908 he attended the Czernowitz Conference on Yiddish and joined other prominent writers in establishing standards in

Yiddish grammar, spelling and diction; also in the assertion that Yiddish was the national Jewish language and in placing the question of Hebrew for later determination.

Zhitlowsky's two-volume work, *Philosophy: What It Is and How It Was Developed*, was published in 1910–1911. His complete writings were later issued in ten volumes. Exerting a marked influence on the intellectual life of the Jewish community, he continued for years to write philosophical and polemical articles for newspapers and magazines. When communism and fascism began to agitate society in the 1920s, he asserted that socialism could not exist without democracy. Later, however, when the Nazis rose to power, he tended to favor Soviet Russia—accepting the extenuating circumstances used by its apologists to acquiesce in the Stalin dictatorship.

Mention must be made of two other writers who came to this country about the same time. H. Roisenblatt (1878–1956) was only thirteen when he was brought to New York, but his imagination was already aglow with memories and emotions of his Ukrainian childhood. Although he became fairly well Americanized by the time he reached adulthood, his spirit remained rooted in his Jewish past. His best lyrics glorified his childhood memories. Of modest aspiration and consciously self-critical, he wrote ironically, with muted feeling, but with lyrical beauty. Some of his best nature and philosophical verses were written in his old age.

Abraham Liessin (1872–1938) had studied in a yeshiva during his impressionable years, but entered adolescence with a passion for social justice. His fiery lyrics soon made it too risky for him to remain in Russia, and in 1897 he migrated to New York. He joined the group of Jewish socialists and became as previously indicated, a contributor to the *Forward*. In 1913 he irked Cahan with some of his writings and left to edit the *Zukunft*. For the next twenty-five years he made the monthly the most distinguished cultural magazine in Yiddish. While he remained a firm socialist to the end of his life, he was also a deeply conscious Jew. He found emotional release in the Jewish past, and sang of the sages and martyrs of the previous centuries with wisdom and dedication.

"From Worms, Mainz, Speyer, through Prague and Lublin and Odessa," he wrote, "the fire extended itself, one miracle repeating itself." He wrote philosophically, not abstractly or mystically, but with the old Jewish assumption that suffering led to spiritual enlightenment. Suffering by itself, however, he considered a Christian doctrine, a denial of life, and Jews never denied life. "For the greatest triumph is the triumph of the spirit which conquers the body and performs great miracles."

8

The Efflorescence of Yiddish Literature

Around a million and a half Jews entered the United States during the first fourteen years of this century. This hegira was forced upon them by the pogroms of 1903–1905 and continued oppression and poverty. These immigrants, even more than the earlier ones, ranged culturally from the Hasidic pietists to determined atheists, from bare literates in Hebrew to university graduates and sophisticated intellectuals. Unlike the newcomers of a generation ago, they found here a fully established Yiddish milieu: daily newspapers, various magazines, a flourishing theater, and numerous social, economic, and religious organizations. Also improved were the working opportunities: the persistent struggle of unions to eliminate sweatshop conditions was having its favorable effect; working conditions were ameliorated, wages were higher, and there were working opportunities in other than the needle trades. It was therefore easier for many to find their economic groove and to make use of the available cultural facilities.

Not a few of the younger immigrants, forced to take factory jobs to earn their living, were primarily interested in nursing their literary inclinations and took every opportunity to write. They no sooner struck new roots in this country than they began to follow the new developments in modern literature and to emulate the models best suited to their specific talents. Joseph Opatoshu, one of these young writers, later reminisced:

> On arrival, the newcomer, disappointed in the Russian revolution [of 1905], perceived the American rhythm, the American expansiveness, and felt a love for their new home. . . . With the new immigrants came new writers, who entered the shops, the farms, to sow and cut. . . . With his coming to this country the young writer, having burned his bridges behind him, no longer dreamt of returning to the old home. He at once sought to settle in his new home and to create a new Yiddish literature. It was an inner outgrowth, an organic fusion of Yiddish literature with his surrounding environment.

Not all writers fitted this image, of course. L. Shapiro, who came to New York in 1906, was *sui generis.* His stories of pogroms, written while in Russia, possessed a controlled anger and epic strength that charged them with emotional acuity. "The Cross," "The Kiss," "Silence," and other stories were powerful in their tragic effectiveness and tense verbal economy. In New York he wrote of Jewish life on the lower East Side—workers and petty merchants adapting themselves to their new environment to the best of their ability—but the narratives lacked the literary power of the earlier stories. Soon Shapiro stopped writing, and years later he stated: "The real source of my early writings were stubbornness and stoicism, in a deeper sense—*to strengthen the heart.* However, having written 'The Cross', I said to myself: 'Enough, no more pogroms! I can no longer live with pogroms in my heart!' " He turned to experimentation with color film, but the inner wound would not heal, and in despair he sought relief in alcohol—then a rare resort for a Jew. It was only in 1931 that he had managed to write enough material for a volume, *New Yorkish.* Thirteen years later he issued his last volume, *The Writer Goes to School,* a medley of essays, reminiscence, and critical reflections. All the while, in New York and Los Angeles, he lived mostly by himself and had little contact with other writers—as if nursing his traumatic wound and oblivious to the excitement agitating the Yiddish literary environment of his day.

Joseph Rolnick, who came to New York in 1907—after an earlier brief visit in 1899—was not quite the loner Shapiro was.

Yet he was a dedicated individualist, a confirmed worrier, a singer of solitude and loneliness. He worked at first in a factory and later as a proofreader on a newspaper. Unable to adjust to his environment, he wrote mostly about himself with a wistful sadness, yet with generic implications. Later he made his peace with the world, and in a series of poems on the Persian poet Hafiz, gave voice to melodic allegory and metaphysical pessimism. Never fully associated with his dynamic contemporaries with whom he was in general sympathy, he asserted: "In the whole world there are only two: I, who speak, and the other—who understands."

Most of the young writers of the time were more gregarious. Freed of the bonds of piety, they were bursting with literary energy and artistic zeal, bent on expressing the art and dreams and visions which for centuries past had been repressed in the cramped life of the yeshiva. A number of them had familiarized themselves with the current trends in writing in both Europe and this country and were eager to mine the golden ore of Jewish folk life and give it the beauty and sparkle of esthetic expression. They sought to free Yiddish literature from the trashy writing of the newspaper serials. Loving the freedom of America, they wanted to praise its greatness. Idealists, they disdained lack of talent, lack of respect for and responsibility to literature. They did not wish to see belles lettres serve as means to education or reform; they insisted on its being solely an artistic medium. The rhetoric and didacticism of the older writers repelled them. As one of them later declared, they turned away from the "prosey sweatshop verses" favored by the *Forward,* from Yehoash's and Liessin's Hebraic poetry, and sought to emulate the contemporary Gentile esthetes whom they admired.

These literary-inclined newcomers, forced to work at manual labor but dreaming of artistic glory, became rebellious and aggressive. On free evenings they gathered in an inexpensive cafeteria, where they drank tea and read and discussed their latest writings. Among the more active of this group were Mani Layb, Zisha Landau, Reuven Eisland, and M. A. Dillon, with the first being perhaps the most talented. Ten years later Noah Steinberg, in *Young America,* wrote of them:

> Mani Layb is the most gifted among our younger poets. . . . An individualist, incomparable charm emerges from him, and one recognizes that it is not put on, that he was born with it. Mani Layb is one of the first among us who has become absorbed in his own self.

In 1907 they formed *Die Yunge* (The Young Ones) with the aim of bringing their work into print—having been snubbed by the established editors. Lack of funds limited the first issue of their anthology, *Yugend* (Youth), to 24 pages. The older writers reacted critically, even abusively, but the leaders of this first "school" in Yiddish literature defied and ignored this reproof. In 1910 they published *Literatur* in two successive issues extending to 144 pages each. Two years later they produced *Shriften* (Writings) in hefty volumes which continued annually, with interruptions, to 1926. The contributors to these anthologies who later added greatly to Yiddish literature counted among them writers like H. Sackler, I. J. Schwartz, David Ignatov, Joseph Opatoshu, Moshe Nadir, I. Raboy, M. L Halpern, and H. Leivick. The anthologies also enabled Jewish artists to acquaint readers with ideas and trends in the plastic arts. As Glatstein pointed out, "The main achievement of the new group of Yiddish poets resides in their coming out with a demand for the creation of a school, a school permitting the freest possibilities to the true poet."

Simplicity was the first desideratum of these young poets. Reacting against the rhetoric and prolixity of their predecessors, they demanded that the poems should be neither involute nor complex, but possess the refined virtue of simplicity. Thus the verses of Mani Layb or Landau, for instance, were simple, and their moods were a yearning for the peace of one's soul. These lyrics brought new life into Yiddish literature and put an end to the old way of bemoaning everything. As followers of European impressionists and symbolists, the *Yunge* strove to depict the gentle, quiet, wistful movements of the human spirit.

In 1914 the "neo-realists" of the group, spearheaded by Opatoshu, formed their own cluster and issued their own anthology,

Die Neie Haym (The New Home), a volume of over 300 pages, brought out five issues of *Literatur un Leben* (Literature and Life), and the following year Ignatov issued *In and Out of the World,* a similar collection of new writing. By these means, and by individual stories and poems which had begun to be accepted by newspapers and magazines, these "young" writers succeeded in modernizing and enlivening Yiddish literature; their frankness of view and esthetic emphasis brought it into the mainstream of world literature.

After 1914, cataclysmic events, causing chaos and deep suffering within the Jewish community in Eastern Europe, strongly affected most of the Jewish writers in America. By that time the several clusters had begun to disperse; the more talented were already secluding themselves in the production of books that redounded greatly to their reputation.

Toward the end of World War I several newcomers began to contend that the esthetic emphasis and rigid prosody of the *Yunge* tended to stifle the creative impulse. Among these exponents of subjective idealism were Aaron Glantz-Leyeles, Jacob Glatstein, N. B. Minkoff, and B. Alquit. Naming themselves *Insikhisten* (Introspectivists), they published in 1920 the *In Sikh* anthology. These writers also manifested the influence of the latest literary movements. As imagists they disclaimed the presumed restraints of rhyme and rhythm, and deliberately avoided national and social themes. "We Introspectivists," they declared, "believe that free verse is best suited to the individuality of rhythm and therefore, if for no other reason, we prefer it to other forms of verse." As was inevitable, however, time and circumstances brought an end to this literary rationalization on the part of the foursome, and their subsequent work and activity, as those of their immediate predecessors, soon veered toward the main groove of Yiddish writing, especially after they began to be accepted by the prevailing media.

The following brief sketches of the newer writers will indicate their achievement and place in Yiddish literature.

David Ignatov (1885–1954) was a dynamic leader of the *Yunge.* Of Hasidic ancestry and upbringing, he migrated to New

York in 1906 and became a factory worker. When his first literary efforts were rejected by the established periodicals, he led other aspirants in starting *Yugend,* in which his first story was published. His domineering behavior as editor led to a split in 1914. In the anthologies he edited he included stories and poems by fledgling writers, thereby encouraging them to continue writing. His own achievement as a writer hardly measured up to his reputation: his ability sometimes failing to realize his vaulting ambition. Among his early work, *The Hidden Light* (1918) and *Wonder Stories of Old Prague* (1920) were written in the Hasidic tradition: mystically, romantically, sentimentally. Among his other books are *In the Cauldron* (1918), *The Golden Boy* (1921), and *On Distant Roads* (1932). The latter novel, in three volumes, is highly subjective and primarily concerned with social salvation. He also published *To a New World* (1939), a Biblical tragedy, and *Gideon* (1953).

Mani Layb (1884–1953) came to the United States in 1905 and worked for many years in a shoe factory. Boldly imaginative, consciously bohemian, he wrote of his most intimate experiences and feelings with the outcry of a tortured soul. Brought up on folk songs, he injected their rhythm and melody in much of his verse. Although his ballads, sonnets, and songs were largely self-analytical, they often combined national and social themes with folk legends. A man of many moods, he sensed tragedy and mystery everywhere. Insisting that verbal art is the instrument of literary self-enrichment, he strove for mastery of lyric nuance and beauty. Too self-critical to publish his collected work while alive, many of his poems appeared posthumously, as did the article in which he summarized his life and writing:

> An immigrant, bringing with me native landscapes, ideals of socialism and humanity, nebulous artistic impressions of German romanticists and French symbolists, of Russian writers from Pushkin to Blok, and thrust into a sweatshop and poverty, with little time to write, what could I do? But the little I did do is my own, achieved by myself.

The youngest of the group, Zisha Landau (1889–1937), was the most colorful. Born of a distinguished rabbinical family, early imbued with the spirit of Hasidism, he came to New York in 1906 nursing romantic rebelliousness. Handsome, extrovert, impetuous, he soon established his eminence among his fellow rebels. Working as a house painter, he wrote poems in his free time. Influenced by Heine and later European writers, he extolled the doctrine of art for art's sake. A poem, he insisted, must be "a purely artistic song." Although his verse expressed longing, moodiness, and pessimism, it was also playful, ironic, and sensuous. Later, having outgrown his youthful cleverness, he wrote poems of social and spiritual content, some in the form of prayers. While too sophisticated to write prayers with complete sincerity, his lines imparted verbal sensitivity and evocative imagery.

Reuven Eisland (1884–1955) came to New York in 1903. He was the first of the *Yunge* to expound the doctrine of esthetics in opposition to the prevailing emphasis on social content. More the imagist than the lyricist, he described the daily life around him, particularly the drab existence of the factory worker, with picturesque vividness. He also wrote about prominent literary personalities and, later, a good deal of reminiscence. His great emotional experience concerned his love for Anna Margolin, the poet whose life was as adventurous as it was unfortunate, and which Eisland depicted with profound feeling in lyrics of emotional sensuousness and beauty.

I. J. Schwartz (1885–1973) migrated to the United States in 1906. Strongly motivated by the Hebrew poetry of Yehuda Halevi and Ch. N. Bialik, he tended to write with the peace and nobility of the Sabbath spirit. After he had settled in Lexington, Kentucky, he became strongly impressed by the grandeur of the American landscape and the spirit of American poetry. His volume, *Kentucky* (1925), sang of the life of Negroes, Southern whites, and Jews with strong sensuousness, fresh observation, and sympathetic insight. His poem, "George Washington," is a study of a nonchalant, simple Negro, presented as an animated and attractive personality. His verse also extols the American prairie and what it stands for in American life. Returning to New York in 1920, he published translations of *Julius Caesar* and *Hamlet.* A good part of his later writing treats Jewish themes in an American milieu; of interest also was his long autobiographical poem, "Childhood Years." His volume, *The Golden Epoch,* contains translations of poems by Yehuda Halevi, Solomon ibn Gabirol, and other medieval Spanish Jews. Into his late eighties he continued to write and lecture on his chosen subjects.

Isaak Raboy (1882–1944), the least bohemian of the *Yunge,* came to New York in 1904. Life in his native Bessarabia had developed in him a love of the land, and in his early stories he extolled the natural beauty of the life-giving earth. Finding work in a hat factory distasteful, he enrolled in the Jewish Agricultural School in Woodbine, New Jersey, and subsequently worked on farms in the Middle West. His first novel, *Mr. Goldenberg* (1913), depicts farm life in the Dakotas, a subject new to Yiddish literature. *Seaside* (1918) treats Jewish farm life in Connecticut. Perhaps his best work, *A Jew Comes to America* (1926), delineates realistically the efforts of Jewish immigrants at adjustment in the tenements of Delancey Street of New York. *Bessarabian Jews* (1928) and *Nine Brothers* (1936) describe nostalgically Jewish rural life in the region of his birth and childhood. *The Jewish Cowboy* (1942) is the story of a Jewish youth who went to the Dakotas and made good as a cowboy despite the antagonism of the non-Jewish farm laborers. In all his fiction Raboy wrote simply, tersely, yet with an intimacy that verged on the lyrical.

A. M. Dillon (1883–1934) also came to New York in 1904 and was not long in joining the *Yunge.* His verse first appeared in *Literatur* and later in *Zukunft.* Of a pessimistic turn of mind, he was nevertheless romantic enough to court poetically a Brooklyn Dulcinea and praise the ideal of femininity. His best verse deals with death—implying that by dying he would hurt his detractors. In a cycle of eighteen poems he presented his disgust with life and his decision to sell his soul to Satan in order to enjoy worldly pleasures. In his later years, however, his writings revealed a more positive attitude toward the life about him.

B. Lapin (1889–1952) was of a more optimistic temperament. Brought to Argentina in 1895, he was returned to Russia four years later. In 1909 he migrated to the United States, joined the *Yunge,* and exerted himself in the refinement of Yiddish prosody and verbal assonance. Much of his verse has an ethical connotation and deals with the life of Jewish workers. His religious poems are noted for their metaphysical and mystical groping. He has translated much English poetry, and his Yiddish version of Shakespeare's sonnets, which took him eight years to complete, is impressive for its sensitive accuracy and lilting subtlety. *The Full Pitcher* (1950) appeared shortly before his death and evidenced a mastery of neologisms and original rhymes as well as a humane view of life.

Two other writers, more or less associated with the *Yunge* but too independent-minded to be fully classified with them, were Moshe Layb Halpern (1886–1932) and Moshe Nadir (Israel Reiss, 1885–1943). The first was born in Galicia and studied German literature in Vienna before he migrated to the United States in 1908. His work at various manual tasks embittered his spirit, so that his early writings were coarsely pessimistic. Feeling alienated and uprooted in America, and averse to the verbal dexterity and esthetic emphasis of the *Yunge,* he deliberately rebelled against these traits in inelegant lyrics. Yet his outward droll fooling and mocking negation did not conceal his inner suffering to the point of despair. "Much as I struggle with myself to see only what is pure and beautiful," he admitted, "I see only what is repulsive as a piece of rotting carcass, which waits in the sun to become food for worms, fleas, and mice." In the poem, "In the Golden Land," he stated his refusal to acquiesce in the bitterness of his life: "Would you believe me, mother, that everything here is turned to gold, that gold is made of blood and iron, of blood and iron day and night."

To conceal his inner pain he acted the mountebank in public. In *New York* (1919), which includes some of his best poems, he is at once lyrical and gruff, gentle and sardonic, expressing imagistically the turbulence and suffering of his life. In 1922 he became a contributor to the *Freiheit* and was made much of by the communists, but three years later he left it because he was unable to conform to the contraints of proletarian dogma. His best-known book, *The Golden Peacock* (1924), is a collection of poems revealing new forms, new rhythms, new attitudes, but which is also sharp and prickly with mockery and repressed anger. He deliberately tried to control his true feelings: being sardonic when in earnest, coarse when gentle, brazen when shy. Thus he clowned and acted the buffoon to hide his pain and sadness. Indeed, the last eight years of his life were a period of illness, suffering, and neglect. Sickness and indigence dogged him wherever he went in search of relief. Refusing to yield to hostile reality, he kept stumbling to his grievous hurt. In "My Will" he told how he put his poems in his old coat and hung it out of the window, saying: "These are my years that became mildewed between the old wisdom-stink of my wonderful book case." He died of a heart attack, and two of his volumes appeared posthumously. These poems, lyrical and gentle, cry for peace and acceptance.

Moshe Nadir, also a native of Galicia and likewise given to clowning the better to aim his barbs at the smug or submissive behavior of people in his purview, arrived in New York at the age of thirteen and attended American schools. He began to write verse in his late teens. A humorist by inclination, he associated with the *Yunge* and contributed to journals of humor. Wit and satire coming naturally to him, he assumed the pen-name of Moshe Nadir, which implied in common usage, "Here you are, simpleton." His first book, *Wild Roses* (1915), was an irreverent, caustic, yet gently moody collection of verses. About that time he became a regular contributor to *The Day*, and his popularity increased from year to year. A highly dextrous verbal juggler, he made ingenious use of his Galician Yiddish to achieve his incisive humor.

In 1922, eager to be with his friend Halpern, he moved to the *Freiheit*, but his commitment to radicalism was more sentimental than intellectual. When the daily accepted the Stalin-Hitler Pact in 1939, he left it in protest. For years he was obsessed by the fear of death, which finally occurred in 1943. In his work as a whole a vulgarly comic overlay concealed a genuine sensitivity in much of his writing. Soft and sentimental, he shrank from the rigor of discipline. His clever word-play and telling whimsey were often the trappings cloaking spiritual seriousness.

After a decade of rebellious activity the more gifted of the *Yunge* began to be accepted by newspaper editors and Jewish organizations, thereby becoming part of the literary establishment. They also began to publish books of their own, ironically opening themselves to criticism by ambitious newcomers. The latter, as already stated, had soon formulated their own literary philosophy, asserting that the world existed only as it was reflected in each individual and that the esthetic rigidity of the *Yunge* was stifling the creative impulse.

The most articulate of these critical Introspectivists was Aaron Glantz-Leyeles (1889-1966). Born in Poland, he went to London in 1905 and remained there until he migrated to New York in 1912. Having by then become a member of the Socialist-Territorialists, he worked for the advancement of Jewish education and culture. His first verses were printed in 1909, so that he was already a recognized writer when *The Day* started in 1914 and employed him as a regular contributor. His articles appeared under his own name, but for his poems he used the name of Leyeles. Having broad interests, strong convictions, and sudden enthusiasms, he wrote on literary, cultural, and social subjects in a prose that effervesced with verbal vividness and ideational zeal.

Primarily a poet, he in *Labyrith* (1918) and later verse illustrated the tenets of the Introspectivist credo: employ simple, exact language, create new rhythms to express new moods, permit absolute freedom of thematic selection, and present images in clear and definite poetic concentration—all of this adding up to the quintessence of poetry. Later he retreated from this extreme position, but at first it aroused much debate among Yiddish writers. It did, however, serve to free poetry from the constraints assumed by the *Yunge*.

In much of his verse Glantz-Leyeles experimented with its technical possibilities. Ingenious and imaginative, he composed triolets, ballads, villanelles, chansons, sonnets, and études. An ardent admirer of the American democratic spirit, he in *America and I* (1963) sang of his adopted land with affection and gratitude. An intensive Jew, he was deeply moved by the messianic ideal. In the poetic plays *Osher Lemlen* and particularly in *Shlomo Molkhu* he dramatized the conflict between the dream of redemption and unyielding reality. His Shlomo, a Marrano and a favorite of the court, came to believe that he was God-inspired to be the Messiah. His tragic end was caused by his refusal to act cautiously—proclaiming boldly his inspired mission. Although the ten scenes sparkle more with crackling rhetoric than with poetic luster, the work as a whole possesses dramatic distinction.

Jacob Glatstein (1896–1971), born in Lublin, was a highly gifted poet. He came to New York in 1914 and studied law. His classmate Minkoff influenced him to write in Yiddish, and in 1919 he joined him and Glantz-Leyeles in announcing their adherence to Introspectivism. His first collection of verse, *Jacob Glatstein* (1921), presented him both as a person of keen intellect and as a warm exponent of Jewishness. In the years that followed he published a number of volumes of both prose and poetry. In 1926 he became a regular contributor first to the *Morning Journal* and then to *The Day*. He also wrote for *Der Yiddisher Kemfer*. His literary gifts were early recognized as of superior merit, and his mastery of diction and prosody, expressed in a pure musical Yiddish, soon placed him among the prominent Yiddish writers.

In 1938 he visited his native Lublin and was deeply perturbed by the acute hatred toward Jews in Eastern Europe. In his prose trilogy—*When Yash Traveled* (1938), *When Yash Arrived* (1940), and *Emil and Karl* (1942)—he related his depressing experiences and reflections, weaving into its pages fictional speculations of Hasidic affirmation that highlighted his own foreboding while stressing the unique faith of pious Jews in their certainty of survival. In the third volume he treats the nature of Nazi brutishness. His deep disgust with a society that permitted the genocide of his people is expressed in his famous poem, "Good Night, World."

The Holocaust seared his mind, and in "Millions Dead" he exclaimed: "When the earth will be plowed and sowed, it will yield pitch black bread, the wheat and corn will ever smell with millions dead. . . ." All his affection for the victims he revealed in his love of Yiddish. In *The Joy of the Yiddish Word* (1961) he sang of the tragedy of his generation and of his pride in Israel. The lyrics became ecstatic when they concerned Yiddish: "You are not merely my mother tongue, the speech of my cradle, but the seal on all my thought." On the occasion of his seventieth birthday he was honored with the Leivick Award for Literature.

N. B. Minkoff (1893–1958) was born in Warsaw and arrived in the United States in 1914. Although a law graduate, he earned his livelihood as lecturer and teacher, giving courses in English and Yiddish literature. He was for a time managing editor of the *Zukunft.* His first Yiddish poems were printed in 1918 and evidenced the imagist influence of the period. His later verse possessed the firmness of intellectualized emotion. A nay sayer and profoundly ethical, he ever searched for order, but his abstract images and ideas were not always articulated with the required clarity. Aware of this shortcoming, he stated in one poem, "You wrote that clarity is the essence. This thought perturbs me—at times hatefully—because our time is drunk with insanity and shudder." Subsequently his studies of Yiddish writers—*Six Yiddish Critics* (1959) and *Pioneers of Yiddish Poetry in America* (3 volumes, 1956)—are acutely sensitive works of literary criticism.

The survey thus far has dealt selectively with some of the more important Yiddish writers—Opatoshu and Leivick excepted—who had come to the United States before or soon after the outbreak of World War I. Scores of others were of course contributing to the enrichment of Yiddish literature—especially critics and publicists who have added much to the range and diversity of Yiddish writing. Shmuel Niger, for instance, was a critic of sensitive perceptiveness and broad sympathy who for more than forty years evaluated and guided the work of Yiddish writers. He and numerous others are not dealt with merely because the emphasis here is on creative writing. What follows therefore are sketches of a few poets and storytellers who had achieved recognition after 1914.

A. Almi (Sheps, 1892–1963) was born in Warsaw and came to New York in 1912, where he worked on the *Tageblatt* and other newspapers. His several volumes of poetry are noted for their humor and satire. His book on *Chinese Philosophy and Poetry* (1923) was a novel addition to Yiddish literature. Also of importance are his polemical literary criticism and memoirs. Of an unhappy disposition, he ended his life by suicide.

Jacob Glatstein was a leading poet and journalist whose love of Yiddish enhanced his deep spiritual Jewishness.

Ephraim Auerbach (1893–1973) was born in Bessarabia and went to Palestine in 1911 to join a kibbutz. Four years later he came to the United States, where he taught in Jewish Schools and contributed verse to various periodicals. *Caravan* (1918) was a collection of poems about Palestine. *The Red Thread* (1927) contains fine lyrics on social and natural themes. *Clear Is the Old Spring* (1940) and *Jacob's Tents* (1953) deal with national Jewish life, and *White City* (1954) is devoted to life in Tel Aviv. In his final volume, *The Steppe Is Awake* (1962), he returned nostalgically to the land of his birth.

M. Bassin (1889–1963) was drafted into the Russian army in 1907. Caught indoctrinating fellow soldiers with his radical ideas, he escaped to the United States. Of a literary bent, he wrote poems and articles for various periodicals. He is best remembered for *500 Years of Yiddish Poetry* (2 volumes, 1917) and *American Yiddish Poetry* (1940).

B. J. Bialostotsky (1893–1962) was born in Kovno and came to New York in 1911, where he taught in Jewish schools. In 1922 he joined the staff of the *Forward*. Inwardly perturbed, he expressed in his poems the turbulence of his seething agitation. At one time he stated: "It is possible if I were the son of normal people, I might not have become a writer. The longing for the normal, healthy life made me impatient, and it was this restlessness which made me seek an outlet through writing." If this restlessness characterized his several volumes of verse, it is absent from his comprehensive and competent book of literary criticism.

Menakhem Boraisho (Goldberg, 1888–1949) came to New York in 1914. In addition to his work as a journalist he wrote poems of distinction, among them *A Ring in the Chain* (1916) and *Sand* (1920). *Zavel Riemer* (1923) is a long epic poem about a poor worker who learns to play the violin, told with lyrical felicity and benign realism. For years an employee of the American Jewish Congress, he completed *The Walker* in 1943—a work of 500 pages which seeks to ascertain the essence of Jewishness; lyrical yet reflective, the poem flows from fear to faith.

Barukh Glazman (1893–1945) reached the United States in 1911, where he worked as a house painter until he was able to study at Ohio State University. Although he began to write in English, he soon turned to Yiddish. In 1924 he went to Russia and Poland, but returned in 1930, having in the interim published a number of stories. In *Lands and Lives* (2 volumes, 1935) he depicts the life of a Jewish family from its origin in Russia to its establishment in America with a realism that evidenced the influence of the newer fiction of the literary world. One of the most Americanized of Yiddish writers, he delineated mostly uprooted and perturbed Jews on both sides of the Atlantic.

Isroel Goikhberg (1894–1970) arrived in the United States in 1913 and entered an engineering school in a Midwestern university. On graduation, however, he decided to become a teacher of Yiddish. He wrote many poems for children but even more for adults. In them he depicted city sounds and sights, the swiftness of urban pace, the majesty of skyscrapers, and the human turmoil within it all. *Songs of Our Generation* (1925) is a work of translation from the Russian; *Good Morning* (1929) and *Verticals* (1935) contain popular poems for juveniles. *Nemerov* (1946) consisted of poems steeped in the tragedy of the Holocaust.

Eliezer Greenberg, born in 1896 in Bessarabia, came to the United States at the end of World War I and worked for a time in a leather factory. He early began to study the works of eminent world poets and critics, thereby attaining wide familiarity with the art of versification and literary theory. In 1928 he published *Streets and Avenues*. His later volumes of verse are *From Everywhere* (1934), *Fisher Village* (1938), *The Long Night* (1946), *Night Dialogue* (1953), and *Eternal Thirst* (1968). These poems possess a quiet lyricism and refined reflection. He has also written sensitive studies of several Yiddish writers, and together with Irving Howe edited anthologies of Yiddish stories, poems, and essays in English translation.

Abraham Lutsky (Zuker, 1894–1957) reached New York in 1914 and had difficulty earning a living. His early poems failed of acceptance, but later his verses were published first by the *Forward* and later by *The Day*. In 1921 he began to act out his poems before audiences, and his improvisations proved popular. "A Valse," "At the Rabbi's Table," "A Pot of Beans," and other poems gave wide range to his lively histrionics. Highly skilled in the manipulation of words, he wrote with a lilting mockery that hid an underlying artful pathos. Among his books are *In the Beginning* (1932), *Portraits* (1945), and *All that Is Good* (1958).

Sh. Miller (1895–1958), on arriving in the United States in 1912, worked at manual tasks until he learned bookkeeping. He began to write stories for magazines, and also did translating for the *Freie Arbeiter Shtimme.* In 1927 he moved to California, where he associated with other Yiddish writers. His fiction, and particularly his novel, *Red and Black* (1945) is noted for its psychological insight and reflective calm.

Aaron Nissenson (1898–1964), the son of a miller, was brought to America in 1911. The graduate of a pharmacy school, he decided to make writing his career and joined the *Morning Journal.* His several volumes of verse exalt faith and hope and are kindled by sparks of thought. *The Way of Man,* his drama on the life of Eugene V. Debs, is a probing into the depths of human behavior.

I. A. Rontch, born in 1899, came to New York at the age of fourteen. Five years later, having already published some verses, he went to Chicago to teach in a Jewish school. His volume of poems *Winds* (1923) was favorably reviewed by Ben Hecht in the *Chicago Daily News.* He returned to New York in 1924 and continued his career as a writer and editor.

J. I. Segal (1896–1954) reached Montreal in 1911 and worked first as a tailor and later as a teacher. In 1923 he moved to New York, but returned five years later and became a staff member of *Der Keneder Adler* (The Canadian Eagle). He had associated with the *Yunge* in New York, and in 1918 published *Of My World,* poems of warm feeling and universality. In 1945 his *Poems of Praise* was awarded the Lamed Prize and Leivick wrote of him: "Segal, more than others, has woven his love of the Jews with the love of life and love of Yiddish; because the three were discriminated against, insulted and abused, he has lifted them to the greatest height, to the purest substance."

Yoel Slonim (1884–1944) was the most thoroughly Americanized Yiddish writer, having been brought to this country at the age of two and having received his education in American schools. Although he had begun to write in English, his father influenced him toward Yiddish. In 1906 he became a staff member of *Warheit* and continued with *The Day* after 1919. He had associated with the *Yunge* after 1908 and was one of the editors of *Literatur*. An able journalist, he also wrote considerably on English and American literature. His verse was noted for its modern idiom and imagery.

Zisha Weinper (1893–1957) came to New York in 1913, where he worked as a house painter and later taught in a Jewish school. He early began to associate with other young writers, and his poems were printed in various anthologies. In the course of time he published several volumes of verse and a fine critical work on Yiddish writers. There was a lyrical freshness about his early poems, with the impress of the esthete; later his verse became more narrative in form and social in theme. His love of the American landscape is inherent in much of his writing, and *At the Grand Canyon* (1947) contains one of the best descriptions of American scenic grandeur. A founder of YKUF, an organization for furthering Jewish culture, he was one of its active leaders to the end of his life.

Yoneh Rosenfeld (1880–1944) was early orphaned and suffered extreme poverty in childhood. For ten years he worked as a carpenter, but in 1905 he began to write stories. "Competitors" and the collection *In the Quiet* (1912) gained him considerable prominence. He came to New York in 1921 and began to write for the *Forward* and other periodicals. His fiction delineated with psychological acuity characters who behaved irrationally and futilely. Yet out of the dark depths of human behavior he sought to produce a logic out of illogical circumstances. *All Alone* (1940) vividly describes his early suffering. In several other books his creative fantasy enriched his analysis of character, but his work also suffers from verbosity and a tendency to vulgarity.

Yoneh Rosenfeld was only one of a number of important writers to settle in America after the efflorescence of Yiddish literature had begun to wane. Melech Ravitch, born in 1893 in Galicia, brought out his first volume of poems, *At the Entrance,* in 1912. The following year he went to live in Vienna and was drafted into the Austrian army during World War I. In 1921 he moved to Warsaw and participated in the editing of *Literarishe Bletter* (Literary Pages) and wrote a perceptive study of Spinoza. Again on the move, he sojourned in various parts of the world before he settled in the United States in 1934. In a number of later poems he extolled the American environment. In 1964 he published his volumes of reminiscence.

Kadia Molodowsky (1894–1974) was one of the most distinguished of Yiddish women poets. Highly sensitive to the poverty around her, she expressed her personal distress in a number of poems. Her first volume, *Heshvon* [Autumn] *Nights,* was a work of poetic maturity. She wrote tenderly beautiful verses for children, and her later adult poems possessed imaginative, pictorial, and metaphysical qualities. In 1935 she came to New York and soon wrote, in addition to poetry, three novels imbued with nostalgic wistfulness. During the years of the Holocaust, grieving for relatives and friends, as well as for the Jewish martyrdom, she wrote elegies of dolorous lament. Her collection of these poems, *Light from the Thornbush* (1965), also contains a long paean to Israel. In 1943 she began to publish *Seviva* (Environment), a high-level quarterly devoted to literature and criticism.

I. I. Trunk (1887–1961) was born in Warsaw of a rabbinic family. Spending his childhood in Lodz, he later traveled widely. Inclined to radicalism, he expressed his views and experiences in verse, story, and criticism. He did not reach the United States until 1941. Of a philosophical turn of mind and a highly gifted critic, he produced some of the most penetrating writing in both fields. His book, *Poland* (1946–1943), extended to seven volumes. He also published *Leaves in the Wind* (1944), *Fig Trees and Other Stories* (1922), *Josephus Flavius of Jerusalem and Other Stories* (1930), *Wise Men of Chelm* (1951), *The Happiest Man in the World* (1955), and *Messiah Storm* (1961).

Aaron Zeitlin (1898–1975), the son of a distinguished Hebrew scholar and writer, published his first Yiddish poem at the age of sixteen. During the next several years he wrote essays, critical reviews, and a major work on Byron. His novel, *Shadows on the Snow* (1922), and a play on Jacob Frank, the pseudo-messiah, were well received. At the outbreak of World War II he reached New York and became a regular contributor to *The Day*. Highly admired as a writer and as a person, his collected poems, published in three volumes, were awarded ten literary prizes.

Chaim Grade, born in 1910, spent his early years in a yeshiva. When he began to write Yiddish verse in 1932, his superior poetic talent was at once recognized and brought him wide praise. A leading member of the remarkable "Young Vilna" group of writers, he published his work in Yiddish journals the world over. Shmuel Niger wrote of his poetry: "Chaim Grade's poems are ecstatic nature hymns. He humanizes nature. . . . He loves to portray it in its turbulent and stormy state." Grade's authentic poetic voice is best manifested in *A Mother's Will* (1949). During World War II he found refuge in Soviet Russia. At its conclusion he went to Paris, where he helped organize the surviving Yiddish writers who had gravitated to the French capital. In 1948 he settled in New York, and has since written lengthy poems, fiction, and reminiscences. The first story in *Mother's Sabbath* (1955), "My Quarrel with Hersh Rasseyner," is essentially a philosophical-religious dialogue between the author, who is religiously enlightened, and his fellow Yeshiva student, an intense *Musser* fanatic, on the nature of Judaism and its relation to the Holocaust.

Itzik Manger (1901–1963), a word magician and a subtle artist, was born in Rumania, where he was early apprenticed to a tailor. In 1918 he began to write verse, and *Stars on the Roof* (1929) placed him among the prominent young Yiddish writers. *Lantern in the Wind* (1933) added to his fame as a balladist with a humorous turn of phrase but with a serious undertone. *The Book of Paradise* (1939) is a droll prose fantasy, later issued in an English translation. Escaping from Paris to London just before the Nazis occupied the capital, he in 1943 published *Clouds Over the Roof*, a collection of poems. On his arrival in New York in 1951, he was honored on his fiftieth birthday by the publication of *Songs and Ballads*. *Intimate Persons and Other Writings* was issued on his sixtieth birthday. In all his writing Manger combined pathos and soft satire with remarkable felicity. A highly personal poet, he possessed the spontaneous flow of the folk bard with the purity of lyricism and musicality of sophisticated prosody.

Many other writers might be listed if this book attempted to be encyclopedic. Those included, however, while the more significant, make evident that in the early decades of this century Yiddish writing in America flourished with remarkable energy and creativity. The scores of books published annually were only a small part of the stories and verse and criticism printed in newspapers and magazines. The writers, for the most part, came to this country in the flush of youth, deeply grounded in Jewish lore and tradition, but also influenced by the literary trends in world literature. It was natural for them to express the hopes and woes, the joys and sorrows of their fellow immigrants who were adjusting themselves to their new environment as best they could—which they did with the freedom and felicity of the creative impulse. Years later, when they learned of the massacres and persecutions in Eastern Europe during and immediately after World War I, and still later of their kin dying in Nazi crematories, they lamented these tragedies with their heart's blood. Chaim Grade spoke for all of them when he wrote: "It was not a third of our people who were murdered but rather that a third was cut out of the flesh and soul of every Jew who survived."

On the whole, however, they were oriented toward America and wrote about its beauty and grandeur and personal freedom with admiration and affection. More and more of their writing appeared in English translation, so that it is no longer an esoteric phenomenon. Thus, when Yiddish literature written in America is viewed as a whole, its ethical import and esthetic form are readily obvious. B. I. Bialostotsky expressed this view well:

> American Yiddish literature includes not only rebelliousness and realism but also an emphasis on the dignity of the common man, an insistence that human value should not be measured by material success but rather by a person's spiritual resources. In part, the idea came from the socialistic tendencies then current, but in greater part it derived from the ancient Jewish phrase expressed in Psalms of "He that raises the poor from the dust."

9

Some Major Yiddish Writers

In a book on Jewish publishing in America, one must necessarily be limited to writers who at one time or another had made their home in it. Although Yiddish writing had gone on for centuries in Eastern Europe and was particularly active in the nineteenth century—with Mendele Mocher Sforim, Sholom Aleichem, and I. L. Peretz as the great founders of modern Yiddish writing—the first literary aspirants to migrate to the United States, men like Rosenfeld, Yehoash, and Pinski, rooted creative Yiddish writing in America. They were followed by numerous gifted writers who came with the second wave of immigrants. Over the years they achieved literary prominence, as was made evident in the brief sketches in the preceding chapters. Some of them were obviously of major significance, and these are reserved for more extended treatment. The choice is of course subjective and open to disputation, but there is no denial of their important stature both historically and artistically.

Abraham Reisen (1875–1953), born in Lithuania of an impecunious but cultivated merchant family, received a traditional Jewish education plus a little study of Russian and German. After serving four years in the Russian army he, already aglow with poetic fervor, went to Warsaw in order to be near the active group of Yiddish writers headed by Peretz. In 1902 he brought out a 48-page volume of verse entitled *Current Songs*. The work was well received by his fellow writers, and Abraham Cahan reprinted some of the poems in the *Forward*. To earn his living Reisen did some tutoring.

At the outbreak of World War I he left for New York and became a regular contributor to Yiddish periodicals. From time to time he collected his poems and stories into volumes. His characteristic themes were poverty, longing, love, and sympathy, and all were expressed with a simplicity that masked deep feeling and thought. His verse in particular was written with conscious artlessness. When he wrote of Jewish Lithuanian life in all its penurious nakedness, his very soul sang in wistful sympathy. His gentle reflections, impressionable melancholy, ironic sentiment, social radicalism, pensive yearning, and feeling of precariousness—all found expression in song and story with lyric spontaneity. Sometimes sorrow brought forth tears, or love lifted his spirit into blissful ecstasy; his melancholy plaint reverberated in both.

At its best his poetic voice was soft and still and unpretentious. Even when aroused rebelliously, he sang in a muted key. His lyrical response to the cross-currents of Jewish life was made with the empathy and directness of the true bard. In his early work, when his subject was the Lithuanian milieu, he wrote of his fellow Jews with love and lenity; in the United States, aware of the deterioration of Orthodox wholesomeness among immigrants, he tended to write of their behavior with critical irony. To the end of his life, however, he wrote with a simplicity of form and salutary sadness that made him the most appreciated of Yiddish lyricists.

In his stories Reisen was more the humorist. His smile was usually ironic, saturated with pathos, motivated by repressed poignancy. His tales of poverty were written with exceptional fidelity and pensiveness. It was a life he knew intimately, and he described it with plaintive reality. He felt keenly the suffering caused by hunger and need, and their victims were depicted with warm sympathy. His emphasis was not on incident but on one's reaction to it. The manner in which he revealed how men and women were being intimidated by grim poverty into humble, docile, dispirited creatures constituted the essence of his fictional art.

Unsatisfied love ranked next to poverty in Reisen's city stories. Himself a bachelor until middle age and markedly, if mildly, nympholeptic, the sight of an attractive woman often excited his pliant and impulsive heart to ecstasy; when his attentions met with indifference or rebuff, his heart ached sorely. All this he expressed in humorously pathetic fiction. Many of his early stories concern young intellectuals who long for love and remain unrequited. Their poverty keeps them from conjugality, but in their yearning for feminine affection they flirt at every opportunity. Although the girls they meet are not averse to the attentions of young intellectuals, they favor men who are ready to marry them.

In the United States his own poverty was lessened and a satisfactory marriage decreased his interest in unrequited love. What concerned him more was the spiritual slackening of the Jews around him. Once they began to enjoy material comforts, they did not realize the price they were paying for their fleshpots. They had to work hard, and the strenuous hours in the shops and stores sapped their vitality more readily than their previous indigence. Reisen perceived them bereft of their Sabbath serenity, of their faith in God. Yet he expressed his disapproval gently, ironically, with an inner melancholy, as if fearful of looking too deeply into the souls of his characters. This literary unease in time caused him to resort to reminiscence, and the three volumes which depicted his life up to 1910 possess the beauty and gentleness of his best efforts.

The brevity of some of his stories gives them an anecdotal form. As a gifted storyteller, however, he was in unerring control of the pattern he was following. Like finely carved cameos his stories emerged skilfully etched, with great verbal economy. He knew exactly the effect he wanted, and proceeded with simple directness to his goal. His style lacks brilliant imagery and apt metaphor, but it fits well his natural restraint. Character and incident occasionally combine to produce a contrived dénouement, but this is a shortcoming rarely evident. Indeed, within his limitations he had created a large number of living characters. Regardless of the theme, the people in his stories are humanly convincing. For he dwelt not on poverty or love or spiritual laxity but on their psychological effects. Keenly aware of human frailty, he tended to smile ironically yet compassionately when circumstances distended or distorted the behavior of his characters.

Sholem Asch (1880–1957) was in a sense the antithesis of Reisen: handsome, spirited, self-confident, bold of outlook, the writer of world-renowned novels and dramas. Born in a small Polish town, he was the first Yiddish writer to become a prominent literary figure the world over. He early felt the urge to write, and with Peretz's encouragement published his first story in 1900. Three years later he brought out a collection of his stories.

His first relatively long work, *A Shtetl,* appeared in 1905 and immediately placed him at the head of young Yiddish writers. It was in essence a prose poem. The medieval milieu of his native town was delineated with the ecstasy of first love. The simple, wholesome Hasidim of his childhood recollection appear as idyllic folk: firmly founded in the revered faith of their fathers, inured to their static social customs and economic practices, endowed with the carnal robustness of their peasant neighbors, yet spiritually childlike in their placid naivété. Here Asch also revealed a love of nature as novel to his Yiddish readers as his romanticized townsmen.

Asch next began to experiment with dramatic writing, and his play, *Downstream,* was produced in Polish translation. In it he propounded the self-evident truth that once one is infected with doubt, faith is doomed—even when there is nothing to replace it. This futile faith-seeking was imputed more effectively in *The Messiah Period* (1906) and *The Inheritors* (1913). In both plays Asch was at pains to demonstrate the spiritual bankruptcy of the middle generation, and to point out how desperately the Jewish youth were in search of a new religion.

In 1907 he completed *The God of Vengeance,* a drama that was widely produced but remained controversial for many years because of its moral complications. The theme is essentially spurious. The action concerns the protagonist Yekel's attempt to strike a bargain with God for the preservation of his daughter's moral purity. Asch might have legitimately pitted Yekel against a vengeful God who visited the sins of parents upon their offspring if Yekel, a hardened sinner, had taken every precaution to preserve his daughter's innocence. But Yekel kept his daughter in the same house as his brothel and in close contact with its inmates. Yekel's placing a Torah in his apartment above the brothel as a sort of amulet is of course of no avail.

The following year Asch treated the conflict between carnal lust and spiritual dedication in *Shabbati Zevi,* a drama suffering from a similar defect. The erotic impulse was depicted with oriental cadence, but sexual exaltation in a dedicated messiah could not but lead to tragic disaster.

Asch was by now a featured contributor to the New York *Forward,* and in 1909 he visited the United States. His observation of Jewish life in America gave him material for another unsuccessful play, *The Landsman,* and a number of stories.

In 1913 he published *Wealthy Reb Shlomo,* a more mature version of *A Shtetl.* The magic of his glowing prose transformed the homely environment of his rustics into an idealized community—in sharp contrast to the towns depicted realistically by other Yiddish writers. In the same year he completed a rather feeble Biblical drama, *Jephthah's Daughter,* in which Moloch triumphed over the bellicose Hebrew warrior. Also in 1913 he published *Mary* and its sequel *The Road to One's Self,* in which the current revolutionary agitation in Russia is shown to affect the lives of Jewish youth. Influenced by Artzibashev's *Sanin,* Asch molded the action into *tendentz* fiction. To the same period belong *Our Faith, The League of the Weak,* and *Prestige,* all three dramatic attempts in a minor key.

With war raging in Europe in 1914, Asch decided to make his home in the United States, and in time became an American citizen. As the leading contributor to the *Forward* and as the recipient of royalties from plays, he was able not only to live in comfort but to indulge his penchant for collecting works of art and Jewish rare books and artifacts. In 1916 he serialized *Mottke the Thief* in the *Forward* and later turned the novel into a play. The novel contrasts the wholesome life of the *shtetl* with the grimy gaudiness of the Warsaw slum. The youthful Mottke is drawn with Rabelaisian strokes, and his attachment to his mother is etched with rare tenderness. His behavior lacks conviction, however, when he leaves for Warsaw, becomes a pimp, and sheds his appealing traits in the process.

As a New York resident Asch was strongly stimulated by the life he saw on the lower East Side, especially the often pathetic attempts of immigrant Jews to adapt themselves to American ways and practices. His inclined sympathy notwithstanding, he tended to be repelled by the crass and vulgar behavior of a number of them. In *Uncle Moses* (1918), he made critically clear that in the process of Americanization a good many Jews discarded the traditions and faith of their fathers. Unlike in *Wealthy Reb Shlomo,* which deals with the same Polish Jews, the characters are described in their sweatshop environment, to whom the serenity of the Sabbath had become a troubled memory. Consequently they are portrayed with the bluntness of uninspired realism.

The persecution and pogroms during the World War I period profoundly perturbed Asch. He exerted himself in gathering funds for relief and sought in his writing to exalt the spiritual faith and perseverence of the victims. *A String of Pearls* (1916) is a drama set in the Russian war zone, in which Jews are forced to evacuate their village within twelve hours. The action concerns the miraculous transformation of a young girl into an old woman when she puts on her grandmother's pearl necklace as a means of avoiding defilement by the army leader. A false note, however, is struck in the allegorical antagonism between Jew and Gentile.

In *The Sanctification of the Name* (1919) Asch achieved an artistically profound work. In his delineation of Jewish life in Poland during the brutal massacres of the mid-seventeenth century he implied that the Jews were then, even more than in 1918, on the brink of annihilation, and that now, even as before, their undying faith would save them from extinction. Asch's compassionate spirit gave the tragic situation the poignant quality of imaginative art.

His next three novels deal with Jewish life in America. *The Mother* (1925) is a loosely told story, first of life in Poland, then in New York, with the main character struggling for artistic recognition. *Electric Chair* (*Judge Not* in English, 1926) concerns a successful Jewish banker who has a fortuitous affair with the mistress of an elderly Kentucky colonel, and the latter dies in the ensuing scuffle. Feeling so guilty that he refuses any defense, he was sentenced to be electrocuted; he also rejects any attempt at clemency because he had become aware of the futility of his past life. *Chaim Lederer's Return* (1927) tells of a manufacturer who retired at 60 in order to resume the intellectual life he had abandoned in his youth for the lure of riches—only to discover that his early ideals were unrecoverable. To these novels may be added *God's Prisoners* (1933), a sensitive study of eccentric love. While all four works have flashes of fine writing, the overall effect is of fiction written for popular reading.

A work of large scope and artistic breadth is *Three Cities* (3 volumes, 1929–1931). This novel depicts the three significant aspects of the Russian political drama which ended in the triumphant Bolshevik revolution. *Petersburg* deals with the commercial and industrial expansion at the turn of the century; *Warsaw* presents a sympathetic delineation of the social unrest and political turmoil prior to the outbreak of war in 1914; and *Moscow* provides a liberal's view of the social forces released by the revolution in 1917. Here Asch is the keen social historian, but even more the imaginative novelist. He made clear the elements of national decay and dissatisfaction which, aggravated by disastrous war, hastened the downfall of the Romanov empire. Simultaneously he depicted the part played by Jews in this epic drama. The novel was translated into numerous languages and became a best seller in this country and in England.

In a sense a sequel, *The War Goes On* (1937) continues the story of social upheaval from the savage civil war in 1918 to the economic and spiritual collapse in Germany in the 1920s. The work towers as a work of historical fiction, portraying with notable effectiveness the suffering, pathos, chaos, and the unmitigating despair which spawned the Nazis in Germany. Again and again the narrative flares forth with the passion of the proud Jew, and over the whole hovers the artist's wistful and compassionate insight into human vicissitudes.

Asch's romantic imagination had from early childhood been fascinated by Jewish piety, the whole-souled adoration of God, and the devout observance of Judaic precepts. With the rise of Hitler, he sought an antidote in the moral beauty of Jewish piety. This aspect of Judaism he presented most effectively in *Salvation* (1934). His description of the piety and mystical aspirations of the Jews in the early nineteenth century, epitomized in the life of Yechiel, is both vivid and veracious. Their pathetic and at times pathological behavior assumed inherent reality in their sincere yearning for spiritual beatitude. Yechiel is shown to believe that not erudition but faith led to salvation, that the love of God ennobled the human spirit. With Nazi brutality in mind, Asch concluded the narrative with the pious hope that "each generation will see its own righteous man. For is it not written that the righteous man is the cornerstone of the world?"

Deeply troubled by the millennia-old antagonism between Jews and Christians, yet strongly attracted to the personalities and fervor of the founders of Christianity, Asch was very eager for amity and reconciliation between the two religious faiths. In time he persuaded himself that by retelling the story of Jesus as he believed him to have been, he would clearly demonstrate that the enemies of the Jews were in truth defilers of the Christianity Jesus stood for. In his new novel he depicted Jesus as a pious Jew who had been falsely accused by his Jewish detractors. In the narrative Jesus emerged as much the God-lover as Yechiel, but in addition he was also the son of God. "*Salvation*," Niger pointed out, "was actually nothing else but an introduction to *The Nazarene; The Nazarene* is first of all the realization, the completion and crowning of *Salvation*."

The Nazarene (1939) combined sound research with intuitive art. Jesus is depicted as a righteous Jew bringing faith in God to its ultimate goal. When he reveals himself to his disciples and proceeds to Jerusalem to exhort the populace, he openly courts apprehension and execution as a rebel and blasphemer. Asch stressed the fact that guilt lay with Pilate and not with the High

Priest. The book was quickly translated into numerous languages and was read by millions of Christians and Jews.

This laudatory portrayal of Jesus, coming at the height of Nazi persecution, shocked many of Asch's erstwhile Jewish admirers and brought abuse and obloquy on his head. Cahan was the first to react inimically. He refused to serialize the narrative, so that it was not published in Yiddish until 1943. Others joined in the attack, and to the end of his life Asch was disdained by many Jews as an apologist for Christianity. Deeply perturbed by this abuse, he defended himself in interviews, articles, and in *What I Believe* (1941), insisting that he was a devoted Jew but that as an artist he had the right to express himself according to his ability and conscience.

Undeterred by criticism, much as he resented it, Asch continued to probe into the origin of Christianity, to some extent no doubt stimulated by the worldwide success of *The Nazarene*. In 1943 he published *The Apostle,* which makes clear how Paul gradually emerged as the apostolic founder of Christianity—tracing his life from the zealous persecutor of Jesus's followers to his conversion and his anti-Jewish exhortation. The novel did not appear in the original Yiddish. The English translation was hailed by reviewers and read widely. Jews reacted to it either plaintively or violently, according to their nature. With gas ovens in Auschwitz and other concentration camps in full blast, no sensitive Jew could read with equanimity Paul's fanatical tirades against his fellow Jews. Asch, having portrayed Paul with artistic empathy, could not believe that the novel was anti-Jewish in character. It seemed to him that he was no more pro-Christian than Rembrandt was pro-Jewish in his paintings of rabbis. In *One Destiny:* An Epistle to Christians (1945) he eloquently discussed his views on the relations between Jews and Christians over the many centuries and concluded that the two faiths were inextricably interrelated.

Mary (1949) is the third of the Christological novels. The simplest and least controversial of the three, it portrays the mother of Jesus with loving piety and pastoral artlessness, so that she is in a sense one more of his fine Jewish mother creations.

In 1946 Asch published *East River,* a novel posing the problem of antagonism among the nations and religions, and intimating that amicable relations are possible among them. The question of intermarriage is treated sympathetically. Deftly conceived, the narrative nevertheless lacked the freshness of some of his earlier fiction. Also in 1946 he brought out a collection of stories dealing with Nazi atrocities. *A Passage in the Night* (1954) concerns a wealthy Jew who, having gotten his start to wealth by stealing a purse from a Pole, became eager in his old age to find the man and compensate him generously.

As if to expiate for the Christological writings, Asch produced *Moses* (1951) and *The Prophet* (1955). Moses emerges as through a misted glass mystically, a noble human being, a seeker of truth and justice, but no son of God. The narrative follows closely the story in the Pentateuch, but with the grandeur of an epic: with the Israelites fearful and grumbling, unable to throw off their slavish spirit, but with Moses serving and exhorting them with selfless devotion and inexhaustible sympathy, so that he emerges ennobled as the founder of Judaism and God's exalted prophet. In *The Prophet,* Deutero-Isaiah humbly sings God's word because he cannot silence the chant within him. Consumed by love of God like Yechiel, he is so eager for the return of the exiles from Babylon and for the restoration of the Temple that he feels impelled to go to them and preach the word of God. The wealthy, situated comfortably in Babylon, denounce him as a false prophet and seek to stone him, but the poor Jews heed his word and follow him.

Asch next began to write the story of Jacob and Rachel, but death put an end to his work in 1957. He remains a leading Yiddish writer. In possession of a lyric flow and emotional intensity, Asch was able to suffuse his best writing with poetic beauty. No formal stylist nor master of verbal refinement, he excelled in the expression of rich, sensuous feeling. When in love with his characters his prose began to sing. In the description of the earthy behavior of pious Hasidim or the wretched existence of the poor, his ardent empathy flowed fresh and pure. In a real sense he was one of the major novelists of the present century.

Peretz Hirschbein (1880–1948), a contemporary of both Reisen and Asch, differed markedly from both in personality and artistic expression. Unlike Reisen he was an esthete, a mystic, at once worldly and self-centered; unlike Asch he was at his best as a writer of dramatic idylls.

Born in a house adjacent to his father's mill, Hirschbein grew up in the haunting loneliness and pristine beauty of the Lithuanian countryside. In his thirteenth year he left home for a house of study in a nearby town, and for five years pored devotedly over tomes of Hebrew lore. Through an itinerant bookseller he learned of Yiddish publications, and that in turn led him to the study of current literature in other languages.

Having begun to write in Hebrew at the age of fifteen, he now turned to composing dramas in Yiddish, which seemed to him the medium best suited to his prospective audience. His early plays were naive in conception and quite sentimental and didactic in treatment. In 1904 he went to Warsaw and was encouraged by Peretz to continue writing. His newer plays—*The Carcass* (1905), *Where Life Passes* (1905), *Lonely People* (1906), and *'Twixt Day and Night* (1906), dealt with what was termed "cellar poverty"; the treatment was still stilted, but the characters began to emerge as individual creations.

In 1908 Hirschbein went to Odessa and organized a troupe of actors for the purpose of producing plays of merit. For two years he directed them in a repertoire of the best available Yiddish plays. In 1910 he began to be troubled by his inactivity as a writer and left the actors. The following year he came to New York to see some of his plays produced by an amateur group led by Yoel Entin, the perceptive critic. In the meantime he had written *Eva* (1910), *From Road to Road* (1911), and *The Last One* (1911), all unsuccessful efforts at finding themes suitable to his talent. In 1912 he completed *The Haunted Inn*, the first of his notable folk plays. In that year he also wrote *A Child of the World* and *A Wayside Nook*.

He returned to Europe in 1913, but was soon back in New York, where he became a regular contributor to the newly founded *Day*. He also published some one-act plays in the

Zukunft. Asked by *The Day* to report on the World Exposition in San Francisco, he in 1918 incorporated his sensitive articles in *Travels in America.*

By this time he had written most of his best plays. In addition to *The Haunted Inn* and *A Wayside Nook* he had completed *The Blacksmith's Daughters* (1914), *A Life for a Life* (1914), and *Green Fields* (1916), all being engaging plays about rustic Jews living in Lithuanian hamlets—a milieu in which he had grown up and knew intimately. Absent in them were the turmoil of the city and intellectual vagueness which had weakened his previous dramas. The characters, steeped in the soil they cultivated, had little knowledge of Jewish lore. Strong physically, essentially peasant folk, their piety was sincere and ardent. Having, in a sense, straightened their backs, they had acquired the outward characteristics of their Gentile neighbors. They loved the land and enjoyed the wholesomeness of nature—not with the sensitivity of the poet but with the simple sensuousness of rustics. Although they, as characters, lacked dramatic depth, the atmosphere in which they lived possessed the stamp of authenticity. In every play this effect was achieved by an imperceptive aggregation of intimate detail deftly interwoven with the general action.

When *The Haunted Inn* was produced in English on Broadway, its exotic theme appeared bizarre largely because of a poor translation and inept direction. Yet what perplexed Broadway audiences soon appeared quite natural and engaging on the Yiddish stage. Maurice Schwartz's Yiddish Art Theater began producing the Hirschbein plays in 1918 when it opened with *A Wayside Nook.* It was an immediate and noteworthy success. New York Jews, nostalgic for the bucolic milieu they still remembered or heard about, were charmed by the authentic presentation of the action. Early in 1919 it was followed by *The Blacksmith's Daughters.* Equally popular were *Green Fields* and *The Haunted Inn.* All four plays became part of the theater's repertoire. Subsequently Schwartz produced *A Life for a Life* and *Spirits Know Why* (1923). Bertha Kalish, the noted actress, played in *A Child of the World.* These latter plays, however, proved less popular.

Subsequently Hirschbein made *Green Fields* the first play of a trilogy by adding *Two Towns* and *Levi Isaac,* both having the setting and dramatic pattern of the first. In 1924 he also wrote *The Mouse and the Bell,* a dramatic poem of symbolic mysticism. Several years later he completed his recollections in *Years of Childhood* (1932). These reminiscences he continued in *Process of Life,* which dealt with his life up to 1910 and appeared posthumously in 1948. The earlier book is from a literary standpoint his best work, even more vivid and evocative than his major plays; the latter volume lacks the lyrical eloquence of the first, but provides a clear account of his years of development as a writer.

An inveterate traveler—he was to visit most inhabited countries—Hirschbein spent ten months in the Crimea during the late 1920s. On his return to New York in 1929 he recorded his observations and reflections first in a volume of essays and stories and later in a two-volume novel, *Red Fields,* which was serialized in 1932 and published three years later. He was intensely interested in the way Jews, for centuries excluded from the land, were adapting themselves as tillers of the soil. The novel concerns a group of urban Jews seeking to succeed as farmers. Many are both conscious Jews and devoted communists, and their efforts and conflicts and aspirations are described in detail. Here Hirschbein is much more the social historian than the psychological novelist. Consequently the main action, in which the protagonists struggle emotionally against inherent pride and prejudice, ends in unresolvable conflict.

Babylon, serialized for over three years in *The Day* and issued in 1942 in revised form as a three-decker novel totaling 1400 pages, describes a half century of Jewish life in America. The main characters belong to a family which migrated from Russia in 1883. Semi-emancipated from traditional Orthodoxy, moderately educated, deeply interested in world affairs and Jewish problems, the father and children find their respective places in the scheme of life on the lower East Side. The second generation is shown symbolically manifesting the effects of Americanization upon the Jewish community. The long narrative thus encompasses all facets of Jewish life. Yet the novel gives the impression of prairie flatness: the characters move along the surface, wisely and humorously or foolishly and meanly, without manifesting the vital sluices of fictional art.

In 1940 Hirschbein moved to Los Angeles, and there he wrote *On Strange Roads,* which was serialized in 1947. Two years earlier he, who had long prided himself on his strong physique and expected to become an octogenerian, became invalided and suffered pain until his death not long after.

Joseph Opatoshu (1886–1954) combined in himself the intellectual dedication of his paternal ancestry with the rustic robustness of his mother's heredity. These influences contended in him in a combination of physical dynamism with a passion for righteousness. Born in Poland, he spent his early years in a rustic atmosphere near a forest frequented by horse thieves and other shady characters. At first proud of his native land, he in his late teens realized that the Poles were anti-Semitic and unworthy of his allegiance. By then a student of engineering in France, he also discovered an inner urge to write. Having composed his first story, he managed to submit it to Peretz and was greatly encouraged by his praise.

With his father already in New York, Opatoshu joined him early in 1907. As he stated later, he had decided to burn his bridges behind him and devote himself to write about Jews in their new home in America. To earn his living he took various menial jobs, and one of them brought him close to a number of underworld characters, whom he later depicted with vivid verisimilitude. Later he found work as a teacher of Hebrew, and that gave him time to resume his study of engineering at Cooper Union—a profession he never practiced after his graduation.

Determined to become a writer, he readily joined the *Yunge.* In 1910 he published a revised version of his first story in *Literatur.* His new stories concerned Jews in his slum neighborhood, and his treatment of lawless characters was etched with the acid of satire. These stories appeared in *Schriften* and the *Neie Haym.* Eager for the enhancement of Jewish culture yet attracted to the bold irresponsibility of these characters, he described their life with vivid strokes while condemning their moral laxity. He was

Joseph Opatoshu (left) was a Yiddish fiction writer of great empathy and scholarly insight. Shmuel Niger (right) was the leading Yiddish critic and sponsor of writers.

also perturbed about the futility of teaching Hebrew to boys who would rather play baseball, and his *Hebrew* deplores the spiritual debasement evidenced in some of the religious schools.

With the establishment of *The Day* in 1914 Opatoshu was engaged as a regular contributor, and he remained on it to the end of his life forty years later, thus assuring himself of a steady, if modest, income. The need to provide a story or article each week sent him to the highways and byways of America for human material. With time his sarcasm became less scathing, yielding to irony and sympathetic insight. Many of these early stories dealt with people who worked hard for their sustenance in the face of conditions which oppressed, thwarted, or vulgarized. He described the struggles of class against class, race against race, the old against the young, in their various complex manifestations. *Race* (1923) contains a number of these stories, with "Lynching" being the most memorable.

A writer's indelible impressions come from his youthful experiences. For all his interest in the American scene, Opatoshu drew again and again upon his childhood memories. One of his early stories dealt with the horse thieves whose presumed exploits had fascinated him as a boy. More ambitiously he had the idea of a novel that would embrace the sweep and spirit of Jewish life in Poland during the years of Hasidic decline. A naturally modest if self-confident man, he decided first to test his literary powers with a briefer work having the same setting. The result was *Alone*, which was serialized in 1918 in the *Zukunft* and published the following year. Modest as a work of fiction, it is rich and vivid in the description of forest life; folklore and religious tradition add flavor to the historic setting, and the portrayal of character was already masterful.

He was now ready to write his major work, *The Polish Woods*, and completed it in 1921. It was at once hailed as a work of literary excellence, and its popularity was as great in Poland as in the United States. Translations into several European languages followed, including an English edition in this country some years later. A sequel, *1863*, appeared in 1926 and was received with equal favor. In these two volumes Opatoshu was the artist steeped in Jewish and European history. He delineated graphically a people in time of spiritual flux: Hasidism at the beginning of its disintegration, the *Haskalah* (Enlightenment) movement in its early manifestations, and the factious and futile struggle for Polish independence culminating in the abortive insurrection against Russia in 1863. Of great interest is the portrayal of Rabbi Mendel of Kotsk, who is presented at odds with himself, full of doubt and even despair, angry and bitter, yet a saint withal. Also significant is the wall of prejudice separating Jew from Pole, even though some Jews were dedicated to Polish liberation. The large and variegated canvas of the novel encompassed a Poland in which Jews and Poles lived in close proximity and yet kept deliberately apart, strongly dependent on one another economically and joined in hatred of their Russian oppressors, and yet wholly incompatible socially and spiritually. And the host of characters crowding the action are for the most part vividly drawn and unforgettable.

In 1929 Opatoshu published *The Dancer*, in which he examined the agonized persistence of a disintegrating Hasidism in its American environment. With a realism that cuts to the quick, the novel depicts a group of elderly Hasidim who are as oblivious of the gangsters in their New York tenements as of the politicians in City Hall. Forced to earn their bread as best they could, they remained determined to save their souls. Yet their efforts to observe their religion in godless America are doomed to failure. The weakness of the novel is that it is not so much an organic narrative as a group of related sketches. Yet it has vivid characterization and dynamic action, so that the men and women achieve reality as much in their spiritual striving as in the indulgence of their carnal appetites.

Opatoshu had long been delving into Jewish history, and particularly into the daily life of medieval Jewish towns along the Rhine. He became convinced that this "life was not as shabby and murky as indicated in histories." In 1933 he brought out a volume of two long stories, "A Day in Regensburg" and "Elia Bochur." The first concerns an important wedding within the ghetto. The descriptions of the preparations as well as of the guests and the ceremony, based on close study, revealed an aspect of medieval Jewish life previously overlooked. The second story portrays the German-born author of *The Bovo Buch* as an active intellectual in northern Italy. These and other similar stories are written with fictional grace and realistic gusto. Their vocabulary is ingeniously limited to the Yiddish spoken at the time.

Ever the literary experimenter and keen observer, and most of all the imaginative artist, Opatoshu wrote hundreds of his weekly stories for the *Day*, most of them about Jews in either Poland or the United States. He covered the gamut of human experience and plucked incidents pregnant with emotional vitality. The basic element is usually a conflict of forces, developed with verbal economy, so that the characters emerge vivid and real in the struggle which enfolds them. In the 1930s and even more in the early 1940s the Nazi genocide against Jews agonized his spirit, and in *When Poland Fell* (1945) and *Jewish Legends* (1951) he wrote about the gruesome aspects of the Holocaust.

Hoping to give comfort to his fellow Jews by narrating the heroism of the early Jewish martyrs, Opatoshu chose for the theme of his next major work the uprising against Hadrian's Rome in 132 C.E., spearheaded by the renowned Rabbi Akiba and led by the doughty soldier Bar Kochba. The first volume (*Rabbi Akiba*) was issued in 1948 and was immediately published in an English translation; the second volume (*The Last Uprising*) appeared shortly before his sudden death in 1954. The novel is notable for its sustained literary mastery. Intimating that calamity lay not in defeat but in the fear to fight back, Opatoshu sought to demonstrate that resistance was in itself an act of salvation. Thus Rabbi Akiba is shown seeking to revive confidence in the discouraged remnant after the destruction of the Second Temple. As worldly as he is erudite and sagacious, he encourages his followers covertly to accumulate the sinews of war and persuades Bar Kochba, the estranged scion of the House of David and the head of a Roman legion, to lead the rebellion. In this poignant chronicle Opatoshu has combined historic events with artistic invention to give the stamp of imaginative reality to the narrative. And the work is enhanced by the firmly wrought Yiddish diction and evocative Hebrew aphorisms and precepts.

Leivick Halper (1888–1962), using the signature of H. Leivick, was born in a small town near Minsk, the eldest of nine children. His father, a redheaded *Kohen* and proud scholar, was reduced by poverty to teaching girls how to read and write—to his constant humiliation. Not until he reached adulthood did Leivick understand and even sympathize with his father's choleric outbursts. From early childhood, however, he was tortured to tears by compassion for his mother's nightly kneading of dough in order to bake bread for sale.

Terrorized by his father's temper, young Leivick feared to speak in his presence. An acutely sensitive boy, suffering empathically with those in pain, he was terribly troubled in *heder,* when he read about the sacrifice of Isaac—so much so that he kept returning to it imaginatively to the end of his life. At the age of ten he began five years of study in a yeshiva and often went hungry. While in Minsk he learned of the world outside of his restricted Judaism and became a socialist. He joined the *Bund,* the Jewish socialist organization, and became active in its affairs, so that he was in time arrested and sentenced to four years of hard labor and permanent exile in Siberia. *In the Czar's Prison* (1959) gives a graphically poignant account of his incarceration—an ordeal that seared his soul and plagued his spirit for many years.

While in prison he wrote a dramatic poem, *The Messiah in Chains* (1908), which gave expression to a Jewish legend which had become deeply embedded in his imagination. Another of his poems at that time, "A Soul in Hell or Job the Second," tells of a spirit in revolt against God and impatient for the salvation of his people. In Siberia he wrote a drama, *There Where Freedom,* which explored the deeper aspects of human conflict.

Leivick managed to escape from Siberian exile and reached New York in 1913, where he soon found work as a paperhanger. Continuing to write poetry in his free time, in 1918 he published a small volume entitled *Behind the Lock.* In these verses he depicted his pain, fears, dreams, and visions during his years of incarceration.

Jewish suffering during World War I galvanized his thoughts on salvation. *The Golem* (1920) gave expression to his vision of

H. Leivick was a Yiddish poet and dramatist of rare compassion and spiritual probing.

the Messiah as the redeemer of persecuted Jews. The drama is rich in symbolism, allusions, mystical and legendary intimations—sometimes nebulous and even murky, but always deeply and imaginatively felt. The drama was quickly recognized as a masterly achievement of the poetic imagination. In 1925 it was produced by the Habima in Moscow, and many years later it was performed in English both as a drama and as an opera.

About this time Leivick became ill with tuberculosis and spent a number of years in sanitaria. The dream of salvation did not leave his imagination, and in 1932 he completed *The Salvation Comedy—the Golem Dreams.* Although the work does not equal the poetic fervor of *The Golem,* it is a fine work, with the legendary characters drawn with poetic insight and with the complex symbolism clearly expressed.

All the while he was writing verse for newspapers and magazines, and their collection in *In No Man's Land* (1923) contains the pogrom poems—"He," "The Sick Room," "The Stable," and "The Wolf"—all weighted with symbolism fermenting in his agonized fantasy. He also wrote plays in the hope of earning money. *Rags* (1921) was successfully produced by Maurice Schwartz in the Yiddish Art Theater. Cahan wrote about it with enthusiasm and serialized it in the *Forward. Different* (1922) and *The Impoverished Kingdom* (1923) were also performed in the Yiddish Art Theater. *Bankrupt* (1924) and *The Shop* (1926), like the other prose dramas, lack the insight and intensity of his poetic dramas. In 1927 he completed *Hirsch Leckert,* a romantic drama in verse about a radical worker who refused to become an informer and was proud to die for his ideal. The play was performed in several places, as was his next play, *Chains* (1929), a prose drama generating social conflict and political rivalry.

Leivick's mind continued to seethe with poetic ideas and emotions of anger or affection. He wrote verse to find relief from the agitation of his driven conscience, and its ambiguity often expressed prophetic passion. In "Poems to a Distant Friend" he wrote about his life in America in moody, sad, and reflective verse, stating with painful honesty his difficulty of orientation. He also wrote about his years in sanitaria, and "The Ballad of Denver Sanitarium" reflected a healthy attitude toward himself and the other patients—"one thread of blood binds us all, while wisdom rests on all our lips."

During his years in sanitaria he also wrote four other works: *Sodom* is a dramatic retelling of the destruction of the wicked city. *The Sacrifice* treats the story of Isaac's sacrifice with traditional yet uniquely Leivickian questioning. *The Poet Became Blind* deals with the life of Morris Rosenfeld and alludes to the general lack of appreciation of poets. *Abelard and Heloise* is a poetic drama of intense emotion and lyrical fineness, with the love of the tortured pair a pure flame purged of grossness and sensuality.

In 1936 he was well enough to return to New York, and was engaged as a contributor to *The Day*. Now able to travel, he went to Europe, and what he observed he described in verse. "Hitler Night Motives" is a series of twenty poems on Nazi brutality. "Poems on the Yellow Patch" propounded the thought that he as a Jew should also wear one—and proudly. Soon after his return he published *Who's Who* (1938), a drama about a victim of a pogrom who had vainly sought to escape the ordeal of Jewishness.

During the years of World War II, Leivick could not free himself from the thought that he was safe in New York while millions of his fellow Jews were being tortured and murdered. His earlier acute sense of suffering became an open festering wound again. In poem after poem he expressed this pain of woe, guilt, and death. *In Treblinka I Never Was* (1945) the poems are a long cry of anguish. In the series, "In the Garret the Roof Complains," for instance, he sang wistfully of the Holocaust: "Our people are being murdered, and the world ignores it, and the whole world remains dumb to our outcries."

During these years of agony he also wrote *The Messiah of the Ghetto* (1944) and *Rabbi Meir of Rothenburg* (1945). In the first Rabbi Isaac helps prepare for armed resistance in the Warsaw Ghetto, and the uprising is presented as part of Israel's eternal resistance to evil. The same theme of resistance concerns the second work, with the sainted rabbi opposing the haughty and evil duke of an earlier time of woe with his very life.

With the war over, Leivick counsels against vindictiveness. In the series of fourteen sonnets, "Cycle of Summation," he wrote: "Yet my heart sings thanks—that under the mountains of hangman's decrees there still quivers the dream of true poets: man shall be bright as God's thoughts."

A visit to the concentration camps in 1946 gave Leivick the material for *The Wedding in Fernwald* (1949). The drama relates symbolically and mystically the celebration of a wedding of two survivors—intimating the persistence of the Jewish people by the start of new life among the millions dead.

In 1953 Leivick completed *In the Days of Job*. Nearly all his life he was plagued not only by Isaac, as a possible sacrifice, but also by Job's ordeal. These two "testings" of God are here combined on the assumption that Isaac and Job were contemporaries. The work is at once mystical, imaginative, and philosophical in concept and treatment. Primarily a drama of creative poetry, it achieves distinction by its originality of conception and depth of philosophical insight.

In his last two collections of poems he achieved a certain degree of reflective serenity. In *A Leaf on the Apple Tree* (1955), "The Fire," a cycle of poems, continues his poignant recollection of the concentration camps, and the lines breathe with pain and verbal beauty. His visit to Israel in 1950 is recorded in verse bright with imagery and charged with pathos. The volume also contains a number of fine nature lyrics. *Songs of Eternity* (1959) is distinguished by its sensitive poems of nature. It was as if in the evening of his long literary career, he permitted himself the pleasure of singing peacefully about the earth and the sky and the serenity they afford. Here and there, however, he injects reminders of his painful childhood and of the tragedy of his people.

Leivick's eminence as a poet was recognized early, and his work has been discussed and interpreted more fully than that of other Yiddish writers. Only *The Golem* of his major works is available in English translation, largely because of the difficulty of rendering his poetic imagery and legendary allusions in another language.

A paralytic stroke in 1958 laid him helpless and speechless, and after four years of suffering he died in December 1962.

I. J. Singer (1893–1943), the son of a rabbi, grew up steeped in Hebrew and Hasidic traditions. By the time he was seventeen, however, he had learned about the world outside of his narrow milieu and rebelled against his father's wish that he study for the rabbinate. He went to Warsaw, worked and studied, but also made attempts at writing fiction. Some of his stories were published in a local newspaper. The Russian Revolution in 1917 excited his idealistic zeal and he went to Kiev, where he participated in literary experimentation and wrote two impressionistic plays—*Earth Woes* and *Three*—before he became disillusioned with the revolution and returned to Warsaw in 1921.

In 1919 he had written "Pearls," an impressionistic story of a rich but stingy pawnbroker. Once back in Warsaw he brought out *Pearls and Other Stories* and completed *Earth Pain,* a symbolic drama evidencing his disappointment with the revolution. When Abraham Cahan visited Eastern Europe in 1922 he came upon the volume and was favorably impressed with its literary quality. He obtained permission to reprint some of the stories in the *Forward* and engaged Singer as a regular contributor and correspondent. Singer also became editor of *Literature and Life* and an active member of a modernistic group of writers known as *Die Chaliastra* (The Gang). In 1925 he issued his second volume of stories, some of which dealt with the cruelties of the civil war on the Russian soil.

In the middle 1920s Singer was asked by Cahan to visit Soviet Russia and report on Jewish life under Bolshevik rule. His articles described the changes he found since 1921 and intimated that evidences of anti-Semitism were on the increase. He was also surprised to find intellectual Jews taking an interest in Hasidism. What pleased him was the way young Jews were becoming skilled farmers, and while some of them were enthusiastic about the revolution, others hated the collectives and planned to migrate to Palestine. These articles were issued in *The New Russia* (1927). In the same year he published *Steel and Iron,* a novel of the war, revolution, and civil strife, based largely on his own experiences. Not yet the master of long fiction, the action is replete with melodramatic material and incidents.

Late in 1927, acutely sensitive to the criticism of his writing, he became too depressed to continue. It was only in 1931 that, encouraged by Cahan in a Berlin meeting, he resumed writing and soon produced *Yoshe Kalb.* It was serialized in the *Forward* and in the Warsaw *Haint* (Today). Published in 1933, it soon appeared in English under the title of *The Sinner.* Maurice Schwartz dramatized it for the stage with much success. A work of fictional fascination, it plumbs the depths of Hasidic life, which is treated caustically and not wholly persuasively. Its powerful love story and religious mysticism largely account for its enduring popularity.

Influenced by Cahan, Singer made his home in New York in 1933. Grieving over the death of a young son and viewing life pessimistically, he nevertheless made an effort to establish himself culturally among his fellow writers and concentrated on his writing. In 1936 he finished *The Brothers Ashkenazi,* the first novel he wrote in the United States. Serialized in the *Forward,* it was quickly translated and published in English and several other languages. Everywhere it was praised as an epic masterpiece. The long novel depicts the rise of Lodz from an insignificant village to its leading position as a center of textile production; from its gradual domination by Jewish manufacturers to its ravagement by war, revolution, and Polish anti-Semitism. The upsurge of the Ashkenazi family parallels the rise of the city, and the exploits and downfall of the two brothers dominates the action.

Spring (1937) is a collection of several long stories in which Singer is relatively relaxed and able to write with mild humor and good-natured tolerance. The characters are drawn with sharp, precise strokes, and the action has the merit of the seasoned storyteller.

Unable to forget his morbid disappointment in the Russian Revolution, he injected his bitterness and anger in *Comrade Nachman* (*East of Eden* in English, 1938). The novel contains a poignant and perturbing description of the poverty and slum life in Poland and Russia. The radicalism among the workers and the dedication of some of their leaders are depicted with the cogency of intimate knowledge. The action as a whole, however, suffers from subjective bias. While his arraignment of communist rule has validity, emphasis on its evil aspects and the complete omission of the lingering idealism cannot but weaken the effect of the narrative.

The rise of Hitlerism affected Singer as much as it did other Yiddish writers. In *The Carnovsky Family* (1943) he dramatized the plight of the enlightened German Jews who had been making every effort to be good Germans—only to be coerced and crushed by Nazi brutality. It also makes evident the tragedy of those born of mixed marriages who are rejected as Jews despite their fealty to Germany. The Carnovsky family is forced to migrate to the United States and to undergo the onerous process of reorientation, but the grandson remains a Nazi in spirit and ends his life dismally. For all the tragic reality of the action, the intimation is clear that to discard traditional piety is to risk losing one's Jewishness.

Singer was at this juncture at the height of his popularity. The dramatization of his novels had succeeded beyond anyone's expectation, and their editions in English and other languages brought him considerable income. Yet he remained fundamentally pessimistic—at war with himself. The idols of modern man—and particularly of the modern Jew—had ceased to appeal to him. Much as he knew that the traditional life of his childhood was beyond recall and no longer relevant, he could not help thinking longingly of the beliefs and dogmas of his rabbinical father, in whom he saw a wholesomeness he had not perceived in his rebellious youth. This sentimental reminiscence he described lovingly in *Of a World that Is No More,* a memoir published posthumously. In 1949 a number of his stories were collected in a volume that gave evidence of his literary skill, wry humor, and his firm grasp of human essentials.

As the war intensified in 1943, and news of Jewish martyrdom came out of Europe, Singer's restiveness became acute. He was repelled by the puniness of man in a world of evil and brute force. Thoughts of leaving for Palestine greatly appealed to him. Suddenly all his worries and plans came to naught when a massive heart attack ended his life at the age of fifty.

Isaac Bashevis Singer, eleven years younger than his brother, grew up in a Warsaw tenement where his father held forth as a lay rabbi and where the occupants formed a slum society in miniature. He, like his older brother, was a devoted student of Hebrew lore but without the latter's childhood piety. He was early curious enough to observe the ways and emotional quirks of the men and women who came to his father for consultation and comfort. Years later he described this gamut of human woes and individual foibles in a discursive but telling volume, *In My Father's Court* (1966).

Growing up with little of his brother's idealism and social idealism, he never experienced the latter's bitter disillusionment. What had become part of his outlook on life was a strong cynicism. With a firm eye on the troubled postwar world of the 1920s, he proceeded to train himself as a writer by working as a journalist. His first efforts at fiction dealt with what he knew best—the Hasidic aspects of Jewish life. Unlike most other Yiddish writers, however, he sought not to denounce or romanticize the practices of Hasidic piety but to expose and satirize their eccentric and psychopathic aspects.

Satan in Goray (1935, in English 1955), his first novel, has its setting in a Jewish town in Poland shortly after the dreadful massacres perpetrated by the Bogdan Chmelnitski Cossacks in 1648–1649. The town had been practically demolished, but the few survivors were exerting themselves to rebuild their homes and businesses. Their tragic condition, however, favored the arousal of messianic fantasies. Shifty and deluded visitors stimulated this hope by reporting the oncoming of Israel's restoration. Singer employed his obvious literary talent to depict the pathetic townsmen not as understandably credulous but as queer and foolish eccentrics. He thus presented the epoch of Shabbati Zevi in all its extreme superstitious grotesqueness: its disregard of reason and its exaltation of illusion and its corollary eroticism. This cynicism was the more devastating because it was barbed with the sharp-edged pen of fictional art. As I. I. Trunk has validly pointed out, the novel is "a Jewish Gothic palace, very beautifully built, but without doors and without exits."

In 1935 his brother brought Singer to New York. For a time he wrote as a free lance, but in 1943, upon the death of his brother, he was engaged as a regular contributor by the *Forward*. Thereafter, nearly all his writing, under his own name or under pseudonyms, has first appeared in that daily. His next major work, *The Family Moskat* (1950) covers a half century of Jewish life in Poland during the deterioration of its traditional piety and years of grievous persecution. Its various complex aspects are delineated with fictional authenticity. The range in vivid personalities is from the extremely pious Hasid to the assertive skeptic, from the wealthy businessman to the hapless poor, from the philosophical rationalist to the self-indulgent sophist. It presents the traditional town in the process of disintegration, war, and massacre; also the urban ghetto in all its poverty, grime, intellectual ferment, and idealistic aspirations in the midst of social cataclysm. Despite the artifice of plot and the illogical behavior of certain characters, the novel pulsates with human life and reveals the inner emotional recesses of prominent characters.

Singer is also a master of the short story. *Gimpel the Fool* (1957), *Spinoza of the Market Place* (1961), *Short Friday* (1964), and later collections evidence his skill as a storyteller, but most of the tales stress human queerness and weaknesses, as if he enjoyed disclosing individual foibles and common superstitions. Thus Satan and his minions have little difficulty in causing man to falter and fall. Witches, demons, and evil spirits seem to predominate and thrive on human fears, beliefs, and abnormalities. And his notable talent gives these exotic tales a greater significance than they really have. In *Passions* (1975), however, he achieves greater centrality of human behavior.

The Magician of Lublin (1960) is a picaresque novel of a clever acrobat and magician, told with lustiness and psychological overtones. The characters are portrayed realistically, without affection or sympathy but also without sardonic manipulation. *The Slave* (1962), like *Satan in Goray*, has its setting in pogrom-devastated seventeenth-century Poland. Melodramatic in action, it tells an intense and passionate love story between a Jewish refugee and a Christian peasant girl, with the lovers the most appealing of Singer's creations. *The Manor* (1967) is an epic account of life in Poland during the last third of the nineteenth century. The relations between the defeated Poles and the Jews are described in vivid details. Here, as in earlier works, Singer tends to overstress traits and peculiarities of character, giving his protagonists a somewhat uneven reality. In recent years a number of his stories, many in an American setting, have appeared in *The New Yorker* and other magazines.

Singer has also written several juveniles: *Zlateh the Goat, Mazel and Shlimazel,* and *The Fearsome Inn,* all appealing to the imaginative child. He also turned out a musical, *Yentl the Yeshiva Boy,* which appeared on Broadway.

As the leading living Yiddish novelist, he has had all his work issued in English, thereby giving many Americans an interesting, if not quite typical example, of notable Yiddish literature.

10

Yiddish Book Publishing

Yiddish book publishing in America never became a solid commercial enterprise. Unlike most English writing, for instance, which is written directly for book publication, Yiddish authors print their work first in newspapers and magazines and then seek a means of book publication. Their difficulty in that respect arises from the fact that most Yiddish readers, already familiar with the serials, stories, and poems in their periodicals, are little interested in obtaining the volumes containing them. Consequently only books by the most popular writers command a sale that yields a profit. The publication of most books therefore becomes in large part the author's own enterprise—in the form of a subvention to one of the few available publishers. With authors usually lacking the means of publication, they have come to depend upon an interested group or organization to assume the printing and promotion of their books.

The Hebrew Publishing Company has been from 1901 until recently the one major commercial firm bringing out Yiddish books. Most of its list consisted of religious and practical books, but it early began to issue Yiddish versions of famous and popular books from other languages. D. M. Hermalin, M. Seifert, A. Tennenboim, B. Feigenboim, and others were early engaged as translators and adapters at a low cost, and the volumes were sold at prices under a dollar. Among the Yiddish books the firm brought out were such works as Leon Kobrin's *Yankel Boileh,* Zunser's folksongs, Shomer's popular fiction, stories by Peretz, and all the writings of Mendele Mocher Sforim.

By 1914 the firm was publishing a fairly large list of additional Yiddish writings. Some of Sholom Aleichem's and Peretz's stories were issued separately for as low as three cents a copy. Peretz's collected work in a volume of over 1000 pages was priced at $1.25; a large collection of 75 pieces from Yiddish writers was priced at $2.08; four volumes of Jacob Gordin's plays sold for $2.00; Z. Libin's collected writings in two volumes was listed at 83 cents; a volume of Kobrin's writings of over 1000 pages was priced at $1.50. The firm also published all the work of Yehoash in three volumes, and after his death in 1927 it brought out a collected edition in ten volumes at $15.00—Yehoash having been a relative of the Werbelowskys. These low prices were in part possible because the firm paid little or no honorarium to authors.

From the first the Hebrew Publishing Company issued a number of Yiddish volumes and pamphlets in such fields as history, speech, letter-writing, humor, dictionaries, and popular science, all of it at relatively low prices, so that many immigrants gained an education from these works. With the passing of time, however, many Jews learned English and depended less and less on Yiddish non-fiction. Consequently the firm lessened its activity in Yiddish publishing, and in recent years dropped it entirely. Thus the firm had no part in the efflorescence of Yiddish literature in the early decades of the present century. It still keeps in print its large assortment of Hebrew and Yiddish religious books, but its current list is limited to books in English.

There were no other large commercial publishers of Yiddish books, but several booksellers and printers brought out a number of volumes at their own risk or with a subvention from either the authors or their friends. One of the best-known of the booksellers was Max N. Maisel, a dedicated lover of books whose store was a popular meeting place of literati and who published a good many books. For a time Evalenko's International Bibliotek brought out books in Yiddish—until it was discovered that he was a spy for the Russian government and used his publishing outlet as a means of learning about Russian Jews who were plotting against the Czar's government. Shulsinger Brothers also issued Yiddish books.

This paucity of publishers caused the gradual development of associations and organizations interested in bringing out books by authors whom their leaders admired. Certain groupings of *Landsleit*—former residents of an East European town or area—would feel duty-bound and honored to sponsor the publication of books by authors who were natives of the same place. Yiddish newspapers and magazines also undertook to bring out books written by staff members or friendly associates, sometimes as premiums to new subscribers. Most important as book publishers, however, were the social and literary organizations that devoted themselves to the publication of Yiddish books regardless of commercial requirements. A good many of the books they sponsored, especially before 1914 but also until the late 1930s, were printed in Eastern Europe to minimize the cash outlay. This procedure is now followed by sending manuscripts to Israel and Buenos Aires, where printing Yiddish books costs considerably less than in the United States.

The first, and for years the most active Jewish fraternal organization, was the *Arbeiter Ring* (Workmen's Circle), founded in April 1892. At that time the Jewish immigrant workers were herded in sweatshops and had great need of protection and organization. This brought about the formation of *landsmanshaften* and *Farbanden* as well as labor unions whose aim it was to assist immigrant newcomers in need of help, advice and friendship. Judah J. Shapiro, historian of the Workmen's Circle, stated of it:

> It brought aid and friendship to Jewish immigrants at a time, and in a society, when they were without resources and even without sympathy. The organization has been an inseparable part of the labor movement; it has been involved in every effort for social reform and for extending the public good.

Mutual help became the basis of the organization, and one of its early activities was to educate members both technically and culturally. As early as 1893 one branch had a weekly meeting devoted to education, usually a lecture. This activity was expanded and intensified after 1903, when the newer immigrants were more demanding of cultural improvement. Classes and lectures were provided, and Yiddish books on a variety of subjects were made available. For some time this process was unavoidably diffuse and uncoordinated, but in 1910 an effort was made to organize and broaden the educational program. *The Friend* was started to bring members news of the Jewish world as well as of its cultural developments. "*The Friend*," the editor stated, "should be an educational organ that has light material which is readable, in order that the magazine may become a *family paper* in the home of every member."

A committee was appointed to supervise classes in Yiddish and to make use of available intellectuals as teachers and lecturers. This made possible the publication of *The Universe and Man*, edited in 1913 by Morris Terman and containing twelve popularly written essays on various phases of knowledge based on lectures given the previous winter. Terman declared in the preface:

> The book will not read with the same excitement as a novel. The purpose of the Education Committee, however, is not to supply light reading matter, but to educate and enlighten, and the individual who seeks education and enlightenment must subject himself to some strain.

In time the organization published 22 educational volumes, five on Jewish themes and the others in various fields of knowledge.

Simultaneously the Workmen's Circle started part-time schools for children in order to acquaint them with Yiddish grammar and literature, Jewish history and social problems. Later a teachers institute was formed to prepare instructors for these schools. Arrangement was also made with the New York Board of Education for a series of free lectures to members, and between 1914 and 1916 these lectures were well attended. Another activity was the encouragement of musical and dramatic groups. Thus after 1915 the *Folkbiene* group performed Yiddish plays as well as dramas by Ibsen and other world dramatists in Yiddish translation.

Until 1936 the Workmen's Circle published books individually. That year it formed a publishing division to coordinate its book program. The first volumes brought out under this arrangement were intended for adult members—books the educational committee considered useful. Later it also issued books for children attending its schools. Of the forty-odd volumes published during the ensuing decade, fourteen were on historic personalities. Eight additional books were issued later; also a number of pamphlets for adult and youth groups. Among these publications were such important studies as Shmuel Niger's *The Struggle for a New Education* (1944), H. Bass's *Language and Education* (1950), *A Manual for the Teaching of Jewish History* (1952), and *The History of the Jewish Labor Bund* (3 volumes, 1960, 1962, 1966).

In 1946 Workmen's Circle schools were reorganized to "give a new emphasis to the idea of a *Jewish People,* to which a child's adherence should be developed, and the concept that this People was one, though distributed through many lands." Yiddish was encouraged as a means of enjoying the rich Yiddish literature. This sense of Jewishness was combined with Americanism. The continuing process of assimilation proved stronger, however, than the courses in these schools, and English was used increasingly among members and consequently in the educational curriculum. In 1950 *The Friend* was replaced by the English *Call,* and the number of Yiddish schools declined, now numbering 44 over the entire country. Yet, if the organization itself is somewhat shrunken in membership, it remains active in the development of its various Jewish cultural undertakings.

Jews were always concerned for the proper education of their children. Those not belonging to an organization like the Workmen's Circle usually sent their boys to religious schools or engaged private tutors. The predominant influence of the public schools tended to lessen the effect of incidental Jewish teaching, so that many children were growing up either entirely ignorant of their Jewish background or quite indifferent to it.

In 1910 Labor Zionists, stimulated by Zhitlowsky and others, started what they termed National Radical Schools, with the aim of teaching children Yiddish grammar and literature. Three years later another group formed the Nonpartisan Jewish Folk Schools with the same end in view. When Sholom Aleichem died in 1916 and over one hundred thousand mourners accompanied the body to the cemetery, both groups agreed to honor his memory by uniting their schools in his name.

These schools functioned well, and their number increased throughout the country. In 1919 they brought out a magazine, *Kinder Journal,* edited by Shmuel Niger, with Lippe Lehrer as managing editor. Three years later J. Kaminsky founded *Verlag Matones* (Gifts) for the purpose of publishing books by the Sholom Aleichem Folk Institute. The magazine soon enriched Yiddish literature with new themes and writers, and Matones began to bring out excellently made books by prominent Yiddish writers both for children and adults. From the outset the managers of Matones had agreed that the books must be attractively designed and well illustrated, with the motto: "A Jewish home without books is like a house without windows." Lahrer supervised work on these books with special attention to the purity and clarity of their diction. During the first decade Matones brought out 21 volumes for children and two for adults. One of these books was *Chaver Paver Stories,* illustrated by A. Gudelman, in two volumes. In the same year, honoring Reisen's fiftieth birthday, it published his *Fifty Poems,* illustrated by seven artists. Over the next several decades Matones issued many more books for both children and adults, all by writers of acknowledged merit, including complete works of several prominent authors.

In 1953, forty years after they were founded, the Sholom Aleichem schools had about 40,000 students in their elementary and high school divisions. All the while these schools sought to adhere to four basic principles: "secularity, Yiddish, everywhereness, and child centeredness." Up to 1938 secularity was strictly observed. Thereafter children began to be taught religious aspects of Judaism; still later, in compliance with parental wishes, their children were instructed in Hebrew in preparation for Bar Mitzvah. A new magazine, *Safi Views,* was issued bimonthly to inform Americanized parents about Jewish problems and the most significant events in Jewish cultural life.

At present attendance in the schools is considerably smaller from what it was in peak years, but their achievement within the Jewish community remains notable. To quote Saul Goodman, one of its leaders: "The Sholom Aleichem Schools produced tens of thousands of Jewish men and women who acquired a love for Jewishness, for the Yiddish language, and for Yiddish literature. Many of these Jewish-educated, American-born individuals became better Jews in the process."

The most prestigious Yiddish organization today is undoubtedly the scholarly Yiddish Scientific Institute, whose name was changed in 1956 to YIVO Institute for Jewish Research. Conceived in 1919 in the imagination of Nahum Schtiff, it emerged as a reality in 1925, when it was formally organized with headquarters in Vilna. Its founders, one of whom was Max Weinreich, the scholarly philologist who was its director to the end of his life in 1969, thought of it as an academy or institute for gathering documents, doing research and publishing, and carrying on education within the Jewish community the world over. It consisted of four divisions: history, economics-statistics, philology, and psychology-education. Its three principles were the peoplehood of Jews all over the world, the enrichment of life of that people by means of Jewish scholarship, and application of the most modern methods of social science in the quest for a better understanding of Jewish identity and Jewish group phenomena.

The general response was enthusiastic. Among its early sponsors were Einstein, Eduard Bernstein, Moses Gaster, Simon Dubnow, Edward Sapir, and Sigmund Freud. Branches were established in New York and other Jewish centers. A number of research scholars joined it and were soon gathering valuable material on various aspects of Jewish life. Summaries of this research in New York were written by Chaim Zhitlowsky in 1933 and by Sapir in 1939.

The outbreak of World War II with the invasion of Poland in 1939 put an end to YIVO's existence in Vilna. Fortunately a good part of its material had been sent to New York before the Nazis pillaged the headquarters. Later, after 1945, Weinreich worked hard to obtain the surviving archival material which Alfred Rosenberg had stored in 1941 in what had become the American sector in occupied Germany. The Jewish community in America had in the meantime responded warmly to an early appeal for help, and the transfer of YIVO's activities to the United States was made with the assistance of many sympathizers. For some years now it has occupied its own building in Manhattan, and its work has progressed steadily in outstanding scholarly achievement. Israel Knox, one of its active leaders, defined its particular purpose soon after its establishment in New York:

> Its studies in economics, education and psychology as well as in history and demography and statistics, derive their peculiar significance from their recognition of the Jewish community as a world community; their tone and quality are surely influenced by the fact that they are usually written in Yiddish and addressed to the Yiddish-speaking public.

YIVO Bletter had been started in 1931, and was resumed in New York in 1940. During the next several years the magazine gave much space to the discussion and analysis of the Nazi genocide of European Jewry. Article after article dealt with evidences and interpretations of the calamitous tragedy. In its quarterly issues after 1943 it presented, in both Yiddish and English, information on the activities of YIVO and indicated the Institute's projects and plans in every field. In 1941 YIVO started *Yiddishe Shprach* (Yiddish Language) as a means of informing its members of the philological and other linguistic studies carried on by researchers. *YIVO Annual of Jewish Social Science* was begun in 1946. All the while the YIVO library kept increasing its contents, and now consists of over 300,000 volumes, with many items in Hebrew and Yiddish centuries old, and a large amount of manuscript material.

YIVO also publishes a number of books. It had issued several volumes in Vilna and had a work on psychology and pedagogy ready for the printer when the Nazis invaded Poland. After the Institute was relocated in New York, a replacement of this study was prepared by highly competent scholars. When the material was rescued from the Nazis in 1945, the original manuscript was discovered and several chapters were printed in *YIVO Bletter*.

The following list of books were among those published by YIVO in New York: *The History of the Jewish Labor Movement in the United States* (2 volumes, 1943–1945), edited by E. Tcherikover; Max Weinreich's *YIVO and the Problems of Our Time* (1945), *Thesaurus of the Yiddish Language* (1950); Jacob Shatsky's *The History of the Jews in Warsaw* (3 volumes, 1947–1953). I. L. Cahan's *Yiddish Folk Songs and Melodies,* edited and reissued by Max Weinreich (1957); M. Kosover's *Food and Beverages: A Study in the History of Culture and Linguistics* (1958); *Shmuel Niger Bukh,* memorial volume edited by Sh. Bickel and L. Lehrer (1958); H. Kruk's *Diary of the Vilna Ghetto* (1961); Eliakum Zunser's *Works* (2 volumes, 1964), edited by M. Schechter; Chono Shmeruck's *Peretz's Vision of Despair* (1971); Max Weinreich's *History of the Yiddish Language* (1973); and Sh. Fishman's *Studies in Polish Jewry* (1974).

YIVO has obviously made a singular contribution to Jewish culture. Its late director, Weinreich, had pointed out that its research into American Jewish life gave fresh insights into an appreciation of YIVO's purpose:

> The basic idea underlying YIVO's research is that the social scientist should see Jewish life in the United States in the light of antecedents and cross-influences in the old homes, both in their East European and central European variants. . . . Thus, Jewish history in America, to be sure, is American history, but on the other hand, there is no adequate understanding of the sociological and social-psychological problems of the Jews in America unless these problems are viewed against the background of the Jewish groups in those regions of Europe from which American Jewry stems and in which so many initial patterns were established.

YIVO and other Jewish organizations are either primarily interested in research or in the education of their members. In 1938

Jews concerned for the health of Jewish culture realized that the continuing decline of Yiddish reading was endangering the publication of Yiddish books unless they formed an institution to bring into print writings of merit that could not be published through normal channels. That year they founded such an organization, but political differences soon caused a rift. Those who were of a liberal or conservative persuasion were quickly at odds with participants who were inclined to favor the communist position. The two factions therefore separated, with the latter forming the Yiddish Cultural Association (YKUF), and the former calling their group the Central Yiddish Cultural Organization (CYCO).

YKUF consisted mostly of radicals who still favored Soviet Russia. At first it was joined by a number of Yiddish writers who adhered to the socialist ideal. Zisha Weinper became its director and remained its guiding spirit until his death in 1957. With the Stalin-Hitler pact in 1939, and with Stalin's persecution and murder of leading Yiddish writers and artists, a good many members resigned. The loyal adherents, however, exerted themselves to carry out the original aim of furthering Yiddish culture. One of their first acts was to start *Yiddish Culture,* a monthly devoted to the interests of Jewish cultural activities. Many of the articles were written by prominent Yiddish writers and scholars, and its present editor, Itche Goldberg, has kept the periodical on a high literary plane.

Even more commendable has been YKUF's book publishing program. Over the past thirty-odd years, and in the face of financial straits, it has published over one hundred books—some of them reprints of works no longer available. Among these publications were poems and fiction by leading Yiddish writers in Russia as well as a number living in the United States and elsewhere. Thus in addition to works by Soviet Yiddish writers, YKUF has published volumes by Peretz, Zhitlowsky, N. Maisel, Reuven Brainin, Jacob Milch, Kobrin, Raboy, and Rontch. It also brought out English editions of a half dozen books by such writers as Rosenfeld, Raboy, and Joseph Morgenstern.

CYCO, the more conservative organization, attracted a larger number of adherents and contributors. For nearly a decade it functioned as a non-profit publishing unit, and sought to bring out books by established writers which would otherwise fail to be published. The traumatic shock of the Holocaust and the exhilaration of the founding of Israel combined to stimulate the Jewish community to greater cultural activity. The calamitous destruction of the Jewish centers in Eastern and Central Europe, with their cultural foundations utterly uprooted, caused a number of civic minded Jews from several countries to gather in New York in September 1948 for the purpose of doing what was still possible to restore the cultural heritage which the Nazis had sought ruthlessly to extirpate.

The Congress for Jewish Culture, formed at that meeting, with branches in Paris and Buenos Aires, resolved to mobilize Jewish cultural forces the world over for the continuation of their cultural activities. It decided, among other projects, to publish works of murdered writers and scholars as a memorial to their martyrdom. They further decided to seek out and collect documents pertaining to the Holocaust; to reprint literary works destroyed by the Nazis, and to assist the publication of these and other materials; and to promote the development of curricula and teacher-training for Jewish schools. A fund of money to realize these aims was agreed upon as a basic requirement, and the enthusiastic response was reassuring.

During the first eight years of its activity the Congress, in association with CYCO, published and promoted 35 volumes: eleven selected works by Yiddish writers, Dubnow's ten-volume *World History of the Jewish People*, a two-volume edition of Mani Layb's *Poems and Ballads*, and various other books. The Congress has also taken over the publication of the *Zukunft*. Another of its functions was the encouragement of Yiddish writing by providing annual awards for literary achievement. In addition it holds exhibits of works of art in both the Jewish Museum and the Atran Cultural Center, its headquarters in New York. Still another of its activities was the establishment of a world center for Yiddish schools with a coordinating committee, composed of the three Yiddish-oriented school organizations, assigned to further and improve the teaching of Jewish culture by the publication of pedagogic material and the holding of educational conferences. To this end the committee prepared an *Educational Encyclopedia* and a number of textbooks.

During the past two decades the Congress has published works of great importance to Jewish culture. Outstanding is the ten-volume edition of Israel Zinberg's *History of Literature Among Jews,* a comprehensive scholarly survey of Jewish literary activity over the centuries in many countries. Equally significant are the seven volumes of *The Lexicon of Modern Yiddish Literature,* with the eighth and final volume in preparation. Another important publication is Dubnow's three-volume reminiscences and reflections, *The Book of My Life.* Also of notable merit are the four volumes on topics pertaining to European conditions during World War II. The Congress has honored the memory of Shmuel Niger, the leading Yiddish critic, by collecting a fund for the posthumous publication of his available manuscripts, totaling six volumes. It has also brought out one or more volumes written by about thirty writers, thus making them available to students and general readers. Among them are such works as A. Menes's *Jewish Thought in Modern Times, Anthology of Yiddish Literature,* and Chaim Bass's *Writers and Works.*

An interesting incident concerns the publication of a book by Yeshaye Shpiegel. A resident of the Lodz ghetto during the Nazi occupation, he buried his manuscript of *Licht fun Opru* (Light from Relaxation) as the Nazis approached. On his survival from a concentration camp, he returned to Lodz and dug up the manuscript. The Congress gave him $1000 for it in lieu of royalty and had it published. Shpiegel used the money to make a down payment on a home in Israel. The same sum was paid to Mendel Mann for his memoirs of the war period, *At the Gates of Moscow.*

The Congress, under the direction of the dedicated Chaim Bass, is now at the height of its activity and influence and is determined to keep Yiddish literature alive and widespread.

11

Contemporary Anglo-Jewish Periodicals

The American Jewish Year Book for 1974/1975 lists over 160 Anglo-Jewish periodicals currently being published in the United States—exclusive of student and other unlisted ones. A number of them are mainly of local interest: weeklies or monthlies with a first page and sometimes additional space devoted to Jewish news of general interest, and with the remaining pages chronicling local religious, educational, and social activities. The *Detroit Jewish News,* edited by Philip Slomovits, which devotes considerable space to Jewish events the world over and provides professional reviews of books, is a conspicuous exception. Another local weekly worthy of special mention is the *Boston Jewish Advocate,* which contained much material of general interest when it was edited by Jacob de Haas and is still a superior weekly. In recent years *The Jewish Week* of New York, while similar in format and purpose to the other local weeklies, has attained national prominence in its international coverage and journalistic sophistication.

In a book concerned with the cultural influence of Jewish publishing on American civilization, many of these periodicals have little relevance. A number of other magazines, while of broader scope and solid content, are either organs of religious and educational organizations which have been dealt with in previous chapters or are too parochial to warrant inclusion in the limited space of this chapter.

The American Zionist, originally called *The Maccabean Magazine* and then *The New Palestine*, is the official organ of the Zionist Organization of America. From its beginnings in 1910 to the present this monthly has mainly expounded the ideals and principles of Zionism and reported Zionist events and activities as they occurred. Originally limited to four pages, it kept increasing its size and now extends to 32 pages. In 1922, distributed to the Zionist membership, it claimed to be "the most widely read Anglo-Jewish paper in the country." As the establishment of Israel was becoming a reality, the magazine devoted much space to its birth pangs, difficulties and aspirations. With the passing years the contents of the monthly kept changing to reflect altering conditions and circumstance. From the first, the editors also published articles on Jewish writers and artists as well as their stories and poems.

Hadassah Magazine had its origin in the *Hadassah Bulletin*, which began to be issued in September 1914 as a newsletter of three pages by the Women's Zionist Organization of America. Three years later the name was changed to *Hadassah News Letter* and considerably expanded to include not only local news but also items of general Jewish interest. This periodical was issued bimonthly. In April 1961 it began to appear as *Hadassah Magazine*, and its monthly issues covered the world scene in Jewish life. Popular in both content and style, it has a circulation in excess of 330,000 copies. The current editor is Jesse Lurie.

A most worthy contribution to American periodical journalism was made by *The Menorah Journal*. In 1906 sixteen Jewish students at Harvard, conscious of their heritage and sensitive to the existing prejudice against Jews in colleges and elsewhere, formed the Menorah Society for the purpose of spreading light on the cultural essence of Judaism and on a Jewish philosophy of life. The membership soon included Henry Hurwitz, Horace M. Kallen, and Harry A. Wolfson, and the meetings were efforts at studying "Hebraic culture and ideals."

Jewish students in other colleges were soon attracted to the ideals of the Society, and branches of it were organized on a number of campuses. In 1913 these students met to establish the

Intercollegiate Menorah Association. One of its decisions was to issue *The Menorah Journal,* with Henry Hurwitz as editor. As Kallen has astutely stated, the appearance of the *Journal* became "a seminal event in the cultural life of American Jewry."

Hurwitz (1886–1962), who was brought to Boston from Lithuania as a child of six, was deeply influenced by the humanist philosophy of his teachers William James and George Santayana. From early childhood, also, he was acutely conscious of his Jewish heritage. As editor of the new periodical, therefore, he aimed to develop the humanistic values of Judaism. In the first issue of January 1915 he declared editorially:

> *The Menorah Journal* is under the compulsion to be absolutely nonpartisan, an expression of all that is best in Judaism and not merely of some particular sect or school or locality or group of special interests; promoting constructive thought rather than aimless controversy; animated with the vitality and enthusiasm of youth; harking back to the past that we may deal more wisely with the present and the future; recording and appreciating Jewish achievement and not to brag; but to bestir ourselves to emulation and to deepen the consciousness of *noblesse oblige;* striving always to be sane and level-headed; offering no opinion of its own, but providing an orderly platform for the discussion of mooted questions that really matter; dedicated first and foremost to the fostering of Jewish "humanities" and the furthering of their influence as a spur to human service.

Up to the late 1920s the *Journal* appeared bimonthly; thereafter somewhat irregularly until 1962, when Hurwitz's death resulted in its demise. From the first issue it established itself as a high-level forum for the critical discussion of problems concerning world Jewry. Among its early contributors were Louis D. Brandeis, William Ellery Leonard, Harry A. Wolfson, Max L. Margolis, Solomon Schechter, Israel Zangwill, Horace M. Kallen, G. Stanley Hall, Charles W. Eliot, Mordecai M. Kaplam, Israel Friedlander, and William Osler. Later contributors were, by and large, of equal distinction. With the problem of nationality becoming paramount during and after World War I, Hurwitz obtained articles on the subject by such men as John Dewey, Randolph Bourne, Norman Hapgood, David Lubin, and Alfred E.

Zimmern. With Zionism having also come to the fore at that time, Hurwitz published articles dealing with it pro and con by Morris Jastrow, Viscount Bryce, and Felix Frankfurter. In a similar manner the *Journal* treated such issues as education, religion, civil rights, philosophy, history, literature, and the arts. All of Jewish life was considered impartially and with critical intelligence.

Belles lettres were from the beginning a feature of the *Journal.* Many Jewish writers who later achieved prominence in American literature, were first discovered and encouraged by Hurwitz. As early as the 1920s, when Yiddish writing was still relatively ignored by the Anglo-Jewish magazines, Hurwitz published translations of a good many stories and poems by Yiddish writers. Another feature of the *Journal* were extensive reports on Jewish cultural activities in European countries. Later, after the Holocaust, numerous articles dealt with the tragic catastrophe in graphic detail. Hurwitz also encouraged Jewish artists by reproducing their early work, among them Chagall, Epstein, Rubin, Kisling, Lipschitz, Mani-Katz, Modigliani, and Soutine. In all about 200 writers and artists and musicians appeared in the pages of the *Journal.* Significant books by and about Jews were reviewed at length by leading scholars and critics.

At various times Hurwitz invited eminent thinkers to contribute the results of their research to the *Journal.* Thus, for example, M. M. Kaplan, Wolfson, Kallen, and M. R. Cohen presented their views on Spinoza. George Foot Moore and Louis Ginzberg wrote on the traditional concepts of Judaism. Other scholars were encouraged to express themselves on topics of their choice. Max M. Margolis, Felix Perles, Cecil Roth and Salo W. Baron first appeared in the *Journal.* Kaplan's initial use of the term "Reconstruction," which became the name of his movement's philosophy, appeared initially in the issue of August 1920 in the article, "A Program for the Reconstruction of Judaism."

Hurwitz guided the editorial policy of the magazine throughout its existence. Possessed of a highly cultivated intellect, and a man of taste and imagination, he made it a journal of intellectual distinction and superior literary craftsmanship. The Great Depression of the 1930s and the gradual decline of the Menorah movement in the colleges undercut the support of the magazine; its continued, if somewhat irregular appearance for another quarter century without diminution of its intellectual superiority was the result of Hurwitz's heroic efforts. The 157 issues are therefore a monument to his insight and dedication. Leo W. Schwarz, who was for a time associated with the *Journal,* summarized its worth in the 1963 issue of *The Jewish Book Annual:*

> Whatever the viewpoint or interest of the future historian may be, he will find in the bound files of the *Journal* much to satisfy his curiosity about the character of twentieth century American Jews and their Gentile neighbors, from their follies and flummery to their wiles and wisdom. He may smile at the passing winds of doctrine that perplexed them and he may weep about the realities that were part of their flesh and blood. He will probably bless the fastidious and liberated minds who made possible a publication for men and women who love knowledge and beauty.

Orthodox Jewry published a number of periodicals, among them *The Jewish Forum, Jewish Life, Intercom, Tradition, and The Jewish Observer.* The latter monthly is typical in its aim to promote Orthodoxy. Started by Agudath Israel of America in 1962, it is not rigid in its policy, as its editor asserted in the first issue: "We speak of Jews whose point of view is not monolithic. Some are *Chassidim,* others are *Misnagdim,* while some espouse the Hirschian principle of *Torah im derech eretz.* And they often react differently to the events of contemporary history." Most of its contributors are rabbis, and Orthodoxy is basic to all their writings. Thus the articles look to the past, expound the various aspects of Orthodox ritual, and seek to relate them to current events and behavior. Its editorial policy is strongly pro-Israel.

Jewish Life was first issued as *The Orthodox Union* in the 1930s by the Union of Orthodox Jewish Congregations of America, with Rabbi Leo Jung as editor. A bimonthly, it dealt almost wholly with questions of Orthodoxy and related subjects. In 1946 the name was changed to *Jewish Life* with the following explanation:

> There has been a long-felt need for a mouthpiece of positive Judaism. There is need for an authoritative platform to present the

traditional Jewish viewpoint intelligently and vigorously. *Jewish Life* is dedicated to this program. . . . To publish an Anglo-Jewish magazine with its policy dictated by the Torah.

This program the editors have followed with complete success. The recent issues have been a lively and not too strict espousal of Orthodox views on every aspect of Jewish life in America.

The oldest and most important of these magazines is *The Jewish Forum*. Started by S. T. H. Hurwitz in 1918, two years later, at Dr.Hurwitz's death, it was taken over by Isaac Rosengarten. At the time he stated: "The purpose of the magazine is to disseminate Jewish ideals, to inculcate a taste for Jewish learning." With this aim in view, the monthly printed articles on current events, stories, memoirs, news and views pertaining to Jewish history—all the material serving to further the general status of Orthodox Judaism. The various contributors were serious writers and scholars of middling stature.

In 1935, the monthly having completed its seventeenth year of existence and having attained fairly wide acceptance in the Jewish community, Rosengarten felt moved to restate the magazine's aspirations:

> Aiming ever to be the magazine of quality, it hopes, in greater measure than ever, to render its service for the promotion of Jewish cultural life, to help it become both more intensive and extensive. . . . We have found a tendency to theorize, especially on the part of those who lack experience or whose minds are confused by conflicting ideas. It is the part of a magazine like *The Jewish Forum* to help bring greater clarity of thought to bear on the various problems in Jewish life. To this ideal *The Jewish Forum* continues to dedicate itself.

That year, in line with its broadened policy, the monthly serialized Ch. N. Bialik's reminiscences of his childhood. It also devoted two issues to a discussion of the writings of Maimonides. Another issue was given to a symposium on the nature of social justice. Over the ensuing years the monthly published articles favoring Zionism as well as various views representative of Jewish life and thought in the United States.

When Rosengarten died in 1961, Nathan Kohler became the

magazine's publisher and Charles Raddock its editor. They revamped the format to conform with other current periodicals, and its traditional Orthodox policy was further liberalized and made more controversial—while presenting "the best of its 45-year-old editorial history." The Statement of Objectives continued:

> In these pages, then, from month to month we will provide a home, as it were, for men of letters, scholars and journalists engaged in exploring the topical and historical riches of Jewish life and culture, affording them complete creative latitude and freedom of expression within the ideological framework conceived and defined by the founders.

Although Raddock made a mild attempt to veer away from the groove established by Rosengarten, he made no radical enough change to appeal to current Jewish readers. In a symposium on federal aid to parochial education, in which rabbis, churchmen, and laymen participated, Raddock expressed himself in favor of such aid. Ironically, he was joined by both Rabbi Menachem M. Schneerson, head of the Lubavitcher Hasidic movement, and the late Cardinal Spellman. Despite this controversial liveliness, however, the climate in 1962 was not favorable to a Jewish magazine without dynamic appeal or organizational backing. Consequently, *The Jewish Forum* had to cease publication at the end of that year.

Conservative Judaism was started in 1945 by the Rabbinical Assembly, with Leon S. Lang as editor. It was planned as "a quarterly journal dedicated to research and discussion in the furthering of the development of creative Jewish life in America." Towards realization of this aim, the quarterly prints scholarly articles on Judaism, Jewish history, the rabbinate, as well as more general studies of social content. Every issue also includes serious reviews of books on Jewish subjects. The current editor is Stephen C. Lerner.

Tradition is an important journal of Orthodox Jewish thought. Started in 1958 by the Rabbinical Council of America, with Rabbi Norman Lamm as editor, it for some time appeared semiannually. It printed mostly erudite articles of a religious content, but some dealt with literary, historical, and philosophical material relating to Jewry. These studies are of course Orthodox-oriented. In 1964 the magazine began to appear as a quarterly, and the current editor is Walter S. Wurzburger.

Rabbi Stephen S. Wise was too energetic a person and too independent of mind not to want to give public expression to his ideas and ideals. Eager for a medium in which he could give voice to his views on and reactions to current events, in 1929 he was instrumental in the establishment of *Opinion:* A Journal of Life and Letters. His son James was officially the editor, and the editorial board consisted of John Haynes Holmes, Ludwig Lewisohn, M. M. Kaplan, Maurice Samuel, and Rebekah Kohut. The policy of the monthly, while favorable to Zionism, was independent of view. It was also encouraging to creative writing.

In 1934 Rabbi Wise formally assumed the editorship, and for the next fifteen years he voiced boldly and penetratingly his position on the events and activities which interested him.

Opinion was thus in a real sense his personal organ: his trenchant comments and vigorous editorials were among the most effective pieces of Jewish journalism in a period of calamity for the Jewish people. The remainder of the magazine adhered closely to the promise of its subtitle. Dr. Holmes, Rabbi Wise's close personal friend, contributed a column, "Through Gentile Eyes," which gave expression to the liberal minister's friendly attitude toward Judaism. Every issue included articles by established writers on current problems or on literary subjects. In addition there was usually a story, one or more poems, and some reproductions of the work of contemporary artists.

The years in which *Opinion* appeared having been grim and grievous for the Jews of Europe, its contents of necessity reflected this tragedy in all its gravity. Rabbi Wise's editorials thundered against the outrageous Nazi barbarities with prophetic solemnity, and reports of this savagery covered many pages. When Mrs. Wise in 1936 complained about "the sameness and dreariness of *Opinion*'s pages," Rabbi Wise told her: "It is the facts that are forbidding and tragic and not the reporting. If we can change the tragic facts, *Opinion* can be brighter—not before." As it was, the facts continued to worsen, and at the time of Rabbi Wise's death in 1949 even the miracle of Israel's founding was accompanied by bloody war.

Opinion continued to appear after his death, but the life and vigor with which he had suffused its pages was gone from it, and in 1956 it ceased publication.

A magazine now quite forgotten but in its day a worthy medium was *Reflex,* started in 1927 by S. M. Melamed. A culturally oriented monthly, its goal, as stated in an editorial, was "to report and interpret the realities of modern American Jewish life. . . . It sponsors no creed or doctrine. It pretends to no mission. . . . Every phenomenon of importance, every creative figure will be viewed."

In the early issues the articles were of current interest and written by journalists and scholars who were then in the limelight or who later attained prominence. Among them were Alexander Goldenweiser, Moses Gaster, Marie Syrkin, S. A. Dubnow, Isaac Goldberg, Franz Oppenheimer, Maximilian Harden, and Maurice Samuel.

In 1928 the magazine moved to Chicago, and not long after became a victim of the Great Depression. On the whole the monthly was hardly distinguished either by its editorial liveliness or the depth of its contents, so that now it appears dated with a pleasant nostalgic overtone.

The Jewish Spectator, started in 1935 by Aaron Rosmarin and Trude Weiss-Rosmarin, is a fine example of personal, independent journalism. Its monthly issues contained news and articles, stories and poems, of a Jewish content. From the first, the editors began to publish English translations of the work of Yiddish writers. Their editorial policy was to present Jewish events of the month without glossing over individual or organizational shortcomings—their aim being to further the weal of the Jewish community rather than the reputation of its representatives.

After her divorce, Trude Weiss-Rosmarin became the magazine's sole editor. In time her policy of constructive criticism of Jewish leadership made her the respected gadfly of Anglo-Jewish journalism. Born and educated in Frankfort-am Main, with a doctorate in Semitics, and subsequently the author of several books on Jewish subjects, she has also long been a popular lecturer. Her frank and fearless comments on Jewish activities have gained her wide praise and some criticism. She was, for example, an early advocate of Jewish day schools and strongly urged Jewish Federations to provide adequate means for their functioning.

Her caustic and controversial editorials were widely appreciated, and the contributed contents of the *Spectator* were both solid and highly readable. In a typical issue, that of February 1952, Weiss-Rosmarin's editorials took issue with Abraham Heschel's conception of God and criticized Israel's multi-political parties. Among the articles were discussions of the nature and influence of the *Galut* in various countries, the causes that led to Stefan Zweig's suicide, and the relation of the Talmud to common law; also a fine poem by Uri Zvi Greenberg and Chayim Grade's poetically pathetic re-visit to postwar Vilna. This strong interest in Jewish creative writing was evidenced again in the June issue, which contained several poems by Abraham Sutzkever and a revealing interview with Joseph Opatoshu.

Over the years *The Jewish Spectator* continued to deal forthrightly with current affairs and to print serious articles, stories, poems, and book reviews. The issue of February 1960, for instance, contains informative discussions of the relation between science and religion, the Musar Movement, Auschwitz, education in Israel, the elders of Zionism, Max Brod at eighty, and a reprint of a story by Zangwill. In the May issue Weiss-Rosmarin returned to the subject of Jewish education, and her editorial, "Intellectuals and the Establishment," is highly critical of organizations like B'Nai B'rith for spending money on useless or duplicate investigations and being niggardly toward Jewish education:

> It is hypocrisy to pay lip service to education, as all American Jewish spokesmen do, summoning the community to intellectual excellence, while providing what in many instances does not even amount to a

pittance budget for Jewish education on the level of academic excellence.

Winning the Jewish intellectual of tomorrow for Judaism requires inspiring and firing the Jewish imagination of the Jewish college student of today.

After the Six Day War in Israel she urged peace and conciliation with the Arabs. In the September issue she expressed her belief that Israel would gain by reorienting her position toward Middle East hegemony. "The true character of Israel," she asserted, "can only come into its own as a product of its geography." Subsequently she was also critical of the Jewish fund-raising organizations, accusing them of inefficiency, bureaucratic extravagance, and general incompetence. In her concern for the weal of Israel, which was most affected by the totality of fund-raising, she declared: "Hiding the truth and not facing facts is deadly."

After the magazine became a quarterly in 1974 it was enlarged to provide space for longer articles, written in depth, mostly by rabbis and scholars. Thus the spring issue of 1974 begins with twelve pages of editorial comment, in which Weiss-Rosmarin deplores the waste of national resources in everyday life; she calls attention to Arnold Toynbee's fallacious accusation that the Bible's admonition to "be fruitful and multiply" is responsible for the population explosion; she comments critically on G. C. Oxtoby's *Prediction and Fulfillment in the Bible;* she deals pithily with the telecasts on "Religious America," with the "lop-sided views" of a course on "The New York Jewish Community," the Israeli press, Stanley Milgram's *Obedience to Authority;* her most caustic criticism is aimed at the Arno Press, accusing it of false claims and scholarly "hodge-podge" in its 43-volume publication series, *The Jewish People;* nor does she spare Joachim Prinz for his irresponsibility in *The Secret Jews.* The articles are varied, scholarly, and interesting. The eighty-page issue is thus stimulating, informative, and highly readable.

Congress Weekly, later *Congress Bi-Weekly,* and now *Congress Monthly,* was founded in 1933 as an organ of the American Jewish Congress. The present editor is Herbert Poster, a well-qualified journalist. The periodical was from the first a lively and broad-gauged magazine. Although its policy has been that of the Congress—favorable to Zionism and concerned with Jewish affairs both in America and abroad—it also espoused the causes of civil liberty, racial equality, political liberalism, and kindred issues. It did not hesitate, for instance, to discuss frankly the strained relations between Jews and Negroes when that subject came to the forefront in recent years, and it commented unequivocally on political and sociological events of the day. It also published pertinent reviews of books in every issue.

A topical listing of the more important articles printed in some of the issues during the year September 1974 to October 1975 will indicate the general nature of the magazine: The Negro Attitude Toward Israel, American Labor and Israel, Russia's Treatment of the Jews, American Jewish Identity, Compulsory Retirement, Chomsky's Views on the Middle East, World Jewry in a Changing World, The Spread of Jewish Studies in Colleges, Israel and the Soviet Bloc, The Arabs and Black Africa, The Arab Boycott, The Decline of the Blue Laws, Changing Life Styles and the Jewish Family. Each of these topics is of course dealt with by a person with authoritative credentials and usually from first-hand knowledge.

In 1952 the American Jewish Congress also started to issue *Judaism:* A Quarterly Journal of Jewish Life and Thought. Its editor, the well-known scholar Robert Gordis, stated in the first issue:

> We are committed to the proposition that *Judaism* has positive values for Jews and the world. . . . *Judaism* will be dedicated to the quest for truth in the spirit of freedom. Our columns will be open to anyone who has something significant to say and the ability to say it well. New and unconventional interpretations, whatever their standpoint, will be welcomed from every source, for we share the conviction of the Talmud that "Both these and others are the works of the living God."

As a nonpartisan periodical, encouraged by the basic policy of the Congress "to stimulate an informed awareness of Jewish . . . and generally foster the affirmation of Jewish religious, cultural, and historic identity," *Judaism* sought out contributors who discussed creatively the various concepts of Judaism and their relevance to the problems of modern society. The tercentenary issue in 1954, for instance, contained nineteen essays on American Jewish history and problems by eminent scholars. In 1962, to cite another example, a supplementary symposium on "My Jewish Affirmation" consisted of statements by 21 writers, scholars, and artists in which they identified themselves with some aspect of Judaism. Over the years, therefore, the quarterly published learned expositions of theological or philosophical inquiries affecting the scope of Judaism. Of equal importance were the essays on Jewish culture and Jewish personality which were also published in the periodical.

In 1933, as stated earlier, The League for Labor Palestine, cognizant of the increasing use of English by many of its members, decided to supplement *Der Yiddisher Kemfer* with *The Jewish Frontier*. Hayim Greenberg agreed to edit both periodicals, and stated in the first issue of the *Frontier:*

> In the midst of a growing social and economic awareness among the Jewish masses it aims to present a magazine of character and courage. The pages of *The Jewish Frontier* will attempt to analyze and solve Jewish problems by correlating them to the cultural, political and economic renaissance in Jewish life and to the efforts for creating in Palestine a free society rooted in agriculture and industry. . . . We hope to build up a clearing house for writers who, whether in polemics, poetry, fiction, or criticism, are aware of responsibilities.

Greenberg, then at the height of his journalistic influence, sought to interpret current events in Palestine as well as to comment on the frontiers of Jewish life throughout the world. "We represent," he declared, "that synthesis in Jewish thought, which is nationalist without being chauvinist, and which stands for fundamental economic reconstruction without being communist. Only such a synthesis can answer the need of the disoriented modern Jew." These views governed the character of the magazine in practically every issue. The contributors he attracted furthered his views in their articles on the complex aspects of contemporary

Jewish life. Among these writers were, in the early issues, Kurt Lewin, Marie Syrkin, Nathan Reich, David Ben Gurion, Moshe Shertok (Sharett), Charles Resnikoff, Maurice Samuel. Greenberg also printed numerous stories and poems by Jewish writers and reviews of new books.

As the Nazi brutalities against the German Jews began to intensify in the late 1930s, Greenberg reported them with factual restraint but with an underlying emotional grief. He effectively rejected anti-Semitic utterances and accusations, and published supportive articles by liberal Gentiles. In the early 1940s he printed reports from Poland by escaped refugees who had witnessed the destruction of their Jewish communities. He was also deeply interested in Jewish education in the United States, and encouraged prominent pedagogues to write on its status and prospects. In almost every issue, of course, he discussed the problems of a Zionist homeland in Palestine, and when Israel was established in 1948, he devoted much space to its activities and development.

In 1945 there appeared the *Jewish Frontier Anthology*, a collection of representative contributions over the previous decade. Its contents reflected the successive stages in the development of the major issues emerging during the momentous period. The volume had sections on Zionism, America, Palestine, Europe, and other areas. Of significance was the statement made in the preface:

> Being American Jews, we were particularly concerned with the American scene, in all its aspects. Nor could we fail to react to developments throughout the Diaspora. As Americans, as Jews, as believers in a liberal social order everywhere, it was our function to participate actively in the manifold issues of the period.

Greenberg died in 1953. Twenty years later, commemorating the anniversary of his death, J. J. Shapiro, the current editor, wrote glowingly of Greenberg's editorial accomplishments:

> He emerged as the leading intellectual figure in the Labor Zionist movement in this country during the final thirty years of his life. He dealt with the events, the ideas, and the personalities of the major

periods of this century—the post–World War I era, the Russian Revolution, the flowering of the Zionist movement, the Hitler era, World War II, the destruction of European Jewry, and ultimately the establishment of the State of Israel. Of special concern to him was the Jewish community in America, of which he was a part and with which he identified.

Greenberg's influence in *The Jewish Frontier* has persisted to the present. Although the contents of the articles are more diverse, and more emphasis is given to American Jewish activities and events, the emphasis remains on Zionism and Israel.

In April 1933, with Hitler having gained control of the German government, Jews everywhere became very apprehensive of the fate of their coreligionists under his rule. In New York Professors Morris R. Cohen and Salo W. Baron conceived the idea of a conference on Jewish social studies as a means of assembling reliable data about the world Jewish community in response to Nazi propaganda. The conference was held in 1936, with Albert Einstein as chairman. After considerable discussion the participants resolved to sponsor various research projects and publications, among the latter the quarterly, *Jewish Social Studies,* which began to appear in January 1939. The conference concluded with a declaration of its devotion

> to the idea that sound policies and intelligent action in Jewish affairs must be based on the most accurate and reliable information obtainable. Therefore the Conference is organized to promote, by means of scientific research, a better understanding of the position of the Jews in the modern world.

In the first issue of *Jewish Social Studies* Professor Cohen, as president of the Conference on Jewish Relations, stated that the quarterly "seeks to promote scholarly research in the field of Jewish anthropological, economic, political and cultural problems and to make the results available to a wide circle of serious readers." Among the studies in this issue were Franz Boas's "Heredity and Environment," Salo Baron's "Emphases in Jewish History," M. M. Fagen's "The Status of Jewish Lawyers in New York City," and Joshua Starr's "Italy's anti-Semites." The quarterly also included extensive reviews of new books. Subsequent issues have maintained this high level of scholarship.

A random examination of an issue in 1967 indicated that it contained studies on such subjects as Soviet Jewry and the United Nations, Hermann Cohen and Mordecai M. Kaplan, the Marranos in Spain, Arab-Jewish Relations during the Mandate Era, and Jewish Education in Great Britain during World War II; also several serious reviews of Jewish books. In an issue seven years later, again selected at random, there were among the articles Joseph Blau's report on a trip to Israel, Jewish population statistics, public schooling in Hungary for Jews in 1859–1860, an Arab view of Israel, Latin-American voting on Jews in the United Nations, bureaucratic bias and immigrants, and guilt feelings among concentration camp survivors.

In its 36 years of existence *Jewish Social Studies* has established itself as a distinguished scholarly quarterly.

In 1940 the Board of Jewish Education of New York began to issue what it termed "a magazine for young people." Named *World Over,* the biweekly has been edited by Ezekiel Schloss with a view to attracting American Jewish youth by providing them with reading and visual material intended to instruct as well as entertain. Thus the magazine contains illustrated historical tidbits, articles on Jewish topics of both current and historical content, Jewish news items, material on Israel, as well as comics, a crossword puzzle, sports items, and stories. Fully illustrated and written in a simple and informal style, the magazine has attained a relatively large circulation.

Benjamin Weintroub is a fine example of the truism that Jews are "a people of the book." An immigrant from Russia, he was dedicated to self-education. A resident of Chicago, he worked his way through courses at the University of Chicago, studied law and practiced it for a time. All the while he was in love with knowledge and literature, and found his greatest pleasure in books. In 1942, with the aid of an affluent married daughter, he decided to bring out a monthly magazine. With war then engulfing the world and with the Nazis murdering Jews by the virtual genocide, he became the publisher and editor of *The Chicago Jewish Forum* that fall, eager to make it a periodical in which Jews, and others, could express their views and aspirations. "Our aim," he stated editorially, "is to offer the men and women of this large Jewish community both an adult publication and a medium for the expression of their own views. . . . Ours is a venture in democratic journalism."

Unable to pay more than token fees for contributions, he nevertheless managed to obtain articles and stories and poems from established writers and scholars in and around Chicago. Faculty members from local institutions and able writers who had not yet gained acceptance in the national media gave him their writings for the sheer pleasure of seeing themselves in print. He was thus able to fill the early issues of his monthly with material having literary and artistic merit or scholarly substance. Later he succeeded in attracting writers of national prominence, especially after he found it feasible to make semi-annual visits to New York and meet these writers in person.

Thus, year after year, he devoted himself to the publication of his monthly, always striving to obtain the best writing available—and often succeeding—so that the *Chicago Jewish Forum* in time established itself as a highly respected literary magazine. When Weintroub died in 1969, the monthly died with him.

The American Jewish Committee, which was formed in 1906 for the purpose of defending Jews wherever and whenever they were attacked or maligned, decided in 1938 to issue a bimonthly periodical, *Contemporary Jewish Record* with a view to further its self-imposed activities. Morris Waldman, Harry Schneiderman, and Sidney Wallach, long associated with the Committee, were appointed its editors, and in the first issue they stated in part:

> For some time, the need has been felt also for a regular publication in which important magazine and newspaper articles and significant documents and enlightening editorial comment could be preserved,

and notices of pertinent books, pamphlets, and articles recorded. It was felt that such a periodical publication should include also a day-by-day chronology of events of Jewish interest throughout the world, a knowledge of which is deemed necessary for a clear understanding not only of contemporary history but also of current events in general.

Intended to be read mainly by Jews, but also to appeal to interested Christians, the bimonthly provided a review of current events, documents, articles, a digest of editorial opinion, chronicles, recent publications, periodicals, and supplementary items. Among the early contributors were Learned Hand on Cardozo, Cecil Roth on Italy and the Jews. Subsequently such writers as Hannah Arendt, Ruben Dario, James Darmsteter, Waldo Frank, Louis Ginzberg, Judah L. Magnes, and Jaques Maritain contributed articles on Jewish subjects. Some time later the magazine added a section entitled "Cedars of Lebanon," which included discussions of a historic nature by prominent scholars. In one of its issues the editors published a symposium by young Jewish writers on the nature of their Jewishness.

For reasons best known to the Committee, in 1945 it changed the periodical to a monthly, renamed it *Commentary*, and appointed Elliot E. Cohen as its editor. He also edited the final issue of *Contemporary Jewish Record*, and stated in it that the purpose of the new monthly would be

> to carry forward into larger fields the fine tradition established by this magazine since its founding seven years ago. . . . As a monthly we can raise our sights higher. We shall be able to report more closely the rapidly shifting course of issues and events. We shall have ample opportunity to picture Jewish life in this country and abroad in its rich variety. We shall be able to trace more fully the trends and patterns emerging in the postwar world.

Cohen further promised to present Jewish life not only in its own context but "in its inter-relations with those basic issues of thought, politics and culture that are the concern of all human kind." And he added:

> We pride ourselves of Jewish creativeness in so many fields in the modern world. We need that creativeness of thought and expression

in Jewish life, too. We shall have it, we sincerely believe, if we can offer it hospitality and freedom. To do this is a primary aim of this magazine, as it is of its publishers, the American Jewish Committee.

The first issue of *Commentary* appeared in November 1945. World War II having laid waste the Jewish community in Europe, American Jews felt a "responsibility for carrying forward, in a creative way, our common Jewish cultural and spiritual heritage." Cohen was certain that *Commentary* could be of service in this connection, and he stated in his first editorial:

> We have faith that a good magazine can help—by fairness, by searching out truth, by encouraging fresh and free-ranging thinking, by bringing to bear upon our problem the resources of science, philosophy, religion, and the arts, by seeking out authentic voices and giving them open house in which to be heard.

He further explained that in naming the monthly he and the Committee had in mind the tradition of the commentaries written by the "ancient scribes and sages . . . on the revelation which was the Law." Those commentaries were interpretations which changed with each generation and "became the truth that men lived by." Following this precept, he soon began to devote about half of the magazine to Jewish topics and the remainder to general political and social subjects. His policy was liberal but strongly anti-leftist and non-Zionist. Owing to the prestige of his sponsorship and adequate financing, Cohen was able to attract as contributors prominent Jewish and Gentile writers and scholars. As the monthly broadened its involvement in contemporary events, its influence and prestige increased notably.

Gradually the policy of *Commentary* was modified to make it more of "a journal of significant thought and opinion on Jewish affairs and contemporary issues." In 1950 it began to encourage "diverse points of view and belief . . . original creative endeavor in the various fields of culture." Its aim, no longer distinctly Jewish, still sought "to enlighten and clarify public opinion on problems of Jewish concern." However varied its contents, and every issue had from one to four articles on non-Jewish subjects, it remained essentially a magazine of interest to Jewish readers. Yiddish writing, for instance, received quite full and sympathetic consideration.

In 1953 Cohen edited a volume of selections entitled *Commentary on the American Scene.* The articles were all "by Jews about Jews," chatty, homey, reminiscent of Jewish life as it was experienced by immigrants earlier in the century and by their children. In the foreword he stated:

> Each Jew moves, consciously or not, in the context of a long and special history and a religious-ethical tradition that lays upon him, whether as a burden or a badge of pride, the sense of being "chosen," and so creates in him the tendency, even the obligation, to carry himself, "with a difference." It is this that plays a persistent counterpoint—humorous, pathetic, tragic, farcical—to whatever Jews do and are.

Cohen's political leftism was so strongly anticommunist that he tended to be more concerned with the dangers to freedom from outspoken liberals than from a demagogue like Senator Joseph McCarthy. Thus he permitted Irving Kristol to write: "There is one thing the American people know about Senator McCarthy: he, like them is irrevocably anti-communist. About spokesmen for American liberalism they feel they know no such thing. And with some justification."

Cohen resigned as editor in 1955, and for the next three years the monthly appeared under the aegis of acting editors. In 1959 Norman Podhoretz was named editor, and he has been directing *Commentary* policy ever since. He gradually modified it still further with the aim of making it a highly prestigious commentary on American and world affairs, Jewish in ownership but general in point of view and emphasis. Jewish topics gradually ceased to predominate, but continued to appear importantly. In the issue of April 1962, for example, there was a symposium on "Jewishness and the Younger Intellectuals," and most of the participants indicated that they felt little affiliation with Judaism. The monthly fully reflected this lessening of its Jewish character.

An examination of the issues in 1964 showed that out of the 92 articles only 25 were of Jewish content, but all eight stories were by Jews. Ten years later the twelve issues of *Commentary* printed

94 articles, with only 14 having a distinctly Jewish content. When questioned on this point, Podhoretz made clear that he considered *Commentary* primarily a Jewish contribution to American culture. And, indeed, that it has become: one of the most highly regarded periodicals interpreting and advancing the cultural aspects of contemporary American civilization.

In 1966 *Commentary* and the American Jewish Committee started the Jewish Book Club. Organized on the same principles as other book clubs—with members pledging to buy a minimum of four books a year—the club has been quite successful in attracting a sizable membership. The monthly choices and alternates are selected from the best available nonfiction (and some fiction) books of Jewish content. Occasionally it arranges to bring to life a book of permanent worth no longer in print. Financially quite successful, the club has thus served to stimulate the wider reading of good books within the Jewish community.

With *Commentary* having gradually departed radically from the original aims of *Contemporary Jewish Record,* it is of interest to note that the American Jewish Committee has, consciously or otherwise, found it advisable to start a new periodical devoted to Jewish life. In 1973 it began to issue *Present Tense,* with Murray Polner as editor, a quarterly of worldwide Jewish interest. In its "Statement of Purpose," the committee declared:

> In sponsoring *Present Tense,* the American Jewish Committee aims to meet the need for a journal that would broaden American Jewry's understanding of the conditions of world Jewry. The magazine will publish popular articles and reportage, expressing wide diversity of opinion of the situation of Jews in countries around the world, the special problems of Israel.

In furthering this aim, Polner wrote that he would try to provide information about Jewish life everywhere "which will be indispensable for anyone who wants to be informed, warmed, or just plain nostalgic. Everything we publish will be motivated by one question: What does it mean for the survival of Jews as Jews?"

That he is realizing this aim in the issues already published may be seen from a listing of the topics in the first issue: Watergate from the Jewish angle, Meyer Levin's journey through the Soviet Union, the nature of London's *Jewish Chronicle*, the present condition of the Soviet Jews, a story by I. B. Singer, a memoir of Orthodox Jews in Poland, American Jews in Israel, assimilated Jews in France, an interview with Raul Hilberg on the Holocaust, the Jews in Argentina, the West Bank, and the deserters in Canada. Subsequent issues had a similarly Jewish content. The articles are well organized, written in a popular style, and some are fully illustrated. To a degree, therefore, *Present Tense* is a return to the purport of *Contemporary Jewish Record*, updated and broadened to meet the current needs of Jewish readers in America.

The Theodor Herzl Foundation, an integral part of the American Zionist Federation, in 1955 started *Midstream*, a quarterly dealing with the subjects of Zionism, Israel, and Jewishness. As stated at the outset, it was to provide "a critical interpretation of the past, a searching examination of the present, and afford a medium for considered independent opinion and for creative cultural expression." Shlomo Katz was appointed editor. On the whole the magazine adhered closely to its announced program. When, five years later, Katz edited *The Midstream Reader*, a selection of material from the magazine, he stated in the preface:

> *Midstream* was defined as a Zionist publication, committed to free inquiry, questioning the Jewish *status quo*, and seeking a confrontation of the problems of Jewish existence and the fateful questions that face a world aghast at the threat of self-annihilation. . . . *Midstream* stresses story and poem, and believes the results justify the effort.

Most of the articles published in the magazine were written by serious students of Jewish life. They were largely analyses of current problems from various aspects, with emphasis on Israeli developments. The stories and poems were mostly by young but already noteworthy writers. It thus established itself as a serious literary and cultural periodical, in its quality somewhat reminiscent of the *Menorah Journal*. Its contributors were and are among the better Jewish writers, as may be seen from the following random list: I. B. Singer, Herbert Gold, Isaac Rosenfeld, Judd Teller, Leslie A. Fiedler, Howard Fast, Charles Resnikoff, David Ignatow, and Harvey Shapiro.

In 1965 *Midstream* became a monthly—summers excepted. When Katz resigned his editorship recently, he was succeeded first by Ronald Sanders and then by Joel Carmichael.

In 1946 a group of pro-communists started to issue a monthly, originally called *Jewish Life* but in 1956 changed to *Jewish Currents* to avoid confusion with the Orthodox periodical of that name. The editors aimed to present Jewish activities from the point of view of the radical left. They were acutely conscious of the Holocaust catastrophe and ardently anti-fascist, but their loyalty to the Soviet Union and to Stalin made them apologists for the restrictions and persecution of Jews in Russia. When news began to reach the United States of arrests, imprisonment, and execution of Jewish writers and intellectuals, the editors denounced it as vicious gossip.

It was only in 1956, when Khrushchev had made his historic speech on February 25, 1956, revealing Stalin's criminal activities and the atrocities committed against Jewish leaders, that Morris U. Schappes, who was by then editor-in-chief of *Jewish Currents,* became critical of Soviet Russia's policy of "compulsory assimilation" toward the Jewish population. He has been quite candid about the monthly's dogmatic defense of Russia in the early 1950s. In 1971 he stated editorially: "We have shed many of our illusions but none of our ideals; we have shed many of our dogmas but none of our principles."

Similarly, *Jewish Currents* was at first dogmatically anti-Zionist. When Gromyko in 1947 declared in the United Nations that Soviet Russia favored the establishment of Israel, the monthly dutifully echoed this sentiment. For years, however, it was more favorable to the Arabs than to the Israelis. Numerous articles discussed the issue of racism in Israel, and some of the contributors maintained that Israel was racist because it did not give Arabs equal rights in every respect—cavalierly disregarding the fact that from the day of its establishment to the present the Arabs have been at war with Israel, threatening its destruction, and making it rightly fearful of an Arab "fifth column" within its midst.

With the passing of the years, however, *Jewish Currents* became more tolerant of Israel, and in 1961 Schappes wrote editorially: "While not pro-Zionist, we are therefore decidedly pro-Israel, no matter how much we criticize the Ben Gurion foreign policy or some internal relations inside Israel. We regard Israel's right to exist as unquestionable; we are partisans of the welfare of Israel and its peoples, Jewish and Arab."

After 1967 the monthly again and again criticized Soviet Russia's attacks on Zionism. It was similarly opposed to the curbing of Jewish rights in the Soviet Union, stating: "The persistently troubling situation of the Jews in the Soviet Union is reported and discussed in every single issue . . . which sets itself the task of reporting signs of progress and change without losing sight of the fact that basic problems are still unresolved." As late as the summer issue of 1975 Schappes expressed his indignation at the openly anti-Semitic attacks coming out of Soviet Russia: "We are outraged, as progressive Jewish internationalists, by the propagating of anti-Semitism, reaching its peak in the *Ogonyosik* article." It should be stated that as a consequence of this attitude, Schappes was some years back expelled from the Communist Party and *Jewish Currents* is regarded with disdain by its members.

Over the years *Jewish Currents,* despite this split and its miniscule financial capability—most of those producing it are volunteers—has been a lively and positive source of material of Jewish interest. It published articles, favorable and otherwise, on such subjects as Jewish secularity, Jewish culture, Yiddish literary heritage, intermarriage, and the Jew-Negro dialogue. It devoted much space to the Holocaust, and presented several views on Jewish resistance to Nazi extermination—eager to prove that Jews did fight back despite statements to the contrary. Thus it was particularly critical of Raul Hilberg's assumption that Jewish historical pacifism had kept Ghetto victims from efforts to resist. Also of interest is that certain liberal rabbis are among its contributors. Rabbi R. E. Goldberg, for instance, in an article on Jewish values in a changing world, wrote:

> A Jewish value that is as old as the Torah warns us then and now against idolatry, against the cult of an individual or a nation, against turning anything of the moment into something eternal or perfect, against substituting any religion or ideology for Divinity and surrendering to that our own powers of reason, criticism and self-criticism.

The monthly brought out two collections of its contents: *Jewish Life Anthology: 1946–1956,* which consisted mostly of stories and poems from the Yiddish; and *The Jewish Currents Reader: 1956–1966,* which is devoted to the more significant material published during that decade. Each issue since then contains news of Israel, the editor's diary on events of the month, parents' corner, inside the Jewish community, general articles, a story, poems, and book reviews. On the whole *Jewish Currents* has dealt seriously, if not always favorably, with the variegated life of the Jewish community.

In the late 1960s the social explosiveness in American colleges, resulting largely from student opposition to the Viet Nam war but also from the general social restiveness, has also affected Jewish students. In various colleges they expressed their dissatisfaction with the so-called Jewish establishment. Some sought escape in communes; others, searching for certainty, veered toward Hasidism; a number became political rebels. Those who had the means, or an enterprising member, started informal periodicals to express their views and goals; and although few lasted more than several issues, their dynamism had a pervasive influence. Consequently these literary outpourings, being symptomatic of Jewish student confusion and resentment, must be the concern of their interested elders. The following relatively permanently established magazines are of particular significance;

Response: A Contemporary Jewish Review, began life in the summer of 1967 and is now a full-fledged quarterly. Its editors stated that it is an independent review dedicated to the discussion of problems in contemporary Jewish civilization. The editors believe that "despite commitment to or dissatisfaction with movements, institutions, and organizations, the responsible few must participate in responsible dialogue about Judaism." The magazine is an affiliate of the Jewish Press Service and is a member of the North American Jewish Student Appeal. It does not accept advertisements and depends entirely on subscriptions and donors. Most of the contributors are faculty members and advanced students. Its issues now run to 128 pages.

Among the early articles were such topics as new alternatives to the synagogue, Jewish education, the arts, a symposium on living in two cultures, the Jewish student movement, the Jewish woman, Israel, messianism and modernity, survivors of the Holocaust, and a literary approach to the Torah. It also included fiction and verse.

A more recent issue dealt with the subject of Xenophobia: Jewish fears and American realities—and the reactions of several contributors. Other articles discussed the fictional hero, Duddy Kravits, Richard L. Rubenstein's *Power Struggle,* Rabbi Kook's, *The Pangs of Cleansing,* a provocative letter by Art Waskow on the pursuit of justice, and verses by seven poets. The quarterly is thus in appearance as well as in content little different from other similar periodicals.

Sh'ma: A Journal of Jewish Responsibility, which began to appear in 1970, is a lively biweekly during the academic year and is now edited by Eugene B. Borowitz. A much more modest undertaking than *Response,* it extends to only eight pages and is in constant need of financial assistance. An indication of its independent scope and general position may be gathered from the contents of two typical issues. The one for December 14, 1973, begins with an affirmative response by Arthur J. Goldberg to an inquiry regarding "the attitude of American Jews in relation to detente with the Soviet Union"; the other articles, relatively brief, are on prewar certainties and postwar ambiguities, the historic context of liberation, male and female liturgy, the roles of Jewish women, and a woman's reaction to an *aliyah.* The issue of November 15, 1974, is devoted largely to the problem of abortion in the light of the Supreme Court decision. The remaining articles deal with Israel's problems and difficulties, various Jewish activities, literary criticism, religious practices, and *Havurot* (Jewish communal living). The contributors are fairly prominent.

Interest in Yiddish has greatly increased in recent years. Many volumes of fiction and poetry have appeared in English translation, and much has been written about them by critics. Courses in this language and literature have been established in scores of colleges, and the teachers are now members of an association. In 1973 they started *Yiddish:* A Quarterly Journal Devoted to Yiddish and Yiddish Literature. The editor is Joseph C. Landis of Queens College. In the first issue, which appeared that summer, he stated the purposes of the periodical:

> It aims to provide a bridge between two cultures and two worlds; to make audible in English the voices and judgments of Yiddish writers; critics, and thinkers, past and present, here and on the other five continents where Yiddish is spoken and written; to bring to public notice the lesser known riches of Yiddish literature—those writers and works that have not yet found their way into commercial publication. . . . It aims to provide a resource for faculty and students engaged in the study of Yiddish. And, finally, it hopes to be a stimulating magazine for any reader who is interested in Yiddish language and literature and in the world they have touched.

In the few issues that have already appeared, the editor's hope seems amply realized. Each number is meaty, highly informative, and broad in coverage. The articles are by and about Yiddish writers, and the stories, criticism, and reviews are of intrinsic interest. In the third issue, for instance, Elie Wiesel wrote on Reb Aaron Zeitlin, S. A. Portnoy wrote on the autobiography of a Jewish revolutionary, I. Shmulewitz discussed an obligation to remember; also included are Milton Hindus's introduction to Linetsky's *The Polish Lad* and a selection from it, a Purimshpiel, a fine poem by Jacob Glatstein. The fourth issue began with a piece by Aaron Zeitlin and was followed by Saul Goodman's study of Abraham Heschel, I. L. Steinberg's criticism of I. B. Singer's writings, two articles on Rudolf Rocker, a survey of Max

Weinreich's monumental four-volume study of Yiddish, and a story by Jacob Zipper. Each issue has a department of information exchanges, a list of current articles, reviews, and books of Yiddish interest. The quarterly is thus performing as a highly scholarly survey of Yiddish literature.

In the spring of 1975 Leonard Fein and Elie Wiesel started to publish *Moment*, named in honor of the Yiddish daily in prewar Warsaw. Established as an independent magazine, with diverse sponsors committed to Jewish life, it is designed to speak to and about American Jews. Fein, on the faculty of Brandeis University, stated:

> People tailor their aspirations to their sense of possibility. We intend and expect that *Moment* will help raise the sense of Jewish possibility, hence also raise Jewish aspirations. Until that happy time when we learn once more that we can, if we will, tailor our possibilities to fit our highest aspirations.

Both editors asserted that their aim is to enrich the life of the Jewish community by offering it "as rich a diet of ideas and information as we can." In a news report they declared there was an urgent need for "a new, independent medium to keep up with the growing spirit . . . in the American Jewish community over the past ten years."

In the first issue there were articles on Jacob Schiff and the Galveston immigration experiment, on women, on the Jewish right, on Rembrandt's Jews; also a long story, several departments, and book reviews. The second issue had an article by Gerry Wills on Kissinger and Disraeli; another on the road to peace in the Middle East; also on God and Mentsch at Yale, OPEC, baseball, a Jew in Persia, a story, poems, and departments. One of the latter, Recollections, presented documents and vignettes out of the American Jewish past. *Moment* thus appears to be a welcome addition to the Anglo-Jewish list of periodicals.

12

Jewish Influence in American Publishing

Although American Jews have in recent years been prominent in book publishing, only a few had entered the industry before 1900. One of the first Jewish booksellers-publishers was Benjamin Gomez (1769–1828). Of a prominent Sephardic family, he early opened a bookstore in New York. In 1792 he brought out a 48-page volume entitled *The Christian Economy*, presumably a translation of an ancient Greek manuscript "found in the island of Patmos where St. John wrote his Book of Revelations." Three years later he issued a volume in which Doctor Priestley's "Letters to the Jews Inviting Them to Amiable Discussion of the Evidence of Christianity" were combined with "Letters to Dr. Priestley in Answer to Those Addressed to the Jews" by David Levy. Subsequently Gomez published other books of literary or general interest, 21 in all by 1799, when he gave up publishing for the lottery business. A contemporary of his, Naphtali Judah (1774–1855) also did some publishing in connection with his printing activity, but his impact on the industry was minor.

Benjamin Levy (1786–1860) was a third-generation American Jew, born in New York. Around 1811 he went to New Orleans, and not long after opened a book and stationery store. In 1817 he published his first book. Subsequently he became the most active publisher in Louisiana, having brought out over a hundred books by 1843, when poor investments forced him into bankruptcy. Most of his books dealt with local and regional legal matters. Among them were compilations, references, briefs, appeals, and courtroom pleadings. Other of his books concerned business, politics, and literature. Between 1822 and 1839 he also issued the *New Orleans Price-Current and Commerical Intelligencer*. After his bankruptcy he reorganized the firm under the name of his son Alexander.

Abraham Hart (1810–1885) was one of the leading publishers of his time. The son of a shopkeeper who had settled in Philadelphia in 1804 and died nine years later, young Abraham began to work for the Carey publishing firm in 1823. A business prodigy, he was three years later sent to Boston by Moses Thomas, auctioneer and publisher, with a letter of credit for $5000 to buy books at the annual trade auction. In 1829, when Edward Carey, who operated the bookstore of the family firm, decided to start a separate publishing house, he invited Hart to become his partner. The new company, named Carey and Hart, was enterprising and highly successful during the next two decades. An instance of Hart's ingenuity was evidenced in the way he handled the American edition of Bulwer-Lytton's *Rienzi*. With foreign books uncopyrighted in the United States, American publishers competed with one another in their effort to bring out popular English works at the earliest date in order to gain the advantage of a day or more in the sale of their edition. In this instance both Harper and Brothers and Carey and Hart received copies of the novel on the same day. Thereupon Hart speeded the typesetting by dividing the book into twelve parts and giving each part to a different printer, thereby obtaining printed sheets the following day. That afternoon 500 copies of the bound book were placed in the mail stagecoach for New York, which Hart had reserved for that purpose and was the lone passenger. The novel was thus on sale in New York bookstores a full day ahead of the Harper edition and was sold out within that time.

The firm of Carey and Hart published many books of distinction. Among them were Thackeray's first work, *Yellowplush Correspondence;* Longfellow's *Poets and Poetry of Europe* and an edition of his own *Poems;* R. W. Griswold's *Poets and Poetry of America,* Macaulay's *Critical and Miscellaneous Essays* in five volumes, and the novels of Captain Mariyot.

In 1845 Carey withdrew from the firm, and Hart took as a partner Henry Carey Baird. Four years later Baird left, and Hart remained in full control of the firm until his retirement in 1854. All the while he took an active part in the affairs of the Jewish community of Philadelphia, serving as an officer in educational and charitable organizations and as president of the first Jewish Publication Society.

No other Jewish publisher appeared until the turn of the century. The heads of the leading firms, who in time established themselves as "gentlemen publishers" and dominated the industry, shared a distaste for Jews similar to that of other American intellectuals of the period. It was natural for them not to employ anyone not congenial to them, and Jews during the nineteenth century therefore tended to go into more hospitable forms of employment. Thus while a number of Jews entered the field of journalism after the Civil War, there is no evidence of anyone breaking the barrier of prejudice in book publishing.

Moses Pollock may be said to be a notable exception. Born in Philadelphia in 1819 of a large and enterprising family, he found work in the small firm of M'Carty and Davis, successor to Johnson and Warner, whose bookselling and publishing began in 1788. Davis, the head of the firm, had gradually become fond of young Pollock and before he died had willed him enough money to acquire control of the firm. Pollock was not aggressive as a publisher and brought out relatively few books, among them the popular Pike's *Arithmetic,* Oliver Goldsmith's *Natural History,* and a collected edition of Charles Brockdon Brown's writings.

Before too long the business of publishing ceased to interest Pollock, but he was more and more drawn to rare books. Edwin Wolf stated in *Rosenbach:*

> He was first a lover of books, then a scholar, and finally a seller of books. . . . He was a dealer with acumen. His field was Americana, a young one in those days when an Elzivier was still worth more than a Franklin [imprint]. He believed sincerely that as the country grew

so would the interest in its history and the books which told that history. But he hated to sell what he esteemed. Each encounter with a customer was a case of the buyer turned salesman. The records of the books he was persuaded to sell are not extant, but today in most of the great libraries of the United States are several choice items of Americana, usually fine copies in their original bindings, with Pollock's bibliographic notes inside the front cover.

The source of many of these items was the warehouse of the old firm which Pollock had bought with Davis's money. In it he had found many boxes filled with children's books—most of them first editions. Among them, for instance, were 857 first-edition copies of *The Death and Burial of Cock Robin* (1805), which the original publisher had considered worthless but which subsequently became highly valuable. Indeed, these and other rare items stored in the warehouse later became the nucleus of the rare-book business of Abraham Rosenbach, Pollock's nephew and assistant.

In 1895, having reached the age of seventy-six, Pollock was finally persuaded to sell some of his books at auction. He still hated to part with them—"I have had them so long," he explained—but Rosenbach had continued to urge their disposal and helped with the packing and cataloguing. Among the items sold were fifty Franklin imprints for $1500 and a number of volumes dealing with the Far West.

When he died in 1903 he left no will, so that his estate was shared by his surviving sisters—he had never married—among them Rosenbach's mother. An auction sale was arranged—in effect a "wash sale" to establish the worth of the books. The catalogue was titled "A Collection of Valuable Americana Gathered by the Late Moses Pollock, Esq., the Oldest Bookseller in the United States." Rosenbach bid for most of the items with his mother's money and also obtained the unsold books and fixtures for $1000.

If no other Jews entered book publishing during the second half of the nineteenth century, at least two achieved stellar positions in the field of newspaper publishing. The first was Joseph

Pulitzer, born in Hungary in 1847. Although he had become quite estranged from Judaism, rival publishers kept referring to him derogatorily as "Jew Pulitzer." After serving in the Union Army he became a reporter in St. Louis. In 1874 he acquired the bankrupt *Staatszeitung*, soon sold it at a profit, and in 1878 bought the *Dispatch* and the *Post*, which he later combined into the highly regarded St. Louis *Post-Dispatch*. Five years later he went to New York, bought the *World*, and made it liberal politically and sensational journalistically. In 1887 he launched the *Evening World* and soon rivaled William Randolph Hearst's *Morning Journal* in vulgar "yellow journalism." By now a nervous wreck and practically blind, he engaged Frank I. Cobb as editor and succeeded in making the *World* the most lively and prestigious newspaper of the time.

Adolph S. Ochs, born in 1858, early entered newspaper work in Chattanooga, and in 1878 acquired the bankrupt *Times* and gradually made it an attractive and profitable daily. In 1883 he married a daughter of Rabbi Isaac Mayer Wise. Unlike Pulitzer he remained loyal to Judaism and contributed generously to Jewish organizations.

In 1896 he managed to gain control of the moribund New York *Times*. Making few radical changes, he quickly eliminated inefficiencies of various kinds and strove to give authority to the daily news. He also reduced the price of the newspaper from three cents to one, and was not long in increasing sales and advertising revenues to a degree that resulted in a handsome profit. The recent history of the *Times* is too well known to require detailed elaboration; it is needful to state, however, that it has long been the country's leading newspaper, Jewish owned but strictly American in policy.

A number of other Jews attained prominence in the newspaper field. Among them were, and are, E. P. Adler, whose Lee Syndicate published dailies in several Midwestern cities; Lucius W. Nieman, editor and publisher of the Milwaukee *Journal*, who established the Nieman Fellowships in Journalism at Harvard University; Moses Annenberg, whose various journalistic enterprises brought him more cash than kudos; David Stern, who published the Philadelphia *Record,* and for a time the New York *Evening Post;* Paul Block, who owned several newspapers in Eastern cities; Eugene Meyer, whose Washington *Post* attained national stature and influence; and Samuel I. Newhouse, who controlled a widespread chain of newspapers. All these newspaper owners were both enterprising and devoted to the spread of daily information.

The number of Jewish editors and journalists was also sizable. Their prominence may be gathered from a mere listing of some of their names: Benjamin de Casseres, Louis Wiley, Simeon Strunsky, Fabian Franklin, Herbert Bayard Swope, Franklin P. Adams, Walter Lippmann, Charles Michelson, Arthur Crock, David Lawrence, George Seldes, I. F. Stone, and Lester Markel—not to mention those active at the present time.

Throughout the nineteenth century American publishers continued to bring out books on the Bible and Judaism, usually by Christian writers. Their contact with living Jews was minimal and passively antipathetic. The "gentlemen publishers" in particular, men of sound ethical standards and of relatively intellectual sophistication—among them William Appleton, Henry Holt, Charles Scribner, George Palmer Putnam, and H. O. Houghton—would not employ a Jew and made little or no effort to seek out Jewish writers. Appleton, for instance, did publish the fiction of Grace Aguilar, but only because she was a popular English novelist. As already indicated, however, their attitude toward living Jews merely reflected that of other American intellectuals—to whom Jews were either international bankers or queer, bearded, poor immigrants.

Around 1900 several publishers still conducted large bookstores, but none was more prestigious than Brentano's. In 1897 the Brentanos began importing sheets from England of books dealing largely with the life of high society or with the arts. Having as customers many wealthy society women, the firm managed to sell most of the bound sheets within the store. Some years later, and particularly after 1920, when Lowell Brentano had become the editorial director of the publishing division, the firm brought out a list of general books, including the works of George Bernard Shaw. On the whole, the Brentano publishing policy was fairly conventional, and when financial reverses made it necessary, the firm discontinued its publishing activity.

It must be stressed that American book publishing around 1900 was still genteel and conventional. The only excitement was generated by Frank Doubleday, who founded his house on the basis of aggressive commercialization of the industry. More fundamentally perturbing to the established publishers, however, were the winds of new literary ideas and trends, already blowing in Europe and soon felt by young intellectuals in America. As literary experimentation and social rebelliousness began to find their way into books abroad, their echoes stirred the minds of the then few restless young American writers. They were ignored or rejected by respectable editors, but their voices were heard by the first Jews to force their way into the publishing industry. Soon their publishing began to enliven and modernize American literature. Young, enterprising, with a keen sense of current literary trends, these Jews began to publish authors who were too radical or too unconventional for the dignified houses. They also went to Europe for their books, but more and more they welcomed young American writers who broke away from the genteel conventionality of their elders. Commenting on this situation in his 1937 Bowker lecture, Alfred Harcourt, who was also an open-minded and imaginative publisher, stated:

> While Boston publishers were bringing out sets of Emerson and Longfellow in new bindings, new publishers sprang up in New York, notably Huebsch, Knopf, and Liveright, who began to publish translations of contemporary foreign authors and books by young American authors who had broken away from the Victorian point of view. These books found an audience at once all over the country in cultivated groups with foreign background and among Americans of international training. The older New York houses were quick to recognize the new trend, and New York publishing became international and cosmopolitan.

Mention must also be made that after World War I most publishers based their printings of books on the assumption that the largest body of book readers was to be found within the Jewish community, and that the books that appealed to it were certain of an adequate sale.

B. W. Huebsch was the first of the new Jewish publishers. The son of a rabbi and orphaned while in his teens, he was taken into his older brother's printing shop. Not long after, when the brother left the shop for further study, young Huebsch carried on by himself. Also avid for education and deeply interested in music—in 1899 he was for a year music reviewer for the New York *Sun*—he devoted evenings to lectures and reading. In 1902 E. H. Griggs, whose lectures Huebsch had attended, asked him to print an edition of *A Book of Meditations*. When the volume was printed, Huebsch obliged the author, whom he greatly admired, by helping him place the book in bookstores. Thereafter Griggs had him print two of his other volumes, which Huebsch also marketed. Additional books began to come his way, and by 1905 he was more of a publisher than a printer.

A man of ideals with a keen appreciation of good writing, Huebsch was not long in becoming known among new and radical writers as a publisher hospitable to works unwanted by the established houses. Thus he brought out his first popular book, Gelett Burgess's *Are You a Bromide?*, which other publishers had rejected. At about the same time he added to his list such radical and unconventional works as Maxim Gorki's *The Spy*, John Spargo's *Karl Marx* and *Syndicalism*, Eduard Bernstein's *Evolutionary Socialism*, William Ellery Leonard's *The Poet of Galilee*, James Oppenheim's *Wild Oats*, Gerhardt Hauptmann's *The Weavers*, Tom L. Johnson's *My Story*, and August Rodin's *Venus*. Huebsch was also very much concerned about book censorship, and argued eloquently against it in *Publishers Weekly*.

Having little capital and bringing out books which appealed to him as worthy of publication even though they had a limited sale, he still managed to issue an annual list of books which would otherwise probably have remained unpublished. Thus he brought out the early books of James Joyce, D. H. Lawrence, Sherwood Anderson, and Van Wyck Brooks; also the writings of

George Sorel, Jules Romains, Artzybashev, and other writers who brought new ideas and genuine stimulation to American readers.

When in 1919 he undertook to publish *The Freeman*, which quickly established itself as an excellent liberal weekly, he tended to lessen his book publishing activity. Five years later, when the periodical expired for lack of funds, Huebsch found himself with a shrunken publishing list and very much at loose ends. While in this situation, he was encouraged by friends to join a newly founded firm, The Viking Press. For nearly forty years thereafter Huebsch functioned as its chief editor with a breadth of view and a sympathetic love of good writing that made him one of the most admired American publishers.

Alfred A. Knopf is one of the more distinguished of American publishers. Born in 1892 and graduating from Columbia University at the age of twenty, he obtained, with the help of a friend of his father, a clerical job at Doubleday, Page and Company at eight dollars a week, thus being the first Jew to join a non-Jewish firm. Already interested in books, and having admired Joseph Conrad's *Lord Jim* while a student, he read the manuscript of his new novel, to which Doubleday editors were paying little attention, and became eager to develop a large sale for it. With Doubleday's permission he described the new novel enthusiastically in a lengthy circular and wrote to reviewers and critics to solicit their interest in it. As a result of this personal promotion *Chance* became the first of Conrad's writings to gain a relatively large sale. George Doran later asserted that "to Knopf more than to any person, Conrad owes his fame and popularity." In the meantime Knopf, still in his early twenties, had learned enough of publishing to want to strike out on his own in order to give free reign to his imagination and enthusiasms.

In 1915 he and Blanche Wolf, whom he was shortly to marry, opened their own publishing house. From the first, like Huebsch, they sought out books in which the long-established publishers were uninterested—mostly books by Europeans, and especially Russians. An enormous advantage to a new publisher with little capital then was the fact that most of these books were already

B. W. Huebsch was the first Jewish publisher in the twentieth century; his love of literature exceeded his success as a businessman.

Alfred A. Knopf published more good books than any of the other publishers of his time.

being published in England and could therefore be obtained in printed sheets on credit. Knopf early published volumes by such Russian writers as Gogol, Ostrovsky, Turgenev, Goncharev, Lermontov, Kuprin, and Bunin. He also reissued W. H. Hudson's *Green Mansions,* which no publisher wanted because Putnam had lost money on it a decade earlier; with the literary climate having in the meantime become much more receptive, the work was read widely and became a modern classic. Knopf was also hospitable to young American writers who were breaking away from the traditional mold and had great difficulty getting published. In time he published such authors as Carl Van Vechten, Alfred Kreymborg, Claude Bragdon, Max Eastman, Richard Curle, Joseph Hergesheimer, Willa Cather, Ezra Pound, H. L. Mencken, and Sheldon Cheney. An early important factor in his success as a publisher was the lavish attention he paid to the format and appearance of his books, so that the Borzoi imprint quickly became assurance of esthetic satisfaction.

With the passing of the years the Knopf firm published some of the best books of the time, including works by about a dozen Nobel Prize winners. Blanche Knopf concentrated on European and Latin-American authors and brought many of them to the firm. In addition to much superior fiction, both foreign and native—and also some popular romances and detective stories—the house brought out such scholarly works as Oswald Spengler's *The Decline of the West,* Egon Corti's *Maximilian and Carlotta,* Thomas Beer's *The Mauve Decade,* Egon Friedels' *A Cultural History of the Modern Age,* Charles Seignobos' *The Evolution of the French People,* Mencken's *American Language,* F. O. Mathiessen's *The James Family,* Carleton Coon's *The Story of Man,* and a host of other literary and erudite works of distinction.

In 1923 Knopf arranged with Mencken and George Jean Nathan to edit a new and handsome monthly, *The American Mercury.* The announcement stated: "First and last, its central effort will be to combat all pedantry and pretense, to encourage sound and original work in all intellectual departments, and to offer a quick welcome and hearing to men and women capable of it." The magazine soon became the bible of sophisticated youthful intellectuals, and in less than two years its circulation rose to 74,000 copies. For about a decade the monthly was one of the most lively and polemical periodicals, but the Depression of the 1930s put an end to its eminence.

After 45 years of distinguished activity, the Knopfs sold control of their firm to Random House. Knopf continued his activity as editor for some years thereafter, and his imprint remains to this day highly respected in the industry. Earlier, on the 25th anniversary of the firm's establishment, Huebsch well summarized Knopf's contribution to publishing:

> Until Alfred Knopf blew in, like young Lochinvar, book publishing was a business; he made it a career. Before him, it is true, publishing was a superior sort of vocation because of its implication of culture, and it had its personalities, men who left the impress of imagination on their work; but there was none whose product in a given period of itself contributed a self-portrait. The *corpus* of Alfred Knopf's publications is more than a symbol of his association with poets and thinkers: it is the man himself.

In 1915 Albert and Charles Boni, Harvard graduates, began to publish the Little Leather Library, brief classics reprinted in a small format and bound in simulated leather. Woolworth and other low-priced stories sold them for ten cents a copy. Many of these items were for the first time made available to a large audience of readers who were attracted by the low price and the opportunity to make the acquaintance of world literature. The series proved deservedly popular and widened the potential readership in America.

Two years later the brothers interested Horace Liveright in a proposal to publish modern books in a format that would enable them to market the volumes at the low price of sixty cents. The firm they organized, Boni and Liveright, named the series "The Modern Library: The World's Best Books." It was a timely and propitious venture. By 1917 many young Americans, in and out of college, were experiencing a literary insurgence, largely influenced by the cultural ferment in European literary circles. Inexpensive editions of books highly esteemed abroad were consequently welcomed by many American readers.

Liveright came to publishing from Wall Street, where he had early manifested his daring flamboyance. An imaginative entrepreneur, with a flair for the new and exciting and extravagant in literature, he was not content with merely bringing out inexpensive reprints of established books. In his eagerness to discover new talent, to exploit literary freshness, he made himself a leading publisher of unconventional books touched by genius. More than Huebsch and Knopf he soon sought out authors whom established publishers ignored or rejected. When his impulsive decisions clashed with the views of his more realistic partners, a toss of a coin placed him in sole control of the young firm and the Bonis went their own way.

In 1919 his list of books indicated the direction in which he was going. On it were such authors as John Reed, Theodore Dreiser, Upton Sinclair, Eugene O'Neill, and George Moore. The following year he published, among others, books by Sigmund Freud, Rose Macaulay, Leonid Andreyev, Waldo Frank, Hendrik W. Van Loon, Norman Hapgood, Edgar Saltus, George Lansbury, and H. M. Hyndman. Still later he published books by such writers as Edgar Lee Masters, C. M. Doughty, Robinson Jeffers, Sven Hedin, John Macy, Sarah Gertrude Millin, Anita Loos, Roger Martin du Gard, Paul Morand, and Emil Ludwig—a veritable galaxy unmatched at that time by any other house.

As was inevitable under the circumstances in the early 1920s, Liveright found himself hounded by censors. He fought them openly and boldly, maintaining his allegiance to freedom of the press. He succeeded in defeating the "clean books" bill in the New York legislature by gaining state senator James Walker's support—the latter's peroration against the bill was climaxed by the cleverly effective assertion that "no girl was ever ruined by a book."

Liveright's generous advances to authors and extravagant promotion of his books more than once put him in financial straits. To relieve his plight, he sold vice-presidencies to Bennett Cerf and Donald Friede, and in 1925 he sold the profitable Modern Library to Cerf. His indulgent preoccupation with the theater after 1925 was another financial drain, and by 1929 he was so deeply in debt that he had to yield control of the firm to his creditors. By that time he had become a physical wreck and died four years later.

In Liveright's favor is the fact that more than any other publisher in the 1920s he brought to American literature a lively exhilaration it experienced neither previously nor later. As Donald Friede stated: "His list was during the top years of the firm the most phenomenal list ever assembled by any publisher. And Liveright was responsible for the greater part of it. He seemed to have the ability to smell out good books."

The Bonis and their uncle Thomas Seltzer went their own ways on separating from Liveright. The brothers started their own firm and bought the list of the defunct company of Lieber and Lewis. One of their early ventures was the Cosmos Library, containing studies of popular science. They also initiated the American Library, which included the complete works of Herman Melville, Ambrose Bierce, and other distinguished writers. In 1926 they acquired the Seltzer list—he having struggled for several years as a publisher with little capital, yet managed to bring out books by such writers as Thornton Wilder, Ford Madox Ford, and Georg Brandes. In 1929 they launched the Boni Paper Books by soliciting subscribers who were to receive a book a month for an annual fee of $5.00. The scheme was predicated on a mass market, and they might have succeeded in attracting the required 200,000 members if the financial crash in October had not put a quietus on the project. The ensuing depression forced the brothers, after several years of economic insecurity, to dissolve their firm.

Where the Bonis initiated in the popularization of literature with their Little Leather Library—which reached a sale of 15,000,000 copies—and what Boni and Liveright achieved on a higher level with the Modern Library, Emanuel Haldeman-Julius succeeded phenominally after 1919 with the Little Blue Books. A native of Philadelphia with a socialist upbringing, Julius in his adult years turned into a sensationally enterprising and often unscrupulous merchandiser of reading material. Having married the daughter of a wealthy banker, he adopted her name and made use of her money to buy the financially straitened *Appeal to Reason,* for years a widely read socialist newspaper published in Girard, Kansas. He made that town his home and used his newly acquired printing presses to bring out the *Rubaiyat* and Oscar Wilde's *The Ballad of Reading Gaol* on a 3½ by 5 page format. Bound in blue paper, he marketed these booklets at a quarter a copy. Increasing success—aided by extravagant promotion—enabled Julius to issue new volumes of original or reprinted matter, limited to 15,000 words, at five for a dollar; then at ten cents a copy, and finally, after 1922, at a nickel a copy. By this time he had issued 283 volumes with a total sale of 22,000,000 and boasted of being "the Henry Ford of book publishing." Simultaneously he had also brought out a number of Big Blue Books at fifty cents a copy.

It should be stated that while some of the Little Blue Books were of practical or prurient content, most volumes had literary or scholarly merit and thus introduced millions of Americans to their first acquaintance with good writing and solid information. Of the more than 2000 volumes, those on sex predominated, followed by those on self-improvement, humor, religious skepticism, and general literature. An indication of the worth of many of these booklets may be gathered from the fact that the sketches of outstanding philosophers by Will Durant were later combined into the highly popular *Story of Philosophy.* Julius' flamboyant and at times fraudulent advertising was castigated by spokesmen for the publishing industry, but it did result in sales totaling 300,000,000 copies, and many readers benefited from their availability. In the late 1930s the appearance of the 25-cent paperbacks and the greater sophistication of many readers cut deeply into the sale of Little Blue Books.

The spread of literary culture in America was further stimulated by marketing developments in "remainder" books as well as by the publication and promotion of good but inexpensive books on the arts and self-help. In the 1920s Max Salop operated the Harlem Book Store, which specialized in marketing books which regular publishers were no longer able to sell at the original price. Obtaining these books at a fraction of the listed price he, aided by Norman Blaustein and Sidney Feldman, managed to place them on sale in drugstores, department stores, and other emporia at a low enough price to attract buyers—thus opening a new national market for books. The importance of this innovation in book marketing is that it brought books to towns and villages which had no regular bookstores and thus encouraged people to buy them. Salop and his associates also started Tudor Publishing Company, which brought out reprints of books on music, art, architecture, and similar subjects in an attractive format at relatively low prices and promoted them actively in stores handling "remainders." Later the firm issued finely produced books at low prices. Tudor has also brought out a number of books in Judaica, and in the early 1940s it took over, for a time, the bookstore distribution of books issued by the Jewish Publication Society. In 1973 Blaustein arranged with Keter Publishing Company of Jerusalem for the American promotion of the *Encyclopedic Dictionary of Judaica*, the one-volume edition of *Encyclopaedia Judaica.* He also marketed the series entitled Popular Library of Judaism. In 1974 he sold his interest in the Tudor firm to Louis Amiel. The latter has for some time been specializing in various types of art books, most of them imports from Europe. Among his recent publications are the XXth Century Homage Series, Great Painters and Their Art, Gallery Maeght Publications, and the prestigious periodical, *XXe Siecle;* also a number of volumes of a more general nature. The Tudor backlist will be marketed as an imprint of Leon Amiel, Publisher.

Jacob W. Greenberg controlled the Outlet Book Company, which also specialized in publishers' "remainders." After some years of successful promotion he, in 1934, sold the business to Nat Wartels and Robert Simon. Earlier he had begun bringing out new books under his own name and published a number of popular works by prominent psychiatrists. He also issued the writings of such authors as George Gissing, Tony Sarg, and Robert Graves.

In 1936 Wartels and Simon organized Crown Publishers for the purpose of bringing out books of a practical content. Concurrently they continued to deal actively in "remainders." In 1943 they acquired the list of the defunct firm of Covici-Friede as well as the old house of Lothrop, Lee, and Shepard with its large list of juveniles. By that time the supply of overstock books had dried up—owing to the curtailment of publishing during the war—so that Crown began to concentrate its efforts on the publication and promotion of new books, mostly of a utilitarian content. In addition, the firm issued books on folklore, collections of humor, anecdotes, Yiddish anthologies in English, and the like. After the war Crown resumed handling remainders while continuing actively its publication of new books.

Columbia graduates, interested in music and books, overflowing with energy and ideas, Richard Simon and M. Lincoln Schuster began in 1923 to talk about starting a publishing house. The following year they rented a small office and began looking for publishable manuscripts. Chance brought them a crossword-puzzle manuscript, and they issued it with unexpected success. Their first year's list also included a volume of popular verse by Irwin Edman, a solid biography of Joseph Pulitzer, M. S. Rukyeser's *The Common Sense of Money and Investment,* and William Tilden's *The Common Sense of Tennis*—typical of the "straight" and "novelty" books which these ingeniously enterprising partners were to publish subsequently.

Characteristic of their marketing enterprise was their publication of Durant's *Story of Philosophy.* Schuster had for some time thought that a popular book in philosophy would have a fair sale. When Haldeman-Julius casually intimated that the eleven Blue Books by Durant might be put into one book, the two partners were quick to take advantage of the idea. They figured that if they put these little volumes into one large handsome book and priced it at $5.00—almost ten times their present price—readers would be impressed and attracted by the thought of getting an understanding of philosophy in an enjoyable and respected form. The planned high-geared promotion resulted in a sale of around a half million copies.

Over the years the firm was commercially highly successful, but from the point of view of literary quality it tended to be dichotomous. It brought out a good many books of solid merit, and among its authors were Arthur Schnitzler, Franz Werfel, John Cowper Powys, Leon Trotsky, Bertrand Russell, Walter Duranty, Felix Salten, and Claude G. Bowers. Deservedly popular also were Ernest Sutherland Bates's *The Bible Designed to be Read as Living Literature, A Treasury of Art Masterpieces, A Treasury of the World's Great Letters,* Mortimer J. Adler's *How to Read a Book,* and numerous similar projects. Concurrently, however, the firm published and promoted vigorously such spurious books as *Trader Horn, The Cradle of the Deep,* and *Calories Don't Count;* also such "made" books as *How to Win Friends and Influence People, The Education of a Poker Player,* and *Dr. Dan, the Bandage Man.*

In its half century of dynamic publishing, the firm of Simon and Schuster has brought out around 4000 books, with an extraordinary number of popular sellers. But if the firm had prospered enormously, its great success was built more on ingenious and aggressive methods of promotion than on the quality of its publications. Both founders are dead, and Leon Shimkin, who joined the firm not long after it was started, recently sold it to the conglomerate corporation, Gulf and Western.

Two other young partners, equally intelligent and also eager to make their careers in book publishing, founded Random House in 1925. Bennett Cerf, having bought the Modern Library from Liveright, asked his friend Donald Klopfer to join him in its promotion and marketing. They did a fine job of improving the appearance of the volumes, dropped the slow-selling titles, added many more over the years, tripling the list and promoting it with energy and persistence. In 1931 they added the longer modern classics as Modern Library Giants, and they too sold in large numbers, so that the reprint series became "the keystone" of the firm's business during the early years of its existence.

Shortly after Cerf and Klopfer completed the reorganization of the Modern Library they began to publish books "at random" —which gave the name to their company. Among the first volumes they issued were relatively expensive editions of Voltaire's

Candide and Melville's *Moby Dick,* both illustrated by Rockwell Kent. When the Liveright firm went bankrupt, Cerf approached some of its authors and signed up Eugene O'Neill and Robinson Jeffers among others.

In 1932 Cerf struck a momentous blow against censorship. Joyce's *Ulysses* was still unpublished in the United States after fear of persecution by John S. Sumner had kept Huebsch from bringing it out in 1920. During the twelve-year interim, however, public opinion and court rulings, resulting from such publishers as Liveright and Covici standing up against anti-vice societies, had served to liberalize the prevailing Grundyism. Cerf, therefore, decided to test the current law against obscenity by arranging to import a copy of *Ulysses* through the mails and stand trial. Judge Woolsey's landmark ruling in favor of the novel enabled Random House to publish it in an attractive edition and promote it into best-sellerdom.

The firm made great strides during the 1930s. Among its publications were new editions of Proust's *Remembrance of Things Past,* the literature of the ancient Greeks in the Lifetime Library, Havelock Ellis's *Studies in the Psychology of Sex,* formerly banned and now accepted as a classic, and T. H. van de Velde's books on marriage; also the poems by W. H. Auden, Stephen Spender, and books by Morley Callaghan and Gertrude Stein. The absorption of the young firm of Smith and Haas brought both partners into the firm, and with them such writers as William Faulkner, André Malraux, Robert Graves, Maurice Hindus, Louis Fischer, Isak Dinesen, and Jean de Brunhoff. The firm also published books by John Strachey, Liddell Hart, C. M. Doughty, and Edgar Snow. Harry Maule's coming to the editorial staff brought another group of prominent authors. Random House also published numerous Broadway plays and a popular list of juveniles.

After World War II Random House further increased its aggressive promotion of popular books. Among them were volumes by John O'Hara, Truman Capote, James Michener, Irwin Shaw, Moss Hart, and Robert Penn Warren. By 1959 it was doing a business of around $10,000,000 annually. With Wall Street underwriters having discovered book publishing as a growth industry, they arranged for Random House to go public. The following year headlines proclaimed the merger of the Knopf firm with Random House. Although the two houses remained autonomous, the combination benefited both. In 1961 the company acquired Pantheon Books, which had been started in 1942 by the eminent publisher Kurt Wolff, a refugee from Nazi Germany. Random House absorbed several other small firms in the early 1960s, but in 1965 it was itself acquired by Radio Corporation of America. Fortunately for the book industry, the R. C. A. executives have not interfered with any editorial activities, and both Random and Knopf continue to function successfully as first-rate publishing houses.

A third pair of young partners to enter book publishing in the middle 1920s were Harold K. Guinzburg and George Oppenheimer, who formed the Viking Press. Joined by B. H. Huebsch, the trio determined "to establish a trademark that will be known as a sign of good books in constructive publishing." In this they were eminently successful. From the first Guinzburg was in effect the controlling head of the firm. Having a solid respect for good writing and motivated by sound ethical convictions, he had the ability to pursue a policy that favored Huebsch's editorial predilections and at the same time made the business a profitable enterprise. Huebsch and his young assistant Marshall Best thus had a free hand in obtaining books from leading European writers as well as from a number of American authors, and most of these volumes proved both critically superior and adequately popular. To a number of previous Huebsch authors they added such writers as Lion Fuechtwanger, Arnold Zweig, Carl Van Doren, Erskine Caldwell, Joseph Roth, Franz Werfel, and Elizabeth Madox Roberts. In 1933 George Oppenheimer left the firm for Hollywood. That year Guinzburg engaged Mae Massee to develop a juvenile list, and over the years she did so successfully.

In 1938 Viking was further strengthened by the coming of Pascal Covici as senior editor. In the 1920s he had operated a bookstore in Chicago and published a few *avant garde* books. In 1928 he and Donald Friede became partners in a publishing firm

Harold Guinzburg was a rare combination of businessman and respecter of good writing.

bearing their names. Having a strong interest in the latest literary trends and quite free of conventional restraints, Covici did not hesitate to bring out Radclyffe Hall's *The Well of Loneliness* after Harper and Knopf had decided against issuing it. The resulting court battle with Sumner was ultimately successful, but the financial cost was high, so that the subsequent wide sale recompensed the firm only in part. Covici continued to publish books of literary merit, among them G. M. Priest's translation of Goethe's complete *Faust* and books by Windham Lewis, Richard Aldington, Alexei Tolstoy, Albert Einstein, and John Steinbeck, but in 1938 lack of capital and the depressed economy drove the firm to financial insolvency. In joining Viking, Covici brought with him John Steinbeck, with whom he had developed an extraordinary intimacy.

Over the ensuing years the Viking annual list of books was both prestigious and relatively profitable. Among the new authors of promise it brought out were Saul Bellow, Phyllis McGinley, Siegfried Sassoon, Rumer Godden, Gene Fowler, and Richard Ellman. Viking also issued the popular Lanny Budd books by Upton Sinclair, the abridged Columbia-Viking Desk Encyclopedia, and the series of Portable Library books. In 1956 Huebsch retired as vice-president, but continued to serve actively as editorial adviser until his death eight years later. In 1961 Guinzburg died of cancer and was succeeded as president by his son Thomas. The firm continued to maintain itself as a prestigious house, with Marshall Best as editor-in-chief until his recent retirement. In 1975 cash flow requirements caused the firm to merge with Penguin Books.

Book reading in the United States having been initially stimulated in the 1910s by the Little Leather Library, Modern Library, Little Blue Books, and remainder outlets, was in the 1920s further expedited in a major way by the emergence of book clubs. The first and largest clubs were founded by enterprising Jews. Harry Scherman and Max Sackheim, operating an advertising agency, helped to promote the wide sale of Little Leather library books. In 1923 they thought of the idea of forming a book club in which members would obligate themselves to purchase a book a month on the basis of "convenience, reading fulfillment, guidance by experts, and continuity." Since both were giving most of their time to advertising work, they arranged with Robert K. Haas, who then controlled the Little Leather Library, to organize and direct the prospective Book-of-the-Month Club, started in 1926.

Many publishers and booksellers at first opposed the club, fearing competition, but Scherman soon overcame this opposition by assuring them of his adherence to the published price and by pointing out that the club was primarily aiming to reach areas in this country where few or no bookstores existed. And indeed, before long both publishers and booksellers found that the club's selections served to increase sales in bookstores.

When new members were joining at a slower rate than anticipated, the club permitted members to buy only four books a year. An aggressive campaign of advertising brought the membership to about 100,000. Then, when the depression of the 1930s caused a considerable drop in membership, the acquisition of new members was stimulated by a dividend arrangement whereby a free book was given with every two bought. By this and other means the club maintained itself during the lean years. In the 1940s the membership rose to around 900,000, and the club has continued in active operation to the present. In the interim Haas resigned in 1930 to start a publishing house of his own and Sackheim left the following year. Scherman then engaged Meredith Wood as his associate.

Not long after the Book-of-the-Month was started, Harold K. Guinzburg became interested in the idea of a book club patterned after a German book club. He engaged Carl Van Doren as the judge to select the books, but had to modify the price-reduction feature to mollify booksellers. This process took some time, but by 1934 the Literary Guild was functioning profitably. By then Guinzburg had found creative publishing more to his liking and sold his interest of Nelson Doubleday.

Honorable mention must be made of the Book Find Club, started by George Braziller in the early 1940s. A political liberal, he wanted to bring books of a social and political content to members of labor unions at a price they could afford. Without capital but knowledgeable in the remainder field, he began soliciting members at union meetings, offering books at fifty cents to those who agreed to take a book every month. His rise was at first uphill and slow, but as he obtained members he gave them the month's choice from remainder stock. Service in the armed forces kept the club at a standstill—his wife doing her best to provide books to members. After 1946 Braziller worked hard to increase the membership. He continued to address union meetings and to circularize various lists, and before long the number of members reached close to 100,000 and he was sending out nearly 50,000 copies a month of books specially printed for him. By then he was dealing with publishers and buying the rights to special editions in order to keep the price at the lowest level. For two decades, therefore, Braziller was able to provide members with solid books of a liberal content at a relatively low price. He, too, had to reduce the required number of books to be bought annually to four. In the 1950s he also started the Seven Arts Club, and managed both clubs with energy and success. In 1968, owing to his increased activity in his own publishing enterprise, he sold both clubs to Time, Inc.

During the 1920s and 1930s a number of college graduates interested in books and writing began to find employment not only with Jewish-owned houses but also among the older publishing firms—the prejudice against Jews having lessened considerably during this period. A number of these young men and women became energetic and enterprising editors and tended to further the publication of manuscripts of new and unconventional writers who in time achieved literary prominence. In part with their aid, but even more as a result of the increased market for books by sophisticated authors, all kinds of writers who would previously have been ignored now began to be welcomed by publishers. In the process, a good many books by and about Jews gradually found acceptance.

Books about Jews, especially about Judaism, were of course published throughout the nineteenth century, but very few were by Jewish writers. In the 1890s the books by Israel Zangwill were popular enough to interest The Macmillan Company, but he was exceptional in this respect. After 1900 a number of Jewish immigrants, having mastered the English language enough to want to write in it and bursting with literary eagerness, began to depict the struggles and aspirations of their fellow Jews—their spiritual adjustments and assimilationary allurements, the anti-Semitic barriers confronting them, and the persistence or perversion of their ideals. And those who possessed literary ability sooner or later found an interested publisher.

One of the first to get his books brought out by established publishers was Abraham Cahan, whose *Yekel* appeared in 1896 and whose most important novel, *The Rise of David Levinsky*, came out in 1917. Mary Antin's *The Promised Land* (1913) found wide readership among Americans. Anzia Yezierska was another writer to gain a popular reception with *Hungry Hearts* (1920) and *Bread Givers* (1923), both presenting emotionally charged accounts of sweatshop life.

By this time the number of Jewish writers increased notably. One need only mention Bruno Lessing, Montague Glass, Elias Tobenkin, Samuel Ornitz, Ludwig Lewisohn, Lester Cohen, Irving Fineman, Ben Hecht, and Michael Gold to indicate the variety and richness of Jewish writing in the 1920s. Their number has of course greatly increased during the ensuing decades, so that in 1947 Joshua Bloch, head of the Jewish division of the New York Public Library, could write of the 1946 list:

> So rich is the year's output of Jewish books as to make it possible for every reader to gain from them an exhilaration of reading genuinely delightful works, many of which are of permanent literary merit. Among these books one can find a relatively sufficient number of titles good enough to meet the critical standards of interest, entertainment, enjoyment, without reverting to sensationalism.

And as late as 1975 George Steiner, the eminent critic, stated in *The New Yorker:* "It is a commonplace that recent American fiction and criticism have to a drastic extent been the product of Jewish tone and explosion of talent." Richard Gilman intimated a similar opinion of the "Jewish" era in American literature after

1945. In a review of Bellow's *Humboldt's Gift* in the New York *Times* Book Review he wrote:

What distinguishes his writing from that of the preceding epoch in our literature, and broadly continues to distinguish Jewish writing in general, was its sense of moral and social crisis, its agitated ambivalence toward experience, its furious humor, and cry of mingled warning and enlightenment.

In recent years not a few Jewish writers have been severely criticized by fellow Jews for their distortion of Jewish life out of ignorance and superficiality, for the exaggeration of negative traits, and for over-emphasizing the comicalness of their characters. Critics have pointed out that in their effort to attain popularity, the writers have tended to exploit their vague childhood recollections of their Jewish environment without concern for inner truth or outer reality. As Leslie Fiedler declared in 1963: "We live in a moment where everywhere in the realm of prose Jewish writers have discovered their Jewishness to be eminently a marketable commodity, their much vaunted alienation to be their passport into the heart of Gentile American culture." These writers, born Jews but growing up with no real knowledge of Jewishness, have sought to gain their effects by caricature rather than by insightful characterization. Books like Ben Hecht's *A Jew in Love*, Norman Katkov's *Eagle in My Eyes*, and Philip Roth's *Portnoy's Complaint*, to list but three conspicuous examples, served to distort the true nature of Jewishness. Such writing, Ludwig Lewisohn stated caustically, carried the Jewish motif

to morbid lengths of self-degradation, raging against their residual Jewishness with flamboyant illiteracy, exalting not the noble and elevated aspects of American culture, but its very dregs and sewage at the expense of all that was glorious and sacred in their ancestral tradition.

It should be stressed that a good many Jewish writers deal only incidentally with Jewish themes or characters, writing stories and poems and plays and criticism mainly in the current American idiom. Among such writers are Norman Mailer, Arthur

Miller, Muriel Rukyeser, Lionel Trilling, Philip Rahv, and Paul Goodman, to mention the first that come to mind. Others, more sensitive of their Jewish heritage and deliberately espousing it in their writing, have depicted Jewish life, favorably or critically, with a sincerity and insight that made for authentic art. One of them, Herbert Gold, remarked: "The American Jewish community is most important to me as a writer because it is a mirror in which the rest of America can be seen. Like all mirrors, it invites distortion." Bernard Malamud is equally candid: "I write about Jews because I know them. But more important I write about them because the Jews are absolutely the very stuff of drama."

A good example of this kind of writing is Henry Roth's *Call It Sleep,* which was a failure when published in 1934 but a success when reissued in 1960. According to Leslie Fiedler "it is the best single work by a Jew about Jewishness written by an American, certainly through the thirties and perhaps ever." Others who depicted Jews and Jewishness with serious, if not always favorable overtones are too numerous to list, but the following are typical: Michael Blankfort, Leon Uris, Meyer Levin, Arthur A. Cohen, Louis Untermeyer, Herman Wouk, Saul Bellow, and Louis Zara. It might be said, indeed, that with events such as the Holocaust and the establishment of Israel, few Jews can escape their Jewishness, and those writers who seek to suppress or deprecate it do so at their artistic peril. As one of them has put it recently:

> No Jew in our time can honestly suppress the visceral awareness that he remains a Jew, that to be a Jew means to be tolerated, and to be an object of anti-Semitism; that anti-Semitism politicized and detached from tolerance can mean genocide; that in the face of all this he must be active and self-respecting as a Jew.

After World War I Jews sought participation in every literary endeavor. More and more entered book publishing, most of them with inadequate capital and on a small scale. A sampling will indicate the nature of their activity and interests.

Jay W. Greenberg began to publish books in the 1920s and specialized in works of popular mental hygiene and psychiatry;

but he also brought out a number of other books. Thus in addition to such publications as Alfred Adler's *Understanding Human Nature* and Joseph Jastrow's *Keeping Mentally Fit* and *Freud: His Dreams and Sex Theories,* he brought out books on the theatre, music, the cinema, and do-it-yourself volumes. The firm was merged with the Chilton Company in 1958.

A. A. Roback, a Harvard Ph. D. in psychology whose Jewishness kept him from acceptance as an author by Boston publishers as well as from an academic career, started his own firm in Cambridge. In addition to his own books he published works by Morton Prince, R. B. Cattell, Hans Sachs, Kurt Tucholsky, the *Albert Schweitzer Jubilee Book,* and Schweitzer's *Realms.* He was also actively interested in Yiddish writing and published the first contemporary book on the literature.

Also in the 1920s Henry Schnitkind, a Bostonian, began to publish books under the imprint of the Stratford Press. He brought out a number of books of general interest, but lack of capital and the economic depression of the 1930s forced him out of business.

Because many Jews entered publishing with little capital during the 1920s, they failed to survive the ensuing depression; but while they functioned as publishers they added works of merit to American literature. The Bonis and Seltzer have already been discussed. Another, Henry Schuman, survived in the reorganized firm of Abelard-Schuman. Among the publications were a number of books of Jewish content, such as M. Begin's *Revolt,* E. E. Pilchik's *Hillel,* and books by Sholom Aleichem, and Justice Louis D. Brandeis.

In the 1930s Julian Messner left the bankrupt firm of Liveright and started his own publishing house. One of the Liveright authors who went with him, Frances Parkinson Keyes, was popular enough to give Messner financial stability during the early years. In 1935 he bought the list of the defunct firm of Long and Smith, and ten years later he acquired Veritas Press with its juvenile picture books. By the time he died in 1948 the company was publishing a fairly large list of books and his wife Kitty, who had worked with the firm from the beginning, took over the management and proceeded to develop the list further. Among her new acquisitions were *Peyton Place* and two other books by Grace Metalious. When Mrs. Messner died in 1964, the firm was acquired by Simon and Schuster.

In 1943 Hayward Cirker founded Dover Publications with the aim of bringing out handsome paperback editions of unavailable books having seminal significance. He was thus one of the first to publish quality paperbacks for use in colleges and by serious readers. In time he developed a fine list of advanced works in science, philosophy, and mathematics. Successful promotion gradually enabled him to expand his publishing program to such fields as games, ornithology, the arts, and works by famous scholars in a variety of areas. His list of over 800 volumes became noted for its attractive formats. In recent years the firm has also brought out books and records for the study of languages as well as classical music.

Jacob Steinberg started Twayne Publishers in 1948 with the idea of bringing out books of a serious literary and historical content. One of his early ventures was The Twayne Library of Modern Poetry, with John Ciardi as editor, and the ten volumes in it brought out poets hitherto unpublished. Steinberg's most important contribution was the United States Authors Series, which was started in 1958 and now includes numerous studies of American authors, many of whom are not now remembered but who had made their contribution to American literary history. In 1964 he began the English Authors Series, and two years later he initiated the World Authors Series, thus broadening the scope of his list to books by authors the world over. Other of his series include Rulers and Statesmen of the World, Great Thinkers Series, the Immigrant Heritage of America Series, and books by Rumanian writers in English translation.

From the first Steinberg was strongly interested in Jewish writings and his list includes dozens of books by Jewish authors. Among them may be mentioned Chaim Grade's *The Agunah* and Lamed Shapiro's *The Jewish Government and Other Stories*—both translated from the Yiddish, Menachem Ribalow's *The Flowering of Hebrew Literature,* Abraham Cronbach's *Judaism for Today,* and Henry L. Feingold's *Zion in America.*

In January 1973 Twayne Publishers merged with the firm of G. K. Hall of Boston. Mr. Steinberg is now connected with Bobbs-Merrill Co. He is also the current president of the Association of Jewish Book Publishers.

Jonathan David Publications, which also started in 1948, is a small-size firm which combines general with Jewish publishing. Limiting itself mostly to non-fiction, the company has over the years brought out a number of books dealing with such varied topics having telltale titles such as *Secret Love Affairs, The Shirley Temple Scrapbook, Madmen of History, The Intimate Life of Rudolf Valentino, A Concise Dictionary of Medicine, A Treasury of Witchcraft and Deviltry, Miracles in Medicine,* and a Fun-in-Learning Series which treats mostly Jewish topics but which also includes a discussion of football and computers.

Its specifically Jewish publications consist mostly of books on the Bible, Psalms, humor, the Seder, Judaism and Christianity, Bar Mitzvah, and Sabra Children. These books are written largely for children and young adults who are interested in acquiring knowledge in the fields of Judaism and Jewish history.

Arthur A. Cohen was still in his twenties in 1951 when he and Cecil Hemley formed Noonday Press as a quality paperback house. Three years later they started Meridian Press and began to issue a superior list of paperbacks in religion, philosophy, and literature. Among their authors were Jacques Maritain, Jacob Burkhardt, E. M. Foster, Irving Babbitt, Herbert Read, Joseph Schumpeter, and J. M. Keynes. In 1956 the partners separated, with Cohen retaining the Meridian list. He promoted his books successfully in colleges and libraries. As sales increased he issued Greenwich Editions, Living Age Books, and Meridian Giants—the volumes in each series written by world-renowned scholars and scientists. He also issued a number of meritorious novels. In 1960 he sold the list to World Publishing Company.

The latter firm was started in 1905 by Alfred Cahan, an immigrant bookbinder in Cleveland, when he began to print and bind popular books for sale in ten-cent stores; also as inexpensive premiums for various companies. In 1933 Ben D. Zevin, having married one of Cahan's daughters, joined the firm. His energy and ingenuity advanced him to the presidency in 1945. Six years earlier he had started Tower Books, hardbound reprints at 49 cents a copy. Somewhat later he had launched World Illustrated Editions, reprints of standard art books. During World War II he printed millions of Bibles for the armed services. Concurrently he also brought out various editions of Webster dictionaries. In 1945 he sent William Targ to New York to develop a trade department. The firm also published the Living Library of American Classics, numerous juveniles, Dreiser's *An American Tragedy,* and subsequently new books by Simone de Beauvoir, MacKinlay Cantor, Herbert Gold, Lillian Smith, and numerous other authors. In 1962, owing to family disagreements, the firm was sold to the Los Angeles Times Mirror Company.

Late in 1944 John Farrar, a founder of Farrar and Rinehart and a prominent editor, found himself outvoted by the Rinehart brothers and left the firm. Friends of his helped him to join young Roger Straus in starting a new publishing house bearing their names. The new firm soon attracted a number of established authors, among them Carlo Levi, Ludwig Lewisohn, Theodor Reik, Shirley Jackson, and Alberto Moravia. After 1950 it published such popular books as Gaylord Hauser's *Look Younger, Live Longer,* Quentin Reynolds' *Courtroom,* William Hillman's *Mr. President,* Lionel Trilling's *Selected Letters of John Keats,* Abraham J. Heschel's *Man Is Not Alone,* William Shirer's *Midcentury Journey,* Edmund Wilson's *Classics and Commercials,* Martin Buber's *At the Turning,* and Margaret Yourcenar's *Memoirs of Hadrian.*

By this time Roger Straus had gained enough experience to establish his dominance in the firm. In 1951 he acquired the list of Creative Age Press, and two years later he took over the books published by Pelegrini and Cudahy. In 1955 he engaged Robert Giroux as editor-in-chief, and the latter brought with him several authors with whom he had worked at Harcourt, Brace and Company, among them T. S. Eliot, Robert Merton, and Robert Lowell. Giroux's name was later added to that of the firm.

During the 1950s and later the company was publishing a sizable list of books by authors of quality. Among them were three Nobel Prize winners, books of Catholic and Jewish content, the Great Letters Series, the fiction of I. Bashevis Singer, and Nathaniel West's *Complete Works.* In 1957 the firm acquired the list of L. C. Page and Company with its thousand titles, many of them of abiding popularity. Three years later it bought the Noonday Press.

As the firm expanded its activity, its list increased not only in size but also in merit. Thus, a relatively young house, it has achieved a position of prestige in the industry. It may be said of it, as it was stated of the old Boston house of Ticknor and Fields, and as the Viking Press aimed at, that its imprint on a book gives promise of general excellence.

Although Atheneum Publishers was not started until 1959, its quality publishing over the past sixteen years is similar to that of the Straus firm. Also of note is the fact that it was formed at a time when the industry surged toward merging and going public, which tended to yield literary prestige to the maw of profit. The small independent company was considered by Wall Street brokers who were forcing bigness upon the industry as unworthy of attention. On its face therefore the three partners who had formed the new house—two prominent editors and a sales manager from established firms—seemed to have undertaken a quixotic quest.

The three partners were Simon Michael Bessie of Harper and Row, Hiram Haydn of Random House, and Alfred A. Knopf, Jr. They were no doubt motivated by complex personal reasons, but all three were united in their desire to publish quality books. Haydn, the non-Jew and spokesman, stated: "Each of us had his own version of the same idea. We were concerned with quality. Each of us in his own way felt you could still make a profitable business and adhere to quality."

Experienced in the realities of publishing, they succeeded in attracting wealthy investors interested in good books to begin functioning with about a million dollars of capital. The understanding was that the partners should proceed at their own pace in developing a list of books that would be both prestigious and profitable. It did not take them long in signing up a relatively large number of authors—sixty within the first year. Among the first best-sellers were a novel by André Schwartz-Bart and the initial volume of Theodore H. White's series, *The Making of a President*. In the early 1960s the firm published such meritorious yet controversial volumes as A. J. P. Taylor's *The Origins of the Second World War* and Daniel Boorstin's *The Image: or What Happened to the American Dream;* also books by Frederic Morton, Sergei Tolstoy, Rose Macaulay, E. B. Williams, C. H. Waddington, August Heckscher, and Thomas Sterling; also a number of quality juveniles and paperbacks. Some of the titles attained wide popularity.

In 1964 Haydn differed with Bessie and Knopf on company policy and resigned. The firm's quality standard continued to be maintained during the ensuing decade, but in 1975 Bessie decided to return to Harper, and Knopf assumed full control.

In 1924 Frederick Ungar was a founder of Phaidon Press in Vienna. When the Nazis gained control of Austria, he managed to reach first London and then New York. With no capital, in 1941 he started the Frederick Ungar Publishing Company by bringing out a few books he had originally published in Vienna. After the war ended he began to issue prestigious works of history, philosophy, and literary criticism that were either out of print or had never before appeared in English. At that time he had also acquired the Stephen Day Press and used the imprint for regional and general books.

As his publishing activity expanded, Ungar began to issue the series, Milestones of Thought, which included works by St. Augustine, Boethius, Joseph Butler, John Calvin, Castiglione, and Rousseau. In the field of history he brought out the first English translation of Jacob Burkhardt's *History of Greek Culture* in a one-volume edition; also, in the American Classics Series, books by

Charles Haskins, James Thompson, Francis Parkman, Livingston Farrand, Evarts B. Greene, and Allan Nevins—all previously unavailable. In the area of literature his list is also rich in the works of eminent European writers, a number of them of Jewish origin, as well as multivolumed works of reference, such as the *Encyclopedia of World Literature in the 20th Century*. So appreciative have scholars and librarians been of his efforts to bring out new and updated editions of important out-of-print books in English translation, that one eminent historian referred to him as "a public benefactor," and the organization of translators has recently honored him.

Another firm founded by two refugees from Germany, Walter J. Johnson and Kurt Jacobi, was the Academic Press. They were son and son-in-law, respectively, of the founder of Leipzig's Academische Verlag, and followed the pattern of activity of the original house by issuing magazines and books in the latest areas of science research. The magazines were bound annually and marketed as books to scholars and libraries. Among the early volumes on their list were Sumner and Somers' *Chemistry and Methods of Enzymes* and *Vitamins and Hormones*, edited by Harris and Thiemann. The high quality of the journals in pure and applied science, making available the latest developments in research, enabled the firm to attract world-renowned scientists as contributors and editors. The house also published treatises, monographs, and symposia. With these works in advanced science having a minor language barrier, the demand for them came from every part of the world.

In 1961 Academic Press started a textbook division in science and mathematics and also issued paperbacks in these fields. So successful has it been over the years that by 1965 it was issuing some 300 volumes annually. Not long after, however, the firm was acquired by Harcourt Brace Jovanovich and has since been operating under its aegis.

Several relatively small publishing houses were started after World War II. A. Kagan started International Universities Press and published a fairly large number of books in psychoanalysis and similar subjects. In 1946 Thomas Yoseloff started publishing under his own name. Although he also issued books of general interest, he early concentrated on books of Jewish content. On his list were books by such Israeli leaders as Vladimir Jabotinsky, Abba Eban, Zalman Shazar, and Jacob Tzur. One of his major undertakings was an English translation of Simon Dubnow's monumental history of the Jews, which took six years to complete and was issued in five volumes. Other important multivolumed projects were Eliezer Ben Yehuda's *Dictionary and Thesaurus of the Hebrew Language* and Meyer Waxman's *History of Jewish Literature.* Yoseloff also published the fiction of a number of Jewish novelists and studies of Jewish life by various scholars. After 1958, when he acquired A. S. Barnes and Company, he brought out various volumes in sports and the outdoors. Recently his firm was acquired by one of the large corporations.

Jeremiah Kaplan, with the financial assistance of a friend, in 1947 began to reissue in Glencoe, Illinois, standard works in the social sciences under the imprint of The Free Press. Having only a nominal overhead, he was able to manage on relatively small sales. As his activity expanded, he increased the number of publications from six volumes in his first year to about fifty by 1960. By that time he was also bringing out new studies of scientific import. Then he received an attractive offer from Crowell-Collier, which had just acquired The Macmillan Company, and he joined the corporation in New York as a vice-president.

Three years after Grove Press was formed in 1947 it was acquired by Barney Rosset. He began to bring out American editions of the International Library issued in England by Routledge and Sons, but ceased to do so after 1956. He also issued new editions of several old novels. In 1954 he started publishing Evergreen Books, quality paperbacks, and three years later launched the quarterly *Evergreen Review.* His publication of an unexpurgated edition of Lawrence's *Lady Chatterley's Lover* brought him both notoriety and profit. The following year he started to issue Evergreen Profile Books by an arrangement with publishers from several European countries; also Evergreen Target Books. His publication of Henry Miller's books caused him much trouble and further notoriety, but they swelled the demand for the books. It should be stated, however, that if he sponsored morally questionable books, he also published a number of important literary works, among them the writings of Rolf Hochhut, Eugene Ionesco, Lazlo Nemeth, F. Dürremat, and John Osborne.

Frederick A. Praeger started his publishing house in 1950 with little capital but with a maximum of energy and enterprise. Strongly interested in books of social and economic content, especially as they affected contemporary society, he began by importing from England sheets of works that appealed to him; these he bound and promoted actively, so that his income from their sales enabled him to pay for the sheets as arranged with the British publishers. During the 1950s he published over 500 books, many of them attaining wide interest. He favored books written by anti-communist authors, among them Milovan Djilas. He also became interested in art books, handled the publications of the Graphic Press in this country, and marketed a World Art Series in both cloth and paper bindings. By 1965 his firm had become relatively large and profitable, so that he was able to sell it to the Encyclopaedia Britannica.

In 1950 Harry N. Abrams started the first commercial firm devoted solely to art books. He issued the Library of Great Painters, with volumes on Van Gogh, El Greco, and Renoir as his initial publications. Well designed, fully and carefully illustrated, and energetically promoted, these volumes sold widely as de luxe Christmas books. He next issued inexpensive editions of these and other books, and again managed to create a large demand for them. He also began to work closely with book clubs, and the Book-of-the-Month Club distributed his *Art Treasures of the Louvre* to its large membership. Later he developed the Pocket Library of Great Art, "designed to bring the great art of the past and present" to the average person, which Pocket Books distributed as low-cost paperbacks. Subsequently he produced low-priced books for competing paperback publishers.

After 1953 Abrams managed to sell editions of his books, produced in Europe, to foreign publishers with a view to lowering costs. Some of his important, expensive books had as many as nine different language editions. In 1957 he published Janson's the *Picture History of Painting* and marketed it in cooperation with *Life,* Book-of-the-Month Club, and foreign-language editions. About the same time he arranged for the sale of art textbooks in cooperation with Prentice-Hall. Many of his numerous other publications in the field of art were generally praised by critics for their color superiority and careful editing. In 1966 he sold the firm to the Los Angeles Times Mirror Company, but has remained active as its head to the present.

In 1952 Arthur A. Rosenthal reorganized the Basic Book Club into the Basic Books publishing company in order to expand the activity of the club into cognate areas. One of his first important publications was Ernest Jones's three-volume *Life and Work of Sigmund Freud.* In the process of expansion Rosenthal formed a new book club, the Library of Science. By 1960 the clubs had a combined membership of 150,000, and he stated: "We are being well repaid for concentrating in areas where we believe we would make a contribution to American thought and culture." By this time he was able to publish successfully such a costly work as *American Handbook of Psychiatry.* One of his most popular books was Isaac Asimov's *The Intelligent Man's Guide to Science.* In 1962 he sold the two book clubs to Crowell-Collier in order to concentrate on his own publishing program. After ten years of further vigorous enterprise in his chosen area of publishing, he decided to sell the firm to Harper and Row. When, several months later, he assumed the directorship of the Harvard University Press, he declared: "For many years I have been deeply involved in the publishing of scholarly books, and the move to Harvard is a natural extension of this interest."

After he had established the Book Find Club on a solid basis, George Braziller in 1955 started to publish books under his own name. He knew that he was not in a position to compete with more affluent companies for books by established American authors, and therefore turned to Europe for manuscripts. In France he found an exciting literary ferment. In time he was able to publish the novels of such young writers as Natalie Sarraute, Claude Simon, Claude Mauriac, Yves Berger, and Julien Cracq. Later he also brought out the work of Jean-Paul Sartre and the fiction of several Italian authors. He also interested himself in the fields of general literature and the arts, and issued the *Notebooks of Leonardo da Vinci*, John Peter's *Masters of Modern Architecture*, William Willets' *Chinese Art*, the four-volume *Great Ages of World Architecture*, the collected plays of Sean O'Casey, Albert Magnet's *Albert Camus*, and various other books in these and related fields. As his list increased he was able to obtain books by American writers. He also undertook the publication of the 12-volume *Great Religions of Modern Man*. In 1965 he launched the Culture of Mankind Series, "presenting selections of the writings and works of art from the great periods of world culture." His most ambitious recent venture is the publication of a series of books dealing with every art period from the Middle Ages to the present.

The foregoing account has not, for obvious reasons, included every Jewish publisher and very few of the Jewish senior editors who have contributed to modern developments in American publishing; but those included, I submit, have definitely stimulated the emergence of book publishing from its parochial and genteel smugness at the end of the nineteenth century and brought it into the sophisticated mainstream of world publishing. The Jewish publishers were predominant in encouraging American authors who had broken away from the restraints of Victorian conventions and were expressing themselves freely and creatively. They also led the fight against censorship, and emerged victorious only after much effort and often crippling expense.

One of their great achievements was to bring modern literature from other countries to American readers. While the long-established conventional publishers limited their lists to the works of traditional American and British authors, and ventured to issue translations of only popular foreign authors, the Jewish publishers did not hesitate to bring out the writings of men and women considered radical or immoral or esoteric by their conservative competitors.

Perhaps as great a contribution of the Jewish publishers was their success in stimulating the wide reading of books by Americans. They did this by producing inexpensive books and making them available in towns and villages and on farms which had no previous means of obtaining them. The Little Leather Library, the Little Blue Books, the Modern Library, the remainder books —all sold at very low prices and brought into local drug stores, department stores, stationery stores—served to develop the habit of reading and prepared the more serious readers for the modern literature subsequently published. Very helpful in this connection were the several book clubs, which brought new books to the doors of their members. Another important factor in the spread of reading was the advent of the paperbacks, in which Jews have had a crucial part. Thus the increase in the number of readers, and their cultural enhancement, was initiated and furthered in large measure by the Jews active in American book publishing.

Bibliography

After more than a half century of activity in book publishing and several years of research in the files and libraries of book publishers, plus my study of Yiddish literature, I find it difficult to account for all the sources of information which I used in writing this book. The following books and periodicals are listed as sources I have perused to a greater or lesser extent in the direct preparation of this book.

Abramovitz, Dinah, *Yiddish Literature in English Translation,* N.Y. 1968

American Hebrew, The, various issues

American Israelite, The, various issues

American Jewish Year Book, 1899–1975

American Zionist, The, various issues

Birnboim, I., "The Journal *In Sich,*" *Pinkus,* 1922.

Bloch Book Bulletin, various issues

Bloch, Joshua, *Of Making Many Books,* Philadelphia, 1953

Boston Advocate, The, various issues

Cahan, Abraham, *Pages from My Life,* 5 vols., N.Y.

Chaikin, J., *Yiddish Writing in America,* N.Y. 1946

Chicago Jewish Forum, The, various issues

Cohen, M. R., *A Dreamer's Journey,* N.Y. 1949

———, *Reflections of a Wondering Jew,* Boston, 1950

Commentary, various issues

Congress Monthly, The, various issues

Contemporary Jewish Record, The, various issues

Day, The, various issues

Elbogen, Ismar, *A Century of Jewish Life,* Philadelphia 1944

Epoch, various issues

Epstein, Melech, *Profiles of Eleven,* Detroit 1965

Freie Arbeiter Shtimme, Die, various issues
Freiheit, Die, various issues
Friedman, Th., and Robert Gordis, eds., *Jewish Life in America,* N.Y. 1955
Glatstein, J., S. Niger, and H. Rogoff, *75 Years of the Yiddish Press in America,* N.Y. 1945
Goodman, Philip, "A Chronicle of the Jewish Book Annual in America," *Jewish Year Book,* 1968
Goodman, Saul, *Our First Fifty Years:* The Sholom Aleichem Folk Institute, N.Y. 1972
———, *Tradition and Innovation,* N.Y. 1967
Grinstein, H.B., *The Rise of the Jewish Community in New York,* Philadelphia 1945
Gutterman, Allen, *The Jewish Writer in America,* N.Y. 1971
Heikin, I., 75 Years of Yiddish Press in America, 1945
Hapgood, H., *The Spirit of the Ghetto,* N.Y. 1902
Jastrow, Marcus, *Dictionary of the Targumin, the Talmud Babli, Jerusalem, and the Midrashic Literature,* N.Y. 1903
Jew, The, early issues
Jewish Book Annual, The, various issues
Jewish Culture, various issues
Jewish Currents, various issues
Jewish Currents Reader, N.Y. 1966
Jewish Daily Forward, The, various issues
Jewish Examiner, The, various issues
Jewish Forum, The, various issues
Jewish Frontier, The, various issues
Jewish Frontier Anthology, N.Y. 1945
Jewish Morning Journal, The, various issues
Jewish Observer, The, various issues
Jewish Spectator, The, various issues
Jewish Tageblatt, The, various issues
Jewish Welfare Board Survey Report, N.Y. 1947
Judaism, various issues
Kinder Journal, Der, various issues
Korn, W. B., "Benjamin Levy: New Orleans Printer and Publisher," *The Papers of the Bibliographical Society of America,* Winter, 1960
Levinger, Lee J., *A History of the Jews in the United States,* N.Y. 1954
Madison, C. A., *Book Publishing in America,* 1966
———, *Yiddish Literature,* N.Y. 1968
May, M. B., *Isaak Meyer Wise,* N.Y. 1916
Menorah Journal, The, various issues
Midstream, various issues
Midstream Reader, The, N.Y. 1960
Moment, various issues
Occident and American Jewish Advocate, The, various issues
Opinion, various issues
Orthodox Union, The, various issues
Present Tense, various issues

Proceedings of the Rabbinical Assembly of the Jewish Theological Seminary, various issues
Reflex, The, various issues
Response, various issues
Ribalow, H. U., *Books in American Jewish Life,* N.Y. 1953
Schachner, Nathan, *The Price of Liberty,* N.Y. 1948
Schulman, Elias, *History of Yiddish Literature in the United States, 1870–1900,* N.Y. 1943
Schwartz, L. W., ed., *The Menorah Treasury,* Philadelphia 1964
Shapiro, J. J., *The Friendly Society,* N.Y. 1970
Sidarsky, David, *The Future of the Jewish Community in America,* N.Y. 1973
Sh'ma, various issues
Soltis, M., *The Yiddish Press: An Americanizing Agency,* N. Y. 1924, 1950
Stern, Malcolm H., *Americans of Jewish Descent,* Cincinnati 1960
Wahrheit, Die, various issues
Wolf, Edwin, *Rosenbach,* Waltham, Mass. 1960
Yanowsky, Oscar, Ed., *The American Jew,* Philadelphia 1964
Yearbook of Central Conference of American Rabbis, various issues
Yiddish, various issues
Yiddisher Kemfer, Der, various issues
YIVO Bletter, various issues
Zukunft, Die, various issues

ILLUSTRATION CREDITS

Acknowledgement for the illustrations used in this book is made to the following:

The American Jewish Archives; Hyman Bass; Alfred A. Knopf, Inc.; The Jewish Theological Seminary of America; The New York Public Library; The Viking Press; YIVO Institute for Jewish Research; and *Die Zukunft.*

Index